Vendetta!

Also by William B. Breuer:

An American Saga
Bloody Clash at Sadzot
Captain Cool
They Jumped at Midnight
Drop Zone Sicily
Agony at Anzio
Hitler's Fortress Cherbourg
Death of a Nazi Army
Operation Torch
Storming Hitler's Rhine
Retaking the Philippines
Nazi Spies in America
Devil Boats
Operation Dragoon
The Secret War with Germany
Hitler's Undercover War
Sea Wolf
Geronimo!
Hoodwinking Hitler
Guantanamo
Race to the Moon
J. Edgar Hoover and His G-Men
The Great Raid on Cabanatuan
MacArthur's Undercover War
Feuding Allies
Shadow Warriors
War and American Women
Unexplained Mysteries of World War II

Vendetta!

Fidel Castro and the Kennedy Brothers

William B. Breuer

John Wiley & Sons, Inc.
New York • Chichester • Weinheim • Brisbane • Singapore • Toronto

Copyright © 1997 by William B. Breuer
Published by John Wiley & Sons, Inc.

Library of Congress Cataloging-in-Publication Data

Breuer, William B.
    Vendetta! : Fidel Castro and the Kennedy brothers / William B. Breuer.
       p. cm.
    Includes bibliographical references and index.
    ISBN 0-471-18456-X (acid-free paper)
    1. United States—Foreign relations—Cuba. 2. Cuba—Foreign relations—United States. 3. United States—Foreign relations—1961–1963. 4. Subversive activities—Cuba—History—20th century. 5. Castro, Fidel, 1927–   . 6. Kennedy, John F. (John Fitzgerald), 1917–1963. 7. Kennedy, Robert F., 1925–1968. I. Title.
E183.8.C9B76   1997
327.7307291—dc21   97-5029

Dedicated to
THEODORE SHACKLEY,
who served the United States
with great honor and distinction
as an Army officer and as a
high-ranking CIA official
in times of enormous
world tension

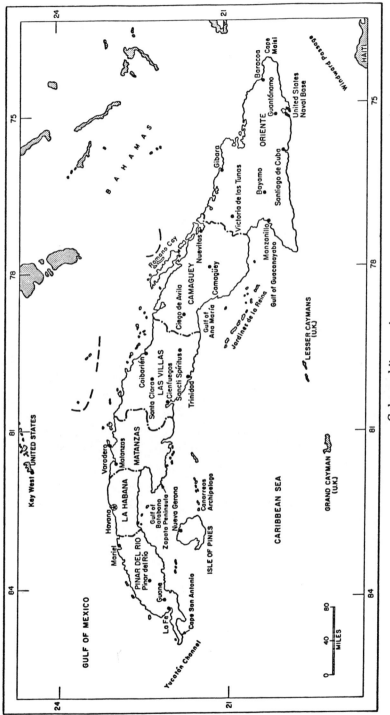

Cuba and its provinces.

Fidel's feelings of hatred for [the United States] cannot even be imagined by Americans. His intention, his obsession, to destroy the [U.S.] is one of his main interests and objectives.

Juanita Castro
(sister of Fidel)
June 11, 1965

Contents

1

Terrorist Plot:
Blow Up New York

A ROSY WINTER SUN was peeking over the Washington Monument and starting its ascent into a clear blue sky on the crisp Saturday morning of November 17, 1962. Lights had been burning all night in the Federal Bureau of Investigation (FBI) headquarters where Alan H. Belmont, assistant to Director J. Edgar Hoover, had been orchestrating a manhunt in New York City to track down a ring of pro–Fidel Castro terrorists before they could blow up or torch several major targets.

Through one or more moles, the FBI had learned that the Cuban group was plotting to explode bombs with timing devices in Macy's, Gimbel's, and Bloomingdale's when these huge department stores were packed with shoppers during the Christmas season. Also on the sabotage target list were several U.S. military installations in the region and oil refineries across the Hudson River in New Jersey.

Since early Friday morning and all through the night, Al Belmont's office had taken on the trappings of a military command post. Using a battery of telephones, he was in contact with the FBI field office in New York and also with the automobiles of special agents who were charging around the city in search of the wanted Cubans.

As is the case in most manhunts, operations were tricky and had to be delicately timed. Belmont's plan was to make the arrests of the three ringleaders simultaneously. Two of them had been located during the night, but Belmont instructed the FBI agents not to pick them up for fear that the third one would learn of his cronies' arrests and go deep undercover or even flee to Cuba.

"Keeping the two Cuban subjects under physical surveillance all night without their knowing they were being watched put an enormous burden on the New York field agents," W. Raymond Wannall, then chief of a section in the Intelligence Division in Washington, would later recall. "They managed to do this with great skill, however."[1]

Wannall had been in Belmont's office during most of the thirty-six hours of the manhunt, providing intelligence information to help locate the terrorist ringleaders. By dawn, both men were haggard and weary. The FBI agents scouring New York were nearly exhausted after twenty-four hours. Mr. Three was still at large.

At 9:00 A.M., John F. Malone, SAC (special agent in charge) of the New York office, telephoned and asked Belmont for a reconsideration of his decision. Mr. Three could not be located, so why not apprehend the two Cuban subjects still under surveillance? Belmont, feeling unspoken pressure from director Hoover, whom he had briefed periodically during the night, stuck to his guns, realizing that if Mr. Three was not found soon, the arrest of the other two subjects might be aborted.

"Those of us in Al's office discussing each problem as it came up supported him completely," Ray Wannall remembered. "But we were happy that we were not the ones making this tough call. If things didn't turn out right, Mr. Hoover would not have been too happy."[2]

An hour later, Belmont received another telephone call from John Malone in New York: Mr. Three had been spotted. Belmont gave the order to arrest all of the ringleaders.

Taken into custody first were the two Cubans the FBI agents had been surveilling all night. They were José Garcia Orelanno, who operated a costume jewelry store, and an employee at his firm, twenty-two-year-old Marino Antonio Estebán Del Carmen Sueiro y Cabrera.

When cornered, Mr. Three, twenty-seven-year-old Roberto Santiestebán Casanova, was belligerent, resisted arrest, and had to be physically subdued by FBI agents. He was carrying a fully loaded Mauser semiautomatic pistol. While being handcuffed, he loudly cursed the FBI men and tried to swallow a piece of paper on which were written notations of formulas for explosives. After arriving at FBI headquarters on Foley Square, Santiestebán kicked a newspaper photographer.* While being questioned by Malone and other FBI men, Santiestebán ranted that he was being illegally detained, claiming that he was an aide to Carlos Lechuga, Fidel Castro's ambassador to the United Nations, and therefore had diplomatic immunity.

Santiestebán had arrived in New York from Havana only six weeks earlier on the same plane with Osvaldo Dorticós Torrado, an

---

*Latins list their father's name (Santiestebán) before their mother's name (Casanova). Hence, Roberto Santiestebán Casanova's "last name" was Santiestebán.

attorney from a wealthy family whom Castro had appointed as a figurehead president of Cuba. Dorticós ostensibly had come to address the United Nations General Assembly. Although the Cuban government had requested diplomatic status for Santiestebán after his arrival, the U.S. Justice Department held that his papers were being processed, and therefore his safeguard from arrest was not yet effective.

As soon as the three Cubans had been collared, FBI agents swooped down on José Garcia's costume jewelry firm, Model-Craft, at 242 West 27th Street, and discovered a large cache of explosives, detonators, grenades, and incendiary devices. Also found were papers explaining how a detonator affixed to an incendiary device and a pushed button would cause an intense flame to erupt in sixty to seventy-five minutes. In a steel safe there were diagrams of areas of ships and railroad freight cars that would be most vulnerable to explosives and incendiary devices.

Hidden in the jewelry store were documents belonging to Santiestebán, who Vincent L. Broderick, U.S. Attorney for the Southern District of New York, declared was "right at the heart of the sabotage conspiracy."[3]

Broderick added, "We are dealing with a man who is a violent revolutionary, charged with exercising aggressive acts."[4]

José Garcia and Marino Sueiro, the other suspected ringleaders, had extensive backgrounds in pro-Castro organizational life in New York City. They both frequented the Casa Cuba Club at 691 Columbus Avenue, identified by the FBI as a hangout for Castro sympathizers. The two men were said to have been active in the *Movimiento del 26 de Julio* (26th of July Movement), the label Fidel Castro had given to his revolution. They also belonged to the Fair Play for Cuba Committee, which a Senate Internal Security Committee had been investigating as a subversive organization.

A few weeks before his arrest by the FBI, Sueiro had sent his pregnant wife back to Cuba because he said he did not want the child to become, by birth, a U.S. citizen. When he was apprehended at Third Avenue and 24th Street, a beautiful, twenty-six-year-old woman with him was taken into custody and held as a material witness. A U.S. citizen, she was described as a schoolteacher and recreation supervisor at the Hudson Guild on West 27th Street, only two blocks from José Garcia's costume jewelry store.[5]

U.S. Attorney Broderick also charged José Gomez Abad, age twenty-one, and his wife, Elisa Monterio de Gomez Abad, twenty years old, with complicity in the terrorist conspiracy. They were suspected of having provided weapons and explosives to the would-be Cuban saboteurs. Because they were attachés in the Cuban delegation at the United Nations, the Gomezes were immune from arrest.

Ten other Cubans connected to the UN were suspected by the FBI of operating a "sabotage school" and were subpoenaed to appear before a federal grand jury in New York City. John Malone asserted that the "school" conducted "informal training in the use of explosives and incendiary devices."[6]

Cuban UN Ambassador Carlos Lechuga was irate over the wave of arrests. He complained bitterly to the media that the FBI agents had been guilty of brutality against Roberto Santiestebán, who had emerged with a black eye after violently resisting arrest.

Santiestebán's attorney, Leonard B. Boudin, charged that the FBI was guilty of a "crime," that his client had diplomatic immunity and therefore had "a right to resist."[7]

Twenty-four hours after the smashing of the terrorist conspiracy was announced in Washington by FBI Director J. Edgar Hoover, an urgent alert went out over the New Jersey State Police radio network. Information had been received that "three or four carloads of Cuban revolutionists" were en route to the huge Esso Bayway oil refinery in Linden and other refineries in New Jersey.[8]

Either the alert was a prank or the quick action of New Jersey law enforcement officers and the FBI headed off sabotage of the refineries. At the same time, military installations in the New York City region stepped up security against rumored sabotage plans by the pro-Castro Cubans.

In Washington, meanwhile, thirty-seven-year-old Attorney General Robert F. Kennedy publicly praised the FBI. He said that Hoover and his men had "acted in continuation of a record that had saved the United States from a widespread Nazi espionage and sabotage network just prior to and during World War II."[9]

In Havana, thirty-six-year-old, bearded Fidel Castro, who had seized control of the Cuban government on January 1, 1959, roundly condemned the arrest of the three Cuban conspirators in New York. He claimed that the arrests were "without foundation" and an "unjustified retaliation" for the arrest in Cuba a week earlier of Miguel Angel Orozco Crespo, whom Castro charged with being operations chief in Cuba for the U.S. Central Intelligence Agency (CIA). Orozco, Castro declared, was plotting to blow up the large Matahambre mines and "murder" four hundred Cuban workers.[10]

THE CUBAN SABOTAGE PLOT was yet another machination in an ongoing vendetta between Fidel Castro and the Kennedy brothers, President John F. Kennedy and Attorney General Robert Kennedy. Supreme headquarters for the United States in the undercover conflict was the CIA complex located in a cluster of World War II Navy buildings off Ohio Drive near the Lincoln Memorial in Washington, D.C. The operations center of the Agency, called Quarters Eye, was housed in a large barracks once home for WAVEs (Women's Navy Auxiliary). It was from Quarters Eye that CIA clandestine missions were coordinated and directed around the world.

Advance headquarters for covert actions aimed at Cuba was the CIA station in Miami code-named JM WAVE. For a decade, it had been small in scope, but in the early 1960s, the station mushroomed into the largest CIA post in the world. Although the funding for JM WAVE was a closely guarded secret, estimates were that its annual budget was about $55 million (equivalent to $550 million in 1997).

JM WAVE was a good-sized city within a city. Its operations center was located in a former U.S. Navy blimp structure on the campus of the University of Miami. The cover name given to the closely guarded, two-story frame building was Zenith Technical Enterprises.

There were more than fifty dummy corporations to conceal CIA activities: real estate firms, a detective agency, charter fishing boats, ocean research vessels, and private yachts, among others. A warehouse stored an amazing array of items for use in clandestine operations, from machine guns and incendiary grenades to walkie-talkies and two-way mirrors.[11]

JM WAVE had a psychiatrist and a polygraph (lie detector) expert to evaluate agents and agent prospects. When medical attention for illnesses or injuries was required, regular civilian clinics were used after doctors and nurses had undergone strict security checks.[12]

At JM WAVE, a group of Spanish-speaking agents wrote instructions in invisible ink and mailed them to undercover operatives inside Cuba. The recipients had previously been told to bring out the writing by placing lemon juice on the paper. Several U.S. military officers were assigned to JM WAVE for specialized tasks, such as training agents in survival techniques and maritime skills.

Most of the four hundred U.S. employees were case officers directly responsible for covert operations. They recruited and controlled perhaps four thousand Cubans, largely recent anti-Castro exiles in southern Florida, as well as many secret agents inside Cuba. A case officer was responsible for seven or eight Cubans (known as PAs, or principal agents). Each PA, in turn, was in charge of between ten and fifteen covert operatives.

JM WAVE had more than one hundred automobiles used by the Americans. Operatives who traveled mostly on the back roads and in the remote regions of southern Florida drove Fords, Chevrolets, and Plymouths, so as not to be conspicuous. Agents in the upper echelons tooled about the Miami area in Pontiacs and Buicks. Theodore "Ted" Shackley, the station chief, drove an Oldsmobile.[13]

One of the most secretive aspects of JM WAVE was the existence of militarylike bases dispersed throughout the Florida Keys: coral island after coral island, with harbors, inlets, and beaches—all facing Cuba. In these secluded camps, relatively free from hostile eyes, a special breed of American agents, under contract to the CIA and known as PM-ers (paramilitary officers), trained Cuban exiles and mounted covert missions against Cuba.

During World War II, General William J. "Wild Bill" Donovan, founder and chief of the Office of Strategic Services (OSS), the predecessor of the CIA, described his PM-ers as "hellraisers who are calculatingly reckless, of disciplined daring, and trained for aggressive action."

Typical of the JM WAVE PM-ers was William "Rip" Robertson, a forty-eight-year-old adventurer who had been a CIA operative behind enemy lines during the Korean War. Six-foot-three, lanky, with a weatherbeaten face, he was a maverick of sorts, disdaining a military appearance. He wore a baseball cap and sloppy clothes. But he was loved by his Cuban exiles, who regarded him as the epitome of the good and the courageous in the United States.[14]

Almost every week for over a year, Cuban teams led by PM-ers departed from the Keys for secret missions in Cuba. "When we didn't go, Rip would feel sick and get very mad," recalled one of his Cuban exile leaders.

Some of these secret operations were to secure intelligence, others took weapons and ammunition to the Cuban underground, but mostly the insurgents were to perpetrate mayhem, much of it intended to crimp Cuba's already fragile economy. Dressed in green fatigues like those worn by Castro's militia, the men carried machine guns with silencers, recoilless rifles, and plastic explosives.

The covert missions were orchestrated with the meticulous planning associated with British commando raids across the English Channel against Nazi-held France prior to Normandy D-Day in World War II. Drawn up by experienced U.S. guerrilla warfare officers assigned to JM WAVE, the operational plans accounted for every minute, from departure in Florida to landing in Cuba to returning to the home base. Most of the intelligence was secured from satellites.

Raiding parties were briefed by CIA case officers on weather forecasts over the Florida Straits and the targeted region of Cuba; they were also shown current aerial views taken by supersecret U-2 reconnaissance airplanes. The U-2s were piloted by U.S. Air Force officers who had been transferred to the CIA payroll, ostensibly as civilians, after an administrative separation procedure known in the espionage trade as "sheep dipping."

The U-2 was a strange bird compared to modern aircraft built for more routine functions. Its stubby fuselage was only 49.5 feet long, its tapering wings stretched 80 feet across. It could fly up to 4,000 miles at altitudes of 14 miles or better on less than 1,000 gallons of fuel. Its vision was better than that of a hawk. Its incredible cameras, aimed through seven portholes in the belly, could photograph a swathe of earth 125 miles wide and 3,000 miles long (a distance equivalent to that between New York and London). The photographs came in 4,000 paired frames, each slightly overlapping the other, resulting in a stereoscopic effect. Photo interpreters from the CIA analyzing the developed and greatly enlarged pictures could make out a newspaper headline 10 miles below.

Because it was loaded with such heavy paraphernalia, the U-2 had no room for a landing gear. So the plane took off from a detachable dolly. On landing back at its base, the wings were shortened by bending down each tip. The pilot then skidded in along the reinforced belly of the plane.

Contingency plans were created for the paramilitary-led ground raiders in case a mission was detected or went awry. If captured, each insurgent had a cover story, weak as it was. Many were furnished phony papers identifying them as employees of a civilian firm (a CIA front) in Florida. If captured, they were to tell Castro's interrogators that they were on a maritime research project and collecting data for that company (which was listed in Florida telephone directories).

Many missions to Cuba were pinpricks, intended to annoy Fidel Castro (which indeed they did) and to keep his regime in a state of semijitters in anticipation of an invasion by U.S. forces. Steadily, however, the infiltration raids grew in scope. The intruders blew up key bridges, set fire to sugarcane fields, and sabotaged Cuban army vehicles. Attacks were made on a huge Texaco refinery (which Castro had stolen from its American owners), a diesel plant at Casilda, a sulfuric acid facility at Santa Lucia, and two Soviet ships unloading materials at a port in far eastern Oriente Province.

Concealing JM WAVE and helping to mask its activities required the cooperation of the FBI, the Justice Department, the Pentagon, the Immigration and Naturalization Service (INS), the State Department, the Coast Guard, and the Treasury at the federal level. Also secretly collaborating were nineteen law enforcement jurisdictions in southern Florida, elements of the media, state political leaders and agencies, and civilian financial institutions.

Most of the JM WAVE agents carried false identification papers and used aliases. Each time one of them obtained a driver's license, a passport, or a bank loan (all legitimate transactions), he illegally used the fake identification and *nom de guerre* (war name), and the institution with whom he was doing business knowingly ignored the violation.

If police officers halted a JM WAVE agent for a minor traffic violation and found a machine gun or explosives in his car, he would be quietly released once his CIA connection was established. Trusted reporters from the *Miami Herald* were given regular access to Ted Shackley and other top JM WAVE officials, who briefed them confidentially on current covert activities. The journalists made certain that they published nothing that might expose CIA operations or endanger lives.[15]

JM WAVE's reach extended around the world. Each CIA station in a foreign country had one or more case officers who focused exclusively on the Cuban situation. In Europe, all intelligence concerning Fidel Castro and his regime was sent to Washington. In Central and South America, each CIA station had specialists to collect information on Castro's extensive efforts to export his Communist revolution to countries there.

THE ROOTS of the often violent vendetta between the Kennedy brothers and Fidel Castro had been planted in Mexico seven years before the Cuban terrorist scheme to blow up New York City. From that time, both Cuba and the United States had created vast espionage and sabotage networks to duel with one another, not only in Latin America but also in other locales around the world.

2

Machinations in Mexico

A CUBANA AIRLINES British-made Britannia glided to a landing at the airport in Mexico City after a 1,000-mile flight from Havana. Among the debarking passengers was twenty-nine-year-old Fidel Castro, a tall, husky, curly-haired man who was coming to Mexico, a historic haven for left-wing dissidents from many countries, to form a trained and disciplined group of guerrillas to "invade" Cuba and overthrow dictator Fulgencio Batista y Zaldivar. It was July 7, 1955.

Twenty-two years earlier in 1933, the swarthy, coarse Batista, then a thirty-one-year-old army sergeant with a fifth-grade education, had led a successful revolt against a corrupt ruler, Gerardo Machado y Morales. Batista promoted himself from sergeant to colonel and emerged as Cuba's newest *caudillo* (strongman). In the years ahead, he made and broke presidents.

Ironically, Castro owed his freedom to Batista, a man he despised. On July 26, 1953, Castro had led a foolhardy attack by a small band of his rebels on an army installation, Moncada Barracks, in Oriente Province in eastern Cuba. The raid to capture arms and ammunition resulted in disaster. Most of the rebels were killed, and the remainder captured, including Fidel and his younger brother, Raúl.

After a short trial in early October, Fidel received a fifteen-year term while Raúl was given a thirteen-year sentence. The prisoners were confined in the national penitentiary on the Isle of Pines off the southern coast of western Cuba. On May 15, 1955, Fulgencio Batista, in the monumental blunder of his life, released Fidel and Raúl in a general amnesty.

Within a week of gaining his freedom, Castro began blasting Batista and other Cuban officials in two Cuban newspapers, *La Calle* and *Bohemia.* Soon word reached Castro that the police in Havana had targeted him for an early demise. According to one account, an automobile had been riddled with bullets—ready for Castro's body to be found within, "killed while fighting police."[1]

SPAWNING UPHEAVALS and engaging in lethal violence was nothing new to Fidel Castro, beginning with his enrollment at the University of Havana at the age of nineteen. Although his wealthy father, Angel, gave him an allowance of the equivalent to U.S.$500 per month (a princely sum for a teenager at the time), Fidel wore shabby trousers and soiled shirts and largely ignored barber shops. His indifference to clean clothing earned him the campus nickname *bola de churre* (dirt ball).

Castro managed to get himself elected president of the University Students Federation, a small but militant clique said to espouse Communist beliefs. Almost at once, he seized on a relatively trivial matter, a slight rise in Havana bus fares, to bring his group into the streets in a noisy protest march.

If Castro's goal was to trigger a confrontation, it succeeded. Police beat the demonstrators, although none were badly injured. Castro emerged unscathed.

Hours later, Castro displayed his sophistication in manipulating public support by wrapping his head in swathes of white gauze and then visiting newspapers and radio stations to disclose the "brutality" of the government.[2]

After Castro announced that the Students Federation would take to the streets again with a much larger number of marchers, Dr. Ramón Grau San Martin, who had defeated Batista's handpicked candidate for president of Cuba in 1944, invited a student delegation to visit the Presidential Palace to discuss bus fares.

At the conference in Grau's fifth-floor office, whose balcony overlooked a plaza, the president was called briefly from the room. Castro, his head still swathed in bandages, whispered to his comrades, "I know how to take power and get rid of that old son of a bitch. When he comes back in the room, let's pitch him off the balcony. When he's dead, we'll proclaim the student revolution and speak to the people on the radio."[3]

The spontaneous plot collapsed. "We came here to discuss lowering bus fares," one horrified student declared, "not to commit murder!"[4]

Later, Castro confided to cronies that his goal was to be elected president of the thirteen-thousand-member student body. In pursuit of that objective, he decided that Leonel Gomez, the highly popular president of the student body at Havana High School Number One, was a threat. Castro reasoned that Gomez was a cinch to enroll at Havana University after graduating.[5]

Castro told his friend Rafael Díaz Balart that Gomez would have to be "eliminated" before he became an "obstacle," and he asked Díaz

Balart to join him in a scheme to murder the high school senior. Aghast, Díaz Balart rejected the request.[6]

Undaunted, Castro enlisted two other young Cubans, and the three men lay in ambush for Gomez outside the Havana University stadium where a soccer game was in progress. When the contest ended and Gomez neared the three men, Castro allegedly fired a pistol shot, striking the high schooler in the lung. Although seriously wounded, Gomez eventually recovered.[7]

Fearing arrest, Castro holed up in the home of General Juan Rodriguez, an exile from the Dominican Republic, who was hatching a plot to sail from Cuba with an armed force and oust Generalissimo Rafael Trujillo, the right-wing dictator who had seized power in the Dominican in 1930.[8]

Castro eagerly accepted an offer to join the general's Caribbean Legion, consisting of some fifteen hundred Cubans, Dominicans, Venezuelans, and Guatemalans. Trained by Communist veterans of the Spanish Civil War, the Legion had $2 million worth of weapons stored at the estate of a conspirator, José Aleman, the Cuban minister of education, who had allegedly dipped into his agency's till for the funds.

The Dominican invasion force would consist of two ships, fourteen warplanes, artillery, bazookas, and hundreds of rifles and machine guns. Aleman's chief agent for the arms buying and smuggling was twenty-five-year-old Manolo Castro (no relation to Fidel), who had been codirector of the dominant political group at Havana University, the Socialist Revolutionary Movement. Police had once accused him of murdering a professor at the university, but he was released for lack of conclusive evidence.

Manolo Castro set up shop in a large luxury hotel in Miami, Florida, bought a large number of arms, and took virtually no precautions to hide his actions. He boasted in bars of his revolutionary activity. Consequently, the *Miami Herald* exposed the invasion scheme.

The U.S. government put heavy heat on President Grau (who reputedly had long known of the scheme). Cuban soldiers surrounded the training camp of the Caribbean Legion and seized most of the guerrillas and eleven planes. Fidel Castro was not among the captives. Eel-like, he had managed to escape.[9]

In the uproar that ensued in Cuba, Minister of Education José Aleman "resigned" but was not charged with stealing the $2 million. He fled to Miami, where he would die years later, reportedly leaving an estate of $10 million.[10]

Less than a year after his Caribbean Legion adventure, Castro, now twenty-one years of age, and a friend, Rafael del Pino, were in Bogotá,

Colombia, where delegates from twenty nations in the Western Hemisphere were attending the Inter-American Conference to discuss mutual problems. Intelligence gained by U.S. secret agents disclosed that Communists planned to ignite bloody riots, force the delegates to flee for their lives, and overthrow the duly elected government of President Ospina Pérez.

Although it was learned that riot leaders planned to murder U.S. Secretary of State George C. Marshall, who would speak at the conclave, this information was not passed along to Washington by the American Embassy staff in Bogotá.[11]

Like a well-oiled military operation, the *Bogotazo* (Bogotá uprising) erupted on April 8, 1948. Mobs armed with weapons, explosives, and Molotov cocktails marauded through the city, firebombing, sacking, looting, and killing.

When the violence was finally brought under control, hundreds were dead or wounded. Once beautiful Bogotá resembled the war-torn big cities of Europe.

That situation delighted Joseph Starobin, a reporter for New York's Communist *Daily Worker*, who exulted in print: "Interruption of the Foreign Ministers' parley is a sock in the jaw to the big business men of the [U.S.] State Department. The world has suddenly seen America's feet of clay."[12]

A few days after the bloody rioting, two Colombian detectives went to the Claridge Hotel to interrogate Fidel Castro and Rafael del Pino, who had been staying at the facility for two weeks. But before the students could be arrested for having been among the instigators of the armed uprising, they had taken refuge in the Cuban Legation, where arrangements had been made to fly them back to Cuba.

Between revolutionary escapades, Fidel Castro found time to pay serious court to Mirta Díaz Balart, a beautiful blonde from one of Cuba's wealthiest families, who was studying philosophy at the University of Havana. She was the sister of Fidel's good friend Rafael Díaz Balart. It was a quite proper courtship: Mirta was always chaperoned when with Fidel.

Soft-spoken, slightly built, with flashing black eyes, Mirta fell deeply in love with the charismatic Fidel. On October 10, 1948, they were married in a lavish ceremony in a Roman Catholic Church in the city of Banes, where her father was the mayor. Mindful that he had generated many enemies and that one or more might try to kill him as he stood at the altar, Fidel had a loaded pistol in his pocket.

As had been the case throughout Castro's life, someone else had to pay his bills. Rafael Díaz Balart Sr., Mirta's father, gave Castro $10,000 (the equivalent of $100,000 in 1997) for a three-month honeymoon in Miami and New York City.

On September 14, 1949, Mirta bore a child who was christened Felix Fidel Castro Díaz—called "Fidelito" by his parents. After receiving a law degree in 1950, Castro plunged even deeper into revolutionary activities. In the city of Cienfuegos, he was arrested and jailed on charges of inciting high school students to launch protest strikes.

CASTRO HAD NEVER had to concern himself with money because it was always provided by his doting father. So on reaching Mexico City in mid-1955, he was shocked to learn that financing a revolution in Cuba would be far more costly than he had anticipated. Weapons and ammunition were very expensive and would have to be bought on the black market. Moreover, because Castro had come to Mexico on a six-month tourist pass, he would have to bribe officials in the Interior Ministry to prevent his deportation after his visa expired.

Writing to a member of the 26th of July Movement in Cuba, Castro complained bitterly: "We don't have one centavo. We have spent everything for stamps, printing, etc. To finance the [revolutionary] campaign through the pittances sent or brought from Cuba has proved impossible."[13]

In countless pitches for money, Castro had boasted that his revolutionary movement did not have a single millionaire or "country-club type." Rather, its strength was in the common man and woman. "It's a matter of morals and principle," he declared. Now he cast aside these lofty traits in favor of ready cash and assumed the role of beggar of wealthy Cuban exiles.

Castro met secretly with Justo Carrillo, a former president of the Development Bank in Havana, in a small town near the Guatemalan border. Carrillo said that a successful revolution in Cuba would have to have the army behind it, and he disclosed that he was conspiring with a group of young, left-wing Cuban officers headed by Colonel Ramón Barquín, the military attaché in Washington.

Barquín and his army conspirators had middle-class backgrounds, were educated at the University of Havana, and trained at military academies in the United States. They resented that Batista's generals, most of whom were largely uneducated and had been elevated from sergeant, were getting rich off the people through bribes and "taxes."

Carrillo said that the young officers had gained many secret allies among wealthy Cuban exiles and that the conspirators planned to surprise Batista, arrest and deport him, then call for general elections.

Carrillo offered Castro the equivalent of U.S.$5,000 to help in the government consolidation after the army officers' successful revolution. Castro could be appointed mayor of Havana, the older man suggested. Castro readily agreed to the offer and made off with the cash under false pretenses; he had no intention of sharing power with anyone in his homeland.

On April 26, 1956, a spokesman for Fulgencio Batista announced that a clique of army officers, led by Ramón Barquín, had been arrested and charged with conspiring to overthrow the government. Eight days later, a trial was held; the verdict was a foregone conclusion. Barquín and two other ringleaders received eight-year sentences, and the other defendants were given four-year terms.

Two weeks later in Mexico, when Justo Carrillo held another clandestine meeting with Fidel Castro, he had changed his tune. Now Castro's revolutionary movement would have to spearhead any effort to eliminate Batista. Consequently, he gave Castro another substantial cash "investment" and provided him with a list of other potential rich contributors who, for a variety of reasons, opposed Batista.

Castro followed Carrillo's advice. From these affluent sources, Castro's empty "treasury" soon contained the equivalent of U.S.$30,000.

Now Castro was ready to organize a force to invade Cuba. From Miami, he imported a Cuban exile, Miguel Sánchez, to be an instructor in guerrilla warfare. Sánchez was known as El Coreano because, though a Cuban, he had fought in the U.S. Army in the Korean War. Also recruited as a military instructor was sixty-four-year-old Alberto Bayo, a Cuban living in Mexico who had been a colonel in the Soviet-backed Republican air force fighting against Generalissimo Francisco Franco's rebel army in the bloody Spanish Civil War in the late 1930s. Something of a soldier of fortune, Bayo also had led guerrilla units in the Moroccan wars.

El Coreano, Bayo, and a Cuban named José Smith began conducting martial arts and guerrilla warfare tactics in private homes and at a firing range in Santa Fe, a suburb of Mexico City. When Castro learned that Mexican police, probably in collaboration with Fulgencio Batista's security officers, were surveilling operations, he shifted training activities to *Santa Rosa*, a large ranch in a remote region 20 miles south of Mexico City. Castro had obtained use of the property by conniving the owner into believing that he was going to purchase the place.[14]

3

A Blueprint for Gaining the White House

O N JUNE 23, 1956, *Excélsior*, Mexico City's largest newspaper, carried a headline on page one:

SEVEN CUBAN COMMUNISTS ARRESTED
HERE FOR CONSPIRING AGAINST BATISTA

One of those jailed was identified as Fidel Castro, who was said to be the ringleader of the plot. Castro, it developed, had become careless in his movements and unaware that he was being tailed by Mexican police. One night, the lawmen followed him to a "safe house," where they arrested him and six others, uncovered a cache of weapons, and found a map of the secret training base, *Santa Rosa*. A day later, forty-one of Castro's cohorts were taken into custody at the ranch.

Far from being spiritually crushed by the adverse development, Castro recognized the situation as a means for gaining widespread publicity for himself and his cause. From his jail cell, he told reporters that he was not a Communist and that he and his men had been kidnapped and some had been tortured. He complained that those taken into custody had been held for nearly three weeks with no charges brought against them. Moreover, Castro charged that the arrests had been a devious plot instigated by the U.S. government, the first of many such accusations he would bring against Washington.[1]

As the wily Castro had hoped, the media stories about the "kidnapping" and the Cuban conspirators being held with no charges brought against them triggered an outcry from sympathetic Mexicans. Anxious to be rid of the mess, Mexican officials, probably influenced by bribes, released Castro and the others. One condition was attached: Castro was to leave Mexico within two weeks and inform the Interior Ministry of the date and place of his departure.

15

Castro agreed to the terms, but he had no intention of leaving the country until an invasion force was ready to sail for Cuba. Bribes and other expenses had again depleted Castro's treasury, so Cuban friends arranged for him to meet with Carlos Prío Socarrás, who had been president of Cuba from 1948 to 1952 and now was an exile in the United States after clashing with Batista.

Prío, a confederate explained, "hates Batista like the devil hates holy water." When Prío fled to Florida to avoid arrest in 1952, he allegedly took with him many millions of dollars looted from the Cuban people while he had been president.

Consequently, in September 1956, Fidel Castro slipped the tail put on him by the Mexican police, made his way northward, swam across the Rio Grande at night, and met with Prío in a shabby motel in McAllen, Texas. Prío was impressed with Castro and agreed to contribute $100,000 (equivalent to $750,000 in 1997) to the 26th of July Movement.

Castro's cause now prospered. More cash donations arrived from Venezuela, Cuba, Mexico, and other Latin American countries, as well as the United States. Now he had money not only to buy weapons but also to bribe the Mexican police to keep away.

With former President Prío's money bulging in his pockets, Castro purchased a 58-foot yacht, the *Granma*, from an American couple named Ericson. Its cost was $15,000. Into this relatively small craft, Castro planned to shoehorn some one hundred persons when he was ready to sail for Cuba.

In Cuba, meanwhile, Fulgencio Batista, through bribes and his own spies and informers, knew everything that was going on in Mexico. However, the Cuban *caudillo* was hardly worried about any threat from the ragtag band of revolutionaries. According to a reliable source, Batista had rejected both an offer to murder Castro and to blow up the *Granma*.

WHILE FIDEL CASTRO was preparing to seize power in Cuba with bullets, far to the north a young senator named John F. Kennedy was laying plans to gain power with ballots. Neither of the two bright, ambitious, and energetic men had any way of knowing that they had embarked on a collision course that one day would take a fearful world to the brink of nuclear destruction.

As time for the Democratic National Convention approached in mid-1956, Jack Kennedy, for one of the few times in his thirty-nine years, was disobeying the wishes of his demanding, strong-willed father, Joseph P. Kennedy Sr. After serving in the U.S. House of Representatives for six years and in the Senate for three years, the younger Kennedy had aspirations for the vice presidential nomination.

Although the sixty-eight-year-old father had never held elected public office, he was an astute politician, convinced that the Democratic standard-bearers were going to be crushed at the polls by the popular Dwight D. Eisenhower, who would be seeking his second term in the White House in the fall.

Never had the United States had a Catholic President or vice president. So Kennedy Senior feared that if Jack gained the number-two spot on the ticket and the Democrats were thumped in November, Jack would be blamed for the debacle.

Kennedy Senior and his wife, Rose, had nine children, four of whom were sons: Jack, Joe Jr., Bobby, and Teddy. For many years, the father's obsession was to have a son become the first president who was a Catholic. His oldest son, Joe Jr., had been designated for that role. But on August 12, 1944, Navy Lieutenant Joseph Kennedy Jr. was piloting an experimental bomber on a mission to wipe out a German buzz-bomb site on the English Channel coast of France when the plane exploded in midair. No remains of those on board were ever recovered.[2]

A few months later, Jack Kennedy returned home from service as a PT-boat skipper in the Pacific, and his father promptly gave him his postwar marching orders: He was to take his older brother's place and get involved in politics. At first, Jack resisted. However, as he later told syndicated columnist Bob Considine: "It was like being drafted. My father wanted his eldest son in politics. 'Wanted' isn't quite the right word. He demanded it. You know my father!"

When thousands of the Democratic faithful descended on Chicago in mid-1956 for the nominating convention, delegates knew that Jack Kennedy had his eye on being the running mate of Adlai Stevenson, who was regarded as a cinch to try his luck once more against Eisenhower, the man who had steamrollered him in the 1952 election. Old-line politicians, including former President Harry S. Truman and king-maker James Farley, warned Stevenson not to select Kennedy, who, in their view, was "too young, too inexperienced, and too Catholic."

Hoping to avoid a bitter squabble over a vice presidential nominee, Adlai Stevenson, instead of selecting his running mate as traditionally had been the procedure, decided to let the convention delegates make the choice. Consequently, after contentious maneuvering by the camps of the hopefuls, Senator Estes Kefauver of Tennessee edged out Kennedy for the nomination.

Stevenson, with an eye to attracting younger voters, asked Kennedy, seventeen years his junior, to make the Stevenson nominating speech. Kennedy accepted. The Illinoisan won on the first ballot. Overnight, the television exposure catapulted Kennedy into national prominence and gave a gargantuan boost to his future political aspirations.

AFTER THE CHICAGO CONVENTION, Kennedy flew to southern France where his father was vacationing at the family villa. There the two men conducted a postmortem of the Democratic conclave and explored in depth Jack's political future. They finally decided that Jack would set his sights on being elected president in 1960, after Eisenhower had completed his two terms.

A blueprint for gaining the White House was drawn up. It called for Jack to win reelection to the Senate in 1958 by such a whopping margin that the wheelers and dealers in the Democratic party, the media, and indeed the entire nation would take notice and regard him as a serious candidate for the presidential nomination.

As most people in Massachusetts had long been aware, Joseph Patrick Kennedy Sr. was the son of an East Boston, Massachusetts, saloon-keeper and ward-heeler politician. After graduating from Harvard in 1912, Joe plunged into the business world with exceptional vigor. When only twenty-four years of age, he gained control of the Columbia Trust Company, a bank in East Boston.

In the years ahead, the saloon-keeper's son accumulated a fabulous fortune. He gambled heavily in the stock market, went to Hollywood to produce grade-B movies, used his high-level political connections to secure the franchise for a lucrative Scotch importing business, and bought and sold real estate. In his business dealings, he was shrewd, ruthless, and unscrupulous. "All successful businessmen are sons of bitches," he often explained.[3]

Joe Kennedy's wife, Rose, a gentle, gracious, devout woman and daily communicant, was the daughter of a fabled Boston politician, John F. "Honey Fitz" Fitzgerald, who was once mayor of Boston and later served in the U.S. House of Representatives. Rose devoted much time to her nine children, each of whom was sent away to an exclusive private school at an appropriate age.

Although away from home much of the time tending to his myriad of business interests around the country and abroad, Kennedy Senior took an intense interest in his five daughters and four sons, setting up $1 million trust funds for each when he or she reached the age of twenty-one. The father encouraged his offspring to excel, planned their educations, and closely monitored their romances, of which there would be no shortage among the sons.

Since Jack Kennedy's first run for the U.S. House of Representatives in 1946, the entire Kennedy clan had worked as a team to get him elected. Campaign manager for Jack's 1952 senatorial campaign in which he defeated Henry Cabot Lodge Jr., a member of a prominent pioneer family long active in state and national politics, had been younger brother Bobby. Tough and ruthless despite his tender years, Bobby would serve in the same capacity in the 1958 campaign.

Bobby had proven to be efficient and effective, not caring upon whose toes he trampled to get the job done. Kennedy Senior was proud of his performance. "Bobby's my boy," he told a friend. "When Bobby hates you, you stay hated!"[4]

While Jack was making innumerable speeches and shaking hands at every crossroads and city across Massachusetts during his campaigns, Mother Rose presided over countless teas that attracted as many as two thousand women to each one. Eunice, the most pugnacious of the sisters, worked long hours almost daily at campaign headquarters.

Kennedy Senior said of Eunice: "If that girl had been born with balls, she'd have been a hell of a politician!"

Patricia and the other sisters appeared at numerous house parties given for the candidate, passed out campaign literature, and made thousands of telephone calls soliciting support.

Jack Kennedy was a highly energetic and charismatic campaigner. His vitality, boyish good looks, and keen sense of humor made an enormous impact, especially on young women. During his run for the Senate in 1952, a worker in his opponent's camp had complained: "What is there about Kennedy that makes every girl between eighteen and twenty-eight think it's a holy crusade to get him elected?"[5]

Kennedy Senior would pour megabucks into Jack's drive for the White House as he had in the past. Moreover, he would continue to play hardball. "They don't pay off for second place," he often declared.

AFTER JOE KENNEDY SR. and Jack had finalized their blueprint for winning the presidency in 1960, the senator flew from France back to Boston and began organizing his 1958 campaign for reelection. As Jack's campaign was beginning to steamroll, in Mexico a series of seemingly fatal setbacks were plaguing Fidel Castro's covert revolutionary movement.

4

A Hoax in the Mountains

TERESA CASUSO, a vivacious Cuban woman who had lived in Mexico City for more than a decade after her husband had been killed fighting in the Spanish Civil War against Generalissimo Franco's Nationalists, met Fidel Castro by chance in July 1956. Like many women before and later, Casuso, who admitted to being "fortyish," experienced an immediate sense of attraction, a feeling that the thirty-year-old Cuban needed someone to watch over him, to tend to all his needs.

Casuso gave Castro her card and, like polite people everywhere, assured him that her house was his house. She never expected to see him again, but within days, he began taking over her home, monopolizing her life. From time to time at night, he brought weapons, cartridges, and equipment, hiding them in closets and other places.

Castro spent many hours alone in the upstairs room of Casuso's residence, examining and reexamining his guns. Often he took his favorite weapon, a rifle with a telescopic sight, and aimed it at the television antenna of the house across the street.[1]

On November 21, 1956, Mexican police, who had been surveilling Casuso for weeks, swooped down on her house and arrested her and two Cuban rebels who happened to be present. The law officers also hauled off the large cache of weapons, 13,000 cartridges, and much equipment that Castro had stashed there.

A few hours later, Castro was advised of the police raid by a friendly Mexican official (meaning one whom Castro was bribing). The Mexican also tipped off Castro that the police knew all about him and his force of guerrillas, and that the Cubans had but seventy-two hours to get out of Mexico.

That night, Castro made the rounds of the safe houses in which his men were living and instructed them to steal out of the city and assemble at a specified point near Veracruz, on the eastern coast of Mexico. Most of them traveled alone and in pairs to the assembly area in dilapidated commercial buses. None was aware that the *Granma* was anchored at a dock in Tuxpan, north of Veracruz.

Castro sent coded messages to alert his underground leaders in Havana. Then, soon after darkness fell on November 24, his automobile began tooling eastward on the main highway to the coast. Suddenly, several dim figures, waving flashlights, leaped into the road, and the car screeched to a halt. These were Immigration Department agents, and Castro had anticipated such a move. After a hefty chunk of cash changed hands, the Cuban continued on to Tuxpan.

Castro didn't realize that two Mexican secret service agents had been tailing his car. Within hours, Fulgencio Batista, at the Presidential Palace in Havana, was advised that the man he had pardoned from the Isle of Pines prison and his guerrilla force were about to sail for Cuba to try to overthrow the government.[2]

At 1:30 A.M. on November 25, the *Granma*, crammed with some ninety persons (the yacht had been built to accommodate twelve), hoisted anchor and headed into the Gulf of Mexico for the thousand-mile trek to Cuba. Six days later, the *Granma*, with seasick, hungry, and thirsty men sprawled about the deck, neared the south coast of Oriente Province. Suddenly, a helicopter swept low over the yacht, then banked and headed for land. Batista's navy and air force had been patrolling in search of the insurgents.

Castro had planned to go ashore at night, but now he decided to land immediately. Climbing over the side of the *Granma*, the rebels began wading ashore, often with water up to their necks. Machine guns, radios, and most equipment had to be left on board.

Reaching shore, the invaders soon ran into a Cuban army ambush. Most of the guerrilla force was killed or captured; the survivors scattered. Only Castro and eleven of his men were able to flee into the nearby Sierra Maestra, a towering wilderness of snarled liana vines, sheer cliffs, and pockets of thick, orange mud. In Cuban mythology, these twelve rebels came to be known as The Apostles.

Others who reached the Sierra Maestra with Fidel Castro were his younger brother, Raúl Castro; a fiery Argentine physician turned Communist revolutionary, Ernesto "Ché" Guevara; a Havana rebel, Faustino Pérez; and a onetime New York dishwasher, Camilo Cienfuegos, all of whom were destined to become future leaders of Cuba.

In the Presidential Palace in Havana, some 450 miles to the west, Fulgencio Batista was unconcerned about the unkempt little band of "outlaws" holed up in the mountains. He put a $100,000 dead-or-alive price tag on Fidel Castro's head.

Batista was convinced that Castro and his men would wither on the vine in their towering refuge, and wither they nearly did. They existed largely on mangos and plantains, and waited . . . and waited some more. The rebels grew beards and shoulder-length hair, partly because of a lack of razor blades, but mainly because the image-conscious Castro wanted to create a trademark for his 26th of July Movement.

ELSEWHERE IN CUBA, Christmas 1956 was greeted routinely. Havana newspaper advertisements hawked presents from El Encanto, the large department store. Rancho Luna, a favorite dining spot for sophisticated citizens, told newspaper readers that 324,000 chickens had been eaten there during the past three years. The *Havana Post* alluded briefly to "revolutionaries in Oriente," whom Batista's army was "hoping to dominate with a minimum loss of life."

At the same time, one of The Apostles, Faustino Pérez, left the Sierra Maestra and made his way past army checkpoints to Havana to contact members of the tiny 26th of July Movement urban underground. Pérez, the son of a Protestant lower-middle-class couple, was to coordinate plans for violent attacks on the "establishment." On New Year's Eve, bombs were placed in several public places in Havana, including the posh Tropicabana nightclub. One blast blew off the arm of a seventeen-year-old girl, injured the daughter of an ex–police chief, and caused extensive damage.

UNDER BATISTA, Havana had earned a reputation as the Western Hemisphere's capital of lust and depravity, a designation that lured rich Americans to flock into the Pearl of the Antilles, as Cuba long had been called. Ribald stage shows of nearly naked women played to full houses. There were some twelve thousand prostitutes, plus an equal number of pimps, doing business in Havana alone. The Mambo Club, opulent and graced by chic, exquisitely groomed young women, catered to the American trade. Cheaper brothels along Virtue Street attracted Cubans.

Gambling in Cuba had become a blue-chip industry. Big-time mobsters from the United States had cut deals with Batista to operate ornate casinos in return for $1.3 million monthly payoffs to the Cuban strongman and his cronies. Diminutive Meyer Lansky was in charge of the glittering casino at the seafront Riviera Hotel. His brother Jake was head man at the International casino. Santo "Sam" Trafficante had control of the gaming rooms at the elegant San Souci, Seville-Biltmore, and Deauville hotels. Nicholas Di Constanzo and Charles "The Blade" Tourine handled matters at the Captril, where Hollywood star George Raft was paid big bucks to greet the wealthy guests at the door.

Government corruption under Batista, although conforming to a half-century of common practice in Cuba, reached new creative heights. It ranged all the way from army sergeants stealing chickens from shirtless peasants to the dictator himself, who shared with his cronies a hefty 30 percent kickback on public works contracts.

Havana merchants who wanted to attract customers by having a bus-stop sign out front could easily obtain one—for a $4,000 under-the-table payoff to traffic officials. Batista's potbellied army chief of staff, General Francisco "Pancho" Tabernilla, pocketed a "fee" for each bottle of Scotch imported into Cuba. Cynical citizens referred to the Scotch as "Old Tabernilla."

Each army regimental commander in the provinces was required to send Batista the equivalent of $15,000 a month from "voluntary contributions" made by various business interests.

Everyone in Batista's government received small paychecks, but the real "salaries" were paid monthly in cash, distributed in plain brown envelopes. Special favors were rewarded by bonuses, also in cash. A bodyguard at the Presidential Palace received $2,500 in cash at Christmastime, but most of the faithful had to settle for considerably less, depending on their work on behalf of Batista.

IN EARLY 1957, Fidel Castro's "army" numbered about eighteen rebels. They apparently had a total of twenty-three weapons—five semiautomatic rifles, four rifles with hand-operated bolts, two Tommy guns, two machine pistols, an air gun, and nine rifles with telescopic sights.

Despondency set in among the guerrillas: They were demanding to go into the towns for some "recreation." Castro cracked the whip, announcing that those guilty of insubordination, desertion, or defeatism would be summarily executed.

Perhaps Fidel Castro himself was being nagged by serious doubts. No one in Cuba or elsewhere, it seemed, was paying any attention to him. In fact, the *Havana Post* had quoted an army colonel as saying that the rebel leader was dead. The only salvation for the 26th of July Movement, Castro apparently believed, was to gain widespread publicity in the media of the United States. Consequently, he sent one of his most trusted rebels, René Rodríguez, to Havana to try to coerce a U.S. journalist to travel to the Sierra Maestra for an interview.

In Havana, Rodríguez called on Felipe Pazos, Cuba's leading economist who had been a governor of the National Bank under President Prío. Pazos's son had been active in an underground network bent on ousting Batista since 1955, and the offspring apparently had talked his father into joining the conspiracy.

Felipe Pazos went to the Havana bureau of *The New York Times* and talked with Ruby Hart Phillips, who had been covering Cuban political events since 1933. She was sympathetic and arranged for Herbert Matthews, a fifty-seven-year-old senior editor at the *Times*, to come from New York to see Castro. Matthews brought his wife to Cuba, presumably as a cover, and left her at the home of two schoolteachers who were supporters of Castro.[3]

On February 15, 1957, the *Times* editor began climbing into the mountain range, and two hours later he reached the designated place for his rendezvous with Fidel Castro. Had Castro not been a born revolutionary, he could have amassed a fortune as a public-relations genius on New York's Madison Avenue. The deception scenario he had created for Matthews's visit was a masterpiece.

Prior to his arrival, Castro had his men make the jungle clearing look like a busy command post, although it was being manned by only two or three guerrillas. Castro was not at the meeting place. A bearded guerrilla explained apologetically that his leader was conducting an important conference with his "general staff." Matthews was impressed.

Suddenly, from out of the mist, the Christlike figure of Fidel Castro emerged. Matthews was even more impressed. Later, he would write exuberantly: "Here was quite a man. A powerful six-footer, olive-skinned, full-faced. The personality of the man is overpowering."

For many hours, shrouded by the thick forest, the experienced journalist from the most influential newspaper in the world and the young revolutionary, who commanded an "army" of eighteen men, sat and talked. Matthews was totally taken in by the shrewd Castro and came to believe that a large force of heavily armed rebels was hovering close by in the jungle or out fighting Batista's troops.

While the two men were talking, a keenly orchestrated skit was taking place. In twos and threes, guerrillas traipsed through the clearing, then disappeared into the foliage. Then they changed into different clothing, came back, and marched past Matthews time after time. As intended, the journalist gained the opinion that Castro had hundreds, perhaps thousands, of guerrillas.

Now came the pièce de résistance. Raúl Castro entered the jungle clearing supporting a seemingly exhausted rebel. They came to where Matthews and Castro were sitting. Raúl saluted his leader smartly and said, "Commandante, the liaison from Column Number Two has arrived."

Fidel seemed annoyed. "Wait until I'm finished with Mr. Matthews!" he snapped.

Matthews seemed to have been smitten by Castro's charm and his views on "democracy and freedom for the Cuban people." After his return to New York, the reporter wrote a series of three articles that appeared on page one of the *Times*. Although the rebel leader and his handful of followers largely had been in hiding, the first of Matthews's articles said Castro had been fighting Batista forces for seventy-nine days and was steadily gaining in strength. He quoted Castro as telling him: "Batista has three thousand men in the [Sierra Maestra] against us. I will not tell you how many we have for obvious reasons. He works in columns of two hundred, we in groups of ten to forty—and we are winning!"

Matthews added: "It was easy to see that his men adored him and also to see why he has caught the imagination of the youth of Cuba all over the island."[4]

In the second article a day later, Matthews wrote: "There is no Communism to speak of in Fidel Castro's 26th of July Movement. . . ."[5]

Matthews's pieces had tremendous impact, not only in Cuba and the United States but around the world. Suddenly, media reporters "discovered" the Fidel Castro–led revolt, and they began descending upon the narrow island in droves. Many of the reporters entered the country incognito to avoid being detained or deported by Batista's secret police force. To get past army checkpoints in their safaris to the Sierra Maestra, newsmen posed as engineers and sugar planters. Castro's couriers, some of them women, escorted the reporters to his hideout, where each was rewarded for his arduous climb with "exclusive" interviews.

Castro was fully conscious of his image. Astigmatic from birth, Castro was seldom caught by outsiders with his spectacles on. ("A leader does not wear glasses," he often told cronies.) His straggly, flowing black beard not only served as a revolution trademark, but it neatly concealed the rebel chief's double chin.

CBS-TV, the foremost network in the United States at the time, sent a film crew, and Castro dispatched his men to tote the nearly three hundred pounds of cameras and sound equipment to the mountain peak where he was ensconced that day. Marcelo Fernández, who had been president of the Engineering School at the University of Havana, trudged up the heights with the two CBS correspondents, Wendell Hoffman and Robert Taber, serving as an interpreter.

During the two days of interviews, Castro impressed upon the reporters that he was fighting for democratic ideals and, therefore,

Batista would "have to go." Shown to a huge audience in May, the CBS piece was titled "The Story of Cuba's Jungle Fighters."

At about the same time, Charles Shaw, news director of WCAU-TV in Philadelphia, sneaked into the Sierra Maestra to pay a visit to Raúl Castro at his headquarters. After returning home, Shaw suggested over the air that the 26th of July Movement might be "essentially a Protestant effort to seize power in a predominately Catholic country."[6]

Another television personality, Ed Sullivan, whose highly popular weekly variety show featured such acts as dancing bears, ventriloquists, and magicians, decided to join the pilgrimage to Fidel Castro's domain. Not renowned for his interviewing skills, Sullivan phrased his questions in a negative slant to elicit the replies he desired. "You are not a Communist, are you, Fidel?" Of course not, Castro replied, stroking his beard. "You are a devout Catholic, are you not, Fidel?" Of course, of course.

United States newspapers, magazines, radio, and television scrambled mightily to outdo one another in heaping adulation upon the Cuban rebel chief. Misty-eyed editorial writers labeled Castro the Robin Hood of the Caribbean and equated him with Abraham Lincoln and George Washington. Almost overnight, the obscure revolutionary was transformed into an international celebrity, one seeming to possess Christlike qualities of omnipotence, compassion, and boundless wisdom.

As a result of this avalanche of media adoration, the ranks of the *barbudos* (bearded ones) grew steadily. So did Castro's bankroll; his "secret weapon" would be money. Some $25,000 each month was pouring in from anti-Batista exiles in Florida. Cuban sugar planters and industrialists operating in rebel-dominated eastern Cuba contributed handsomely via "taxes" levied on them by Castro. The rebel chief also targeted large U.S. corporations on the island, most of which kicked in healthy "voluntary contributions."

A good-sized cash flow from the Soviet Union reached Castro in his mountainous base. These funds were channeled through secret groups in several Latin American countries, including Venezuela, Chile, Costa Rica, and Argentina.[7]

Weapons for his growing rebel army ceased to be a problem for Castro. A twin-engine Beechcraft, loaded with Tommy guns, rifles, and grenades, flew in from Costa Rica, dispatched by that country's leftist strongman, José "Pepe" Figueres. Although guns were costing Castro $1,000 each, his sympathizers in the United States were buying them in large numbers from global arms dealers. By early 1958, airplanes from two Florida cities, Ocala and Lakeland, were regularly bringing Castro weapons and ammunition.

IN A RELATIVELY SHORT period of time, Fidel Castro's political fortunes in Cuba, like those of Jack Kennedy's in the United States, were surging ahead rapidly.

5

Pulling Uncle Sam's Whiskers

I N THIS HONEYMOON PERIOD, it was not just the media that was charmed by Fidel Castro, but also much of Washington. So when Arthur Gardner, the astute and experienced ambassador to Cuba, sent repeated warnings that the rebel leader was pro-Communist, R. Richard "Roy" Rubottom, assistant secretary of state for Latin America, chose to disregard the flashing red lights.

In testimony before the Subcommittee for Inter-American Affairs of the Senate Foreign Relations Committee, Rubottom said, "There is no evidence of any organized Communist element within the Castro movement or that Señor Castro himself is under Communist influence."[1]

In Cuba at the same time, Arthur Gardner suggested to Fulgencio Batista that the FBI or the CIA should be asked to send an operative into the Sierra Maestra to murder Fidel Castro. Curiously, perhaps, Batista replied: "No, no, we couldn't do that! We're all Cubans!"[2]

Meanwhile, State Department leaders had grown weary of Ambassador Gardner's incessant harping about Castro's Communist connections, and the veteran diplomat was bounced from the post. His successor was Earl E. T. Smith, whose gray hair and six-foot-three frame made him look like Hollywood's version of the role.

A descendant of one of Massachusetts's pioneer first families, a boxing champion at Yale, and a wealthy, highly successful stockbroker, Smith glided gracefully through society life in New York and Palm Beach. He was a staunch Republican conservative, a heavy contributor to the presidential campaigns of Dwight Eisenhower, and a gifted infighter if an occasion so demanded.

Arthur Gardner's recall was a curious one. Even though he was probably the foremost U.S. authority on what had been and was transpiring inside Cuba in recent years, he was not invited to the State Department for "debriefing," a radical departure from precedent. The inference was clear: No one in State wanted to hear his views. Nor was Gardner asked to pass along his expert knowledge to his successor, Earl Smith.[3]

ON JUNE 26, 1958, Raúl Castro, at the head of two hundred rebels, came down from the Sierra Cristal area to Moa Bay on the northern coast of Oriente Province. They kidnapped ten U.S. and two Canadian citizens who were working there, including the head of the mineral engineering department at the University of Minnesota.

A day later, 40 miles to the south, Raúl's men abducted Desmond Elsmore, field superintendent of the Ermita sugar mill, and Richard Sargent, Canadian manager of the Isabel sugar mill. Other rebels seized six executives of United Fruit Company, a U.S. corporation, and two officials of Nicaro.

WHILE WASHINGTON was scratching its collective head in indecision about Cuba, Fidel Castro, perhaps intoxicated by the media adulation, the large sums of money pouring into his coffers, and the many recruits now flocking to his banner, decided to pull Uncle Sam's whiskers. His focus was on the mighty U.S. Naval Base at Guantanamo Bay in far eastern Cuba. Since 1903, the United States had leased the 45 square miles from the government of Cuba; a treaty signed that year gave the United States "complete jurisdiction and control" until the end of time. To Castro, the base was a symbol of Yankee oppression.

For decades, U.S. naval personnel on the base, which was divided from Cuba proper by a 26-mile-long, 10-foot-high chain-link fence, traveled to nearby towns on passes for evenings of relaxation. In July, a band of Raúl Castro's rebels, armed to the teeth, leaped into the road and halted a civilian bus carrying thirty U.S. Marines and sailors on pass. All of the Americans were wearing civilian clothes. None was armed. At gunpoint, the captives were ordered off the bus.

It had been a finely tuned scenario. That same day, a letter reached Ambassador Earl Smith from Raúl Castro in which he laid down conditions for the release of the kidnapped U.S. servicemen. Washington must cease sending all weapons and other military equipment to Batista, Raúl decreed. Moreover, the United States must cease supplying Batista's air force with fuel from the Guantanamo naval base. Finally, Washington must secure a firm pledge from Batista that he would not use military weapons already supplied by the United States against the Castro rebels.[4]

This flagrant violation of international law triggered an uproar in Washington. Secretary of State John Foster Dulles told a news conference that the United States could not be blackmailed. Senators William Knowland and Styles Bridges demanded that Castro release the captives "within forty-eight hours" or "effective help will be given to Batista."

Ambassador Smith and the Navy brass in Washington were in favor of sending in a division of Marines—immediately. However, the State Department argued that an armed intervention might cost the lives of the kidnap victims and urged a diplomatic settlement to the minicrisis.[5]

Few in Washington or in Havana realized it at the time, but the kidnapping episode was the beginning of a United States–Castro vendetta that would accelerate greatly when Jack Kennedy became president.

PARK WOLLAM, the U.S. consul in Santiago de Cuba, a city of 200,000 people 70 miles west of the Guantanamo base, under orders from Washington, flew by helicopter to the Sierra Cristal to negotiate with Raúl Castro for the Americans' release. Fidel's younger brother explained that the Marines and sailors were kidnapped because the United States was continuing to help Batista to stay in power. It was a classic case of blackmail—and Uncle Sam caved in.

The State Department's reaction to the Castro brothers' violation of international law was a pledge to cease supplying Batista with the training planes that had been promised him and for which he had paid. The reason given by State was concern of rebel retaliation against the captive servicemen. Only then were the Americans released.

ALL OVER CUBA, the Castro revolution was picking up steam. In Havana and elsewhere, residents closed their windows at night and tuned to the one source of information not controlled by Fulgencio Batista: Castro's Radio Rebelde. Each night at 8:00 and 10:00 P.M. an announcer in the Sierra Maestra called out in a loud voice: *"Aqui Radio Rebelde, transmitiendo desde el territorio libre de Cuba!"*

Libre de Cuba! (Free Cuba!) The pronouncement usually exhilarated listeners, even those who were not necessarily Castro advocates. After the Cuban national anthem and the 26th of July Movement hymn were played, the announcer gave highly exaggerated accounts of the rebels' victorious battles against Batista's army troops.

On occasion, rebels and their sympathizers planted bombs in Havana movie houses, gambling casinos, banks, government buildings, and other symbols of Batista's power and prestige. Heavy industrial nails were sprinkled on the streets to puncture tires, or pieces of chain were thrown over power lines, knocking out electricity for many hours. To keep Havanans on edge, strings of large firecrackers were ignited in various parts of the sprawling city at night. Many civilians were killed or injured in these sporadic nocturnal attacks. Batista's police retaliated by torturing or shooting members and suspected members of the Castro underground and dumping their mutilated bodies on busy street corners as warnings.

When a seventeen-year-old Castro partisan was shot by police while hurling a Molotov cocktail at a building, the rebel propaganda apparatus concocted a scenario to gain support in Cuba and abroad, especially in the United States. The centerpiece of the ploy was a group that called itself the Martian Women. It had been organized by Dr. Martha Frade Barraque, an avowed Communist. The target was Ambassador Earl Smith, who, against the advice of his staff, traveled to Santiago in Oriente Province on July 31, 1958.

Soon after entering the city, Smith's car was halted by some forty Martian Women, all dressed in black widow's weeds, who staged a noisy demonstration. Although only a few were mothers, they unfurled a large banner on which were written in English the words STOP KILLING OUR SONS.

Notified in advance, a score of newspaper photographers and television camera crews were on hand when Batista's police, few of whom were overburdened with common sense, charged up, turned fire hoses on the "mothers," and manhandled several of them.

Photos and stories were circulated throughout the world. It was a propaganda bonanza for the 26th of July Movement and yet another black eye for Batista and his "Nazi Storm Troopers," as one U.S. newspaper branded the police involved in the episode.

IN EARLY NOVEMBER, Fulgencio Batista held an islandwide election to choose a candidate to succeed him as president. The winner was Batista's handpicked candidate, Andrés Rivero Agüero, who received twice as many votes as the other three candidates combined. The president-elect was scheduled to take office on February 24, 1959.

The election had been painstakingly orchestrated. The ballots had been printed in an old frame house in Camp Columbia, the military post outside Havana, under the supervision of honest election officials. At night, when none of the officials were watching, a second set of ballots, using the same paper and presses, was printed and marked by hand for Batista's candidate, Rivero Agüero.[6]

AT ABOUT THE SAME TIME the presidential "election" was being held in Cuba, Massachusetts voters went to the polls and sent Jack Kennedy back to the U.S. Senate by a whopping 859,000 plurality over a formidable Republican candidate. It was the largest margin ever recorded in a senate race in Massachusetts.

At the family's compound in Hyannisport, Joe Kennedy Sr. was exuberant. The blueprint he had carefully crafted with his son Jack in Palm Beach two years earlier was proceeding on schedule. As planned, much speculation began to appear in the media that Senator Kennedy might run for president in 1960 when Dwight Eisenhower's second term would expire.

A SHORT TIME after the Cuban election, the elite of Cuban exile society were dancing in the magnificent ballroom of the Waldorf Astoria Hotel in New York. Billed as the Cuban Gala Night, the event was sponsored by Ambassador Earl Smith. Dressed in a black-tie tuxedo and puffing on a cigar, he smiled broadly and watched the five hundred guests who had paid $40 each to attend the party. For the gala, the astute Smith had managed to blend society, charity, and politics into one glittering package.

A master promoter, Smith had made certain that the event would receive wide media coverage. A *Life* magazine photographer, burdened with gear, roamed about in search of newsworthy shots. The society editor of Cuba's most prestigious newspaper, *Diario de la Marina*, was flown up from Havana. But most significantly, Batista supporters were able to rub elbows and talk with an array of top American politicians, Hollywood stars, and celebrities in the international jet set.

It was a curious milieu of luminaries: Nearly all of them were liberals, and they were unaware that they had paid to benefit the right-wing dictator of Cuba, Batista. David Niven, Merle Oberon, Dina Merrill, and twenty-one-year-old Jane Fonda had flown in from Hollywood. Maria Callas, the acclaimed Italian soprano and one of the world's most widely known opera singers, was there. So were heavily publicized playboys Aly Kahn of Egypt and Porfirio Rubirosa of the Dominican Republic, elegant in their white ties and tails.

Gaining much of the party's spotlight was Jack Kennedy, the forty-one-year-old junior senator from Massachusetts. Nearby, holding a champagne glass was his wife, Jacqueline, wearing a white Givenchy gown. Boyish-faced Teddy Kennedy, younger brother of the senator, and his mother, Rose, were quietly seated near the wall watching the dancers. Ambassador Smith, a staunch conservative, did not agree with most of Jack Kennedy's liberal philosophy, but both men were from Massachusetts, and Smith was a longtime friend of the Kennedy family.

IN EARLY DECEMBER, the anti-Castro maneuvering was still continuing in Washington. William D. Pawley, who had spent thirty-five years of his life as a big-business tycoon and in secret government missions, was meeting in a fourth-floor office in the State Department Building with William Wieland, the director of Caribbean and Mexican affairs, and Assistant Secretary Roy Rubottom. There was tension in the air. Wieland, who had been a junior staff member when Pawley was ambassador to Brazil, considered Pawley an ultraconservative who didn't really understand Latin America. In turn, Pawley regarded Wieland as a sympathizer of left-wing causes.

Bill Pawley had founded Cuba's first national airline in the 1920s (which he later sold to Pan American at a big profit). In the 1930s, he built three airplane factories in China and, after the mighty Japanese war machine invaded that country, helped organize the famed Flying Tigers of American mercenaries. Later, Pawley conducted secret negotiations with Francisco Franco, the Spanish dictator and crony of Adolf Hitler, and arranged for the United States to establish military bases in Spain, much to Hitler's anger. Still later, he had been ambassador to Peru and then Brazil.

Now Pawley explained to Wieland and Rubottom that he had had a late-night meeting in his palatial Miami home with a group of prominent Americans that included Deputy Assistant Secretary of State Lawrence Snow, Assistant Secretary Henry Holland, and Colonel J. C. King, head of the Latin American section of the CIA. They had decided that something had to be done promptly about the Cuban situation or Fidel Castro would surely seize power. Pawley figured he was the man for the job. He would meet with Batista in Havana, coerce him into leaving Cuba, and arrange for a "neutral junta" to take over the government.

Pawley told Wieland and Rubottom that he had briefed Dwight Eisenhower on his plan of installing a "third force" in Havana and that the president, an old friend, "supports my plan completely."

Wieland winced over the word junta and said that group leadership seems to fit the Cuban psyche "like a snowball in hell."[7]

Pawley was angry and explained that the junta would hold power only until the country could be settled down and elections held.

Again looking at Wieland, Pawley added, "This damned thing is all screwed up, and I can straighten it out. I have a lot of influence with Batista, and I'm going to use it. I'll lay it on the line!"[8]

IN LATE NOVEMBER, Raúl Castro's rebel group was bivouacked in the rugged Sierra Cristal hills north of the U.S. Naval Base at Guantanamo. Raúl's band, estimated to number some five hundred armed men at this point, had almost total control of eastern and northern Oriente Province. Batista's army stayed away. More than ten pastures had been turned into runways so aircraft could bring in weapons and supplies, especially from Florida.

Raúl's headquarters was located in the village of Mayarí Arriba, a short distance northwest of Guantanamo, but he careened over the bumpy roads in a Toyota Land Cruiser he had "liberated" from a wealthy Batista supporter to keep in touch with his scattered groups. At age twenty-seven, Raúl was four years younger than Fidel and totally devoted to his brother.

Since 1939, the U.S. Naval Base's only source of freshwater had been from inside Cuban territory at the Yateras River, where a pumping station sent the water through two huge pipes for 4 miles to another pumping station just inside the northeast gate of the facility. From there, it was distributed to homes and buildings throughout Gitmo, as the base has been called by generations of Navy men and women.

Knowing of the base's total dependence on the freshwater pipeline, Raúl Castro had three times briefly shut down the pumping station on the Yateras. Navy leaders at Gitmo were furious and eager to dispatch a battalion of Marines to seize and secure the Yateras pumping station. Permission from Washington was denied.

However, President Eisenhower, who had a short fuse when angered, was livid over the obvious provocation. Through an anti-Batista lobbyist in Washington, a stiffly worded warning was sent to Fidel Castro stating that any future antics of this type would be regarded in a highly serious light.

Apparently the CIA had managed to tap Fidel's or Raúl's telephones. Agents had heard Fidel order his brother to leave the Guantanamo water supply alone. Castro, as future events would disclose, was merely biding his time until his forces were stronger before he made another move against the "symbol of Yankee oppression."

MEANWHILE on December 9, 1958, Bill Pawley arrived in Havana incognito on his secret mission designed to coerce Fulgencio Batista to leave Cuba—and keep Fidel Castro out of power.

6

"One Bad Apple
for Another"

E ARLY IN THE AFTERNOON of December 9, Bill Pawley was meeting
in a private home with perhaps the only American official who
knew he was coming to Havana, Jim Noel, the CIA station chief. Pawley was angry, pacing the floor like a caged tiger. Punctuating his
remarks with blue words, he claimed the State Department had
double-crossed him just as he was leaving for Havana: It had forbidden him to use the name of President Eisenhower in his discussions
with Fulgencio Batista.

Without being able to inform Batista that his plan had the en-
dorsement of the White House, Pawley ranted that the Cuban leader
might simply ignore it as the scheme of only a private citizen.

A few hours later, Pawley met with Prime Minister Gonzalo
Güell, Batista's brother-in-law, at Güell's spacious home in the fash-
ionable suburb of Miramar. As the Cuban sat expressionless and listened, Pawley explained his plan and, ignoring State Department
warnings, implied that it had the backing of President Eisenhower.
Batista would leave Cuba and live in a mansion in Daytona Beach,
Florida. Batista's colleagues in Cuba would not be harmed, and a mili-
tary-civilian junta would prevent Fidel Castro from seizing power.

Pawley ticked off the list of names in the proposed junta: None
were aware that their names were being suggested. None had political
experience or a following. All were pro-American but not linked to either Batista or Castro. The junta would serve as a caretaker government until honest elections could be held.

As soon as the meeting broke up, Güell rushed to the Presidential
Palace, which was ringed by heavily armed soldiers, and told Batista of
Pawley's plan. Batista became angry and refused to even talk with the
American. Güell then hurried to pass the word to Pawley, who was fu-
rious at Batista's rebuff of "President Eisenhower's emissary," as he

put it. Reluctantly, the Cuban strongman changed his mind and agreed to see Pawley.

For more than two hours, Batista and Pawley conferred behind closed doors in the Cuban's private office on the second floor of the Presidential Palace. Suddenly, the doors flew open and Pawley strode grimly from the office. Batista aides, who had been clustered outside, marched in. Usually expressionless, Batista wore a scowl and exclaimed that he had totally rejected the proposal. He was furious at Pawley for suggesting some of Batista's worst political opponents for the junta. "I wanted to kick his ass out of here!" he told Prime Minister Güell.[1]

FAR TO THE NORTH in Washington, President Eisenhower had grown confused over the conflicting accounts he was receiving from various branches of the administration and the media about the true nature of the 26th of July Movement and its leader, Fidel Castro. So he directed Acting Secretary of State Christian A. Herter, a former governor of Massachusetts, to prepare an in-depth analysis of the Cuban situation.

A few days later, on December 23, Dwight Eisenhower—Ike to his friends—was sitting in the Oval Office perusing a four-page memorandum marked ominously "Top Secret" and "Special Handling." It was the analysis of the Cuban situation from Christian Herter. The document stressed that the Batista government was deteriorating rapidly and that the Cuban leader had "alienated some eighty percent of his people."

"Although the Communists are utilizing the Castro movement to some extent," the report stated, "there is insufficient evidence on which to base a charge the rebels are Communist-dominated."[2]

No mention was made of former Ambassador Arthur Gardner's constant warnings that Fidel Castro and his brother Raúl were pro-Communist.

"The [State] Department clearly does not want to see Castro succeed to the leadership of the government," the memorandum continued. "Therefore we have been attempting, without openly violating our non-intervention commitments, to help create a situation in which a third force would move into the vacuum between Batista and Castro."[3]

Herter's analysis concluded: "Any solution in Cuba requires that Batista must relinquish power . . . and leave the country."[4]

On the same day that Herter's document reached the White House, Eisenhower was attending a session of the National Security Council (NSC) to hear Allen W. Dulles, the deceptively mild-mannered CIA director, give his views on Cuba and Castro. Created in 1947 by the

National Security Act that unified the armed forces, the NSC included the secretaries of state, defense, and treasury, the vice president, the Joint Chiefs of Staff, and the CIA director. Unlike his predecessor, Harry S. Truman, Eisenhower relied heavily on the NSC for advice on all aspects of the Cold War.

Allen Dulles, the son of a minister, was a veteran cloak-and-dagger operative. He had made a big name for himself as Office of Strategic Services (OSS) station chief in Switzerland during World War II. His tweed jackets, rimless glasses, and ever present pipe gave the CIA chief a professorial appearance that belied his steel resolve.

Now Dulles told Eisenhower and the NSC that "Communists and other extreme radicals appear to have penetrated the Castro movement. If Castro takes over, they will probably participate in his government."[5]

Eisenhower was angered by the disparity between Allen Dulles's and Christian Herter's views on the Communist influence in Castro's revolutionary movement. A suggestion by an NSC member that the United States support Batista as the "lesser of two evils" was rejected by the president.

"If that fellow [Castro] turns out to be as bad as our intelligence now suggests," Eisenhower declared, "our only hope, if any, lies with some kind of nondictatorial 'third force,' neither Castroite nor Batistiano."[6]

IN LATE DECEMBER, Fidel Castro felt that his revolutionary force was now large enough and the anti-Batista political tide in Cuba was strong enough to launch a military drive westward from the Sierra Maestra stronghold. His objective: Havana and the Presidential Palace.

In sharp street fighting a rebel force of a few hundred men, led by Ernesto "Ché" Guevara, soundly whipped a demoralized Batista garrison of 3,200 troops and seized Santa Clara (population 150,000), the first major city captured by the 26th of July Movement. A trainload of Batista soldiers sent to reinforce the garrison refused even to get out of the railroad cars.

AT THE PRESIDENTIAL PALACE in Havana, Batista was shaken by news of the rebel victory and the refusal of his troops to fight. The dictator knew he was finished. Now it was a matter of saving his own neck. So he rushed his brother-in-law, Prime Minister Gonzalo Güell, to the nearby Dominican Republic to meet secretly with Batista's old crony, aging General Leonidas Trujillo, who offered asylum in his country to the beleaguered Cuban dictator.

WHEN A VEIL OF NIGHT fell over Cuba on New Year's Eve, 1958, a climate of foreboding gripped Havana. Rumors of an impending upheaval had saturated the city that afternoon. Reservations for a gala celebration had poured into the Hotel Riviera's Copa Room, but by dinnertime two hundred of them had been canceled. Most Havanans chose to stay home where they watched *The New Adventures of Charlie Chan* on television.

While the wily Chinese detective was solving perplexing crimes on the airwaves, a caravan of black Cadillacs carrying Fulgencio Batista and his chief cohorts in government and the military was winding through the dark and largely deserted streets of Havana. The convoy was bound for the army's Camp Columbia, outside the city, for a New Year's Eve banquet, Batista's version of The Last Supper.

At Batista's home in the army camp, the atmosphere was grim as some sixty guests milled about the buffet table in the spacious upstairs living room. They stood stiffly in small groups, forcing idle conversation. The military officers were in dress uniforms complete with decorations. Most of the wives wore expensive gowns imported from Paris and New York.

As the clock struck midnight, Batista lifted a cup of coffee laced with brandy and called out, *"Felicidades!"* (Happy New Year!) A chorus of *Felicidades* came from the guests. With that, The Last Supper was drawing to a close. But the grim dictator had orchestrated a final scenario. General Eulogio Cantillo rose and made a solemn pronouncement: "For the salvation of the republic, the military forces have decided that it is necessary for General Batista to withdraw from power."[7]

That was the cue for the departing dictator to carry out his role in the charade. "I will not leave [Cuba] before handing over power," he protested. "A plausible successor must be named." The "plausible successor" was Andrés Rivero Agüero, who had won the rigged election and was to become president on February 24. He was immediately sworn into office. His term as president would be the shortest in Cuban history: two hours.[8]

The theatrics dispensed with, Batista, his guests, and their families began a mad scramble to get out of Cuba before the arrival of Fidel Castro in Havana. At the Columbia airfield, Batista, bogged down with suitcases crammed with a fortune in valuables (including a reputed $40 million), and his wife, Marta, flew to the Dominican Republic. Taking refuge in Jacksonville, Florida, was National Police Chief Pilar Garcia, described by Castro supporters as "the worst of the lot," and General Pancho Tabernilla, who carried off a king's ransom in "fees" from imported Scotch.

An entire national government had vanished between midnight and dawn.

NO ONE IN CUBA was more startled on hearing that Batista and his entire entourage had fled than Castro himself. But the rebel chief felt cheated: He had hoped to mete out "revolutionary justice" to arch-foe Batista, a man Castro for years had called "the beast and assassin."

In Havana on January 1, 1959, pandemonium erupted. Wildly cheering students roamed the campus of Havana University and raced through the streets. Many waved flags of the 26th of July Movement. Rioters sacked two newspaper offices, wrecked gambling casinos, and burned the homes of suspected Batista supporters. Thousands of girls and young women, wearing dresses of black and red (the colors of Castro's revolt), paraded and danced about the streets and parks.[9]

Batista's policemen, who had suddenly found themselves trapped by howling, bloodthirsty mobs, were gunned down. Castroites quickly seized Havana television and radio stations and called out the squad-car numbers of "killer cops."

NOT ALL CUBANS were celebrating or shooting policemen. Thousands of Batistianos were scrambling desperately to get off the island. They jammed into private planes, commercial airlines, yachts and ferries, and assorted boats of all shapes and sizes. At gunpoint, one Cuban Airlines pilot was forced to fly ninety-six escapees to New York City. Hundreds of others reached Miami, Ocala, West Palm Beach, and the Florida Keys. Two aircraft touched down in New Orleans. One contained the two youngest Batista children, Fulgencio, age six, and Marta Marie, four years old.

A clutch of American mobsters frantically chartered three private planes and, lugging suitcases full of loot, lifted off for Jacksonville, Florida. On board were Meyer Lansky, head of the Cuban gambling syndicate; Santo "Sam" Trafficante, operator of the San Souci Hotel and Casino; and Charles "The Blade" Tourine. With them were their wives and girlfriends.

LATE ON NEW YEAR'S DAY, a column of bearded, bedraggled rebels, led by Ché Guevara and Camilo Cienfuegos—two of The Apostles—riding in captured tanks, charged into Havana and took over two key strongpoints, Camp Columbia and Cabanna Fortress. But Fidel Castro remained on the Sierra Maestra until that night, when he came down and entered nearby Santiago de Cuba, the "cradle of the *revolución.*"

Santiago's streets were jammed with wildly cheering men, women, and children. At Céspedas Park, Castro made his first victory speech.

In his high-pitched voice, he told the delirious throng that he was asking nothing for himself, and he promised a free press, free elections, free speech, and land for the landless peasants. The crowd went wild and roared in unison, *"Fi-del! Fi-del! Fi-del!"*

The Messiah beamed and stroked his beard.

EARLY ON THE MORNING of January 2, the Fidel Castro Victory March was rolling toward Havana. His long column of "bearded ones" rode in captured tanks, jeeps, buses, cars, and trucks. The rebel chief himself often covered long stretches between cities by helicopter, relishing it like a child with a new toy. "It's mine! It's mine!" Castro would exclaim gleefully.[10]

A master of high drama, Castro savored every moment of the Victory March. He built suspense by halting repeatedly to give lengthy, rambling orations from balconies and in public parks. Along the way, the caravan drew throngs of frenzied, flag-waving Cubans. Masses of humanity brought the column to a halt in every town. Always the chant "Fi-del! Fi-del!" echoed over the landscape. Castro was modest in victory, folksy and eloquent. Free speech, free elections, free press, he promised each gathering.

Castro's weeklong Victory March reached the outskirts of Havana on January 8. For days, the capital's population had been nearly apoplectic in anticipation of his arrival. Every store and factory was closed, and hundreds of thousands of people poured into the streets, crammed into balconies and onto rooftops. Shouts of *"He's coming! He's coming!"* split the air. Then there was the roar of powerful tank engines and the clanking of steel treads on the pavement. *He* was indeed coming—at last. Behind the path-clearing tanks, the Messiah, a 50-cent Montecristo cigar jammed into his mouth, rolled Caesar-like into Havana in a jeep. The shouting, clapping throngs nearly engulfed him.[11]

Smiling rebels, intoxicated by the mass adulation, used outstretched rifles to force the Castro jeep through the human sea and on to the Presidential Palace. There the rebel leader was tearfully embraced by fifty-seven year-old, colorless Manuel Urrutia Lleo, whom Castro had appointed president of Cuba only a few days earlier. Peering up at the majestic palace that had been the center of Fulgencio Batista's power, Castro quipped over a loudspeaker: "I never did like this place!" The joyous throng laughed uproariously, and its cheers rocked the landscape.

Castro's appointment of Urrutia Lleo had been made with typical impulsiveness. He had barely known the Santiago judge before naming him to be Cuba's president. Urrutia had gained Castro's admiration nineteen months earlier by discharging a group of rebels on the ground that revolution in Cuba was a constitutional right.

After that highly unpopular (to Batista) ruling, Judge Urrutia had been forced to flee the country. He lived quietly in New York City, before rushing back home when the Batista government disintegrated. It would not be long before Castro learned just how serious a blunder he had committed: Manuel Urrutia, who had no inkling of what he was getting into, was both a friend of the United States and a staunch anti-Communist.

Now Castro assured his frenzied followers that he would rapidly form a government and restore constitutional law, rather than run the shop personally. "Power does not interest me," he declared. "And I will not take it. From now on, the people are entirely free."[12]

From the Presidential Palace, the Castro procession moved on to Camp Columbia, where only nine days earlier Batista and his cronies had held their New Year's Eve dinner. A crowd of thirty-five thousand people rendered the rebel chief a tumultuous welcome, then heard him promise "peace with liberty, peace with justice, peace with individual rights." Again, the crowd went wild.[13]

After fifty-six hours of travel, oratory, and basking in the adoration of the multitudes, Fidel Castro made his way to the opulent Havana Hilton, where he bedded down in the Continental Suite shortly before dawn.

AT ABOUT THE SAME TIME, U.S. intelligence picked up a report from a high-grade source that Castro's underground planned to kidnap Ambassador Earl Smith and his key staff members. They intended to hold their victims on the top floor of the embassy, the intelligence report stated, until the U.S. government formally recognized the Castro regime. If that failed to get the job done, the rebels would drop one man after the other to their deaths from the balcony, leading off with Ambassador Smith.

Smith ventured outside embassy grounds only when absolutely necessary, and he was followed at all times by a car with four Marines in civilian clothes armed with Tommy guns. A heavily armed Marine sat in the front seat of the ambassador's limousine. At night, listening devices in Smith's bedroom broadcast and amplified his breathing to armed Marines standing guard outside his door and in the corridors.

FAR TO THE NORTH in Washington, sixty-nine-year-old Allen Dulles was intently studying a report of the shift in Cuban power that had been prepared by his CIA analysts for President Eisenhower. As a gentle snow drifted past his office window, Dulles puffed on his ever present pipe and frowned. He did not like what greeted his eyes in the analysts' document. Fidel Castro's stunning success, it concluded, had resulted largely from the corruption and brutalities of the Batista regime, which had caused widespread anger among the Cuban people. Dulles felt this expressed a simplistic view of the situation.

Before submitting the top-secret report to the White House, Dulles rewrote it. He maintained that Castro's victory was not a natural development that could have been expected in light of Batista's excesses. Rather, he took the view that the Cuban people had substituted "one bad apple for another." Dulles predicted that there now would be a slaughter in Havana that would make the French Revolution look like a tea party. "Blood will flow in the streets," the CIA chief warned.[14]

7

"Two Hundred Thousand Yankee Gringos Will Die!"

O N JANUARY 8, 1959, within hours of Fidel Castro's taking over the Presidential Palace recently vacated by Fulgencio Batista, a 26th of July Movement functionary in the United States contacted the State Department and demanded Ambassador Earl Smith's immediate firing because he was "openly showing his hostility to Dr. Fidel Castro, the national hero of the Cuban people."

In Washington, Congressman Adam Clayton Powell of Harlem also wanted Smith booted out and $200 million in U.S. taxpayers' money sent to Fidel Castro to assist the new regime.

There were also officials in the State Department demanding Smith's scalp, and he was summoned to Washington for "consultations." When the ambassador arrived at the fourth-floor office of Undersecretary Roy Rubottom, he was informed that the Castro regime was going to be officially recognized immediately and that Smith was going to be relieved of his duties as ambassador.

Smith had one final task to perform. He returned to Havana and drove to the foreign minister's office, where he formally presented the note of recognition expressing his country's trust that the Castro regime would "comply with the international obligations and agreements of Cuba."

While being chauffeured back to the U.S. Embassy, Smith brooded, convinced that he had just handed Cuba over to the Communists.[1]

ON SATURDAY NIGHT, January 10, Father Jorgé Bez Chabebe, chaplain of the Catholic Youth Movement in Santiago—the "cradle of the revolution"—was enjoying festivities at a banquet. He looked up to see another priest, Father Rafael Escala, walking toward him. Leaning over, Escala whispered in an urgent tone, "Please come with me, Father. Four Batista officers are to be tried and executed tonight. We will be needed."

43

Grim-faced, Father Jorgé excused himself and prepared to leave the room. He was bewildered by the words "tried *and* executed." How could anyone know in advance of a trial that the verdict would be guilty and the sentence death?

As the two priests entered the municipal court chamber where the trial was ready to begin, Father Jorgé was stunned. The "judges" were five rebels of whom only one had a slight knowledge of the law. The prosecutor and the defense lawyer were also Castro men. Rapidly, the charges were read, a few prosecution witnesses testified briefly; the "judges" chatted with each other, paying virtually no attention to the "trial." Soon, the names of the defendants were read; each was pronounced guilty and sentenced to death.

Father Jorgé and Father Rafael went outside and climbed into an army truck with fourteen prisoners, including the four who had just been "tried." Sentences were to be carried out immediately. It was 2:10 A.M. As the old vehicle bumped and jolted through the dark countryside, the two priests heard confessions and administered final rites.

At the Campo de Tiro firing range in the San Juan hills (up which the famed Teddy Roosevelt and his Rough Riders charged in the Spanish-American War that had won independence for Cuba), the truck halted. The condemned men dismounted, their faces drawn, eyes fearful, hands tied behind their backs. A few of them wept; others pleaded that they had been Castro sympathizers; most stood silent, resigned to their fates.

Father Jorgé saw that there were several other trucks already on the site. About sixty prisoners in all were to be shot. Two other priests were present to hear confessions. One of the condemned men broke away and ran toward a wooded area, but he was caught and dragged back. About half of the men were given blindfolds.

By the glare of truck headlights, a priest led the first two men to the edge of a 40-foot-long, 10-foot-wide, and 10-foot-deep trench. The excavation had been dug earlier by a bulldozer, during the course of the kangaroo trials. After making the sign of the cross, the priest stepped back, and a firing squad of six rebels sent bullets ripping into the two men. The bodies jackknifed into the huge mass grave.

Two more men were led forward, then two more, and two more. Soon the trench was filling with lifeless, bloody bodies. For the next six hours, the priests heard confessions as rifle fire periodically split the air. One condemned man, Enrique Despaigne, whom Castro prosecutors charged with fifty-three murders but whose trial had lasted less than ten minutes, gained a three-hour reprieve shortly before dawn. A

Cuban television crew had asked for the postponement in order to improve the photographic quality of the executions by the light of day.

Attracted by the commotion and the periodic rifle fire, a large number of Cuban civilians gathered on a nearby hill to watch. As each volley rang out over the rugged San Juan landscape, the crowd screamed, "Kill them! Kill them!"

It was 10:00 A.M. when the last shot was fired. As the trucks drove away, Father Jorgé glanced back. He saw a bulldozer methodically covering the bloody corpses in the trench with mounds of earth.[2]

The mass executions had been ordered by Fidel Castro's younger brother, Raúl, whom the rebel chief had appointed military commander in Oriente Province. Raúl, who unlike other rebels could not grow a beard but substituted for its absence with shoulder-length hair, had long been involved in left-wing causes. In his student days, he had been a delegate to a Communist international youth conference behind the Soviet Iron Curtain. When questioned by non-Cuban reporters about the wave of killings at the Campo de Tiro rifle range, Raúl shrugged and replied: "There's always a priest on hand to hear last confessions."[3]

ON JANUARY 12, Fidel Castro strode into the lobby of the Havana Hilton. As usual, an excited mob was on hand, hoping to catch a glimpse of, and perhaps even touch, their liberator. Castro loved the adoration. He threw his arm around the nearest worshipers and, with a broad smile wreathing his suntanned face, cried out: "People! People! Let the people see me—let me talk with them!"[4]

The uproar around the *Líder Máximo* (Maximum Leader), as Castro now called himself, was intense. Bearded rebels, their friends and families, well-rounded girls wearing the olive-green uniforms of the revolution, were pushing, shoving, and clawing to get closer to Castro. Scores of voices were talking simultaneously. But the Maximum Leader's vibrant, high-pitched voice could be heard above the hubbub.

Robert Perez, a reporter for a London newspaper, had squirmed through the crush of people to within a few feet of Castro. Perez, who was born in Puerto Rico but reared in Ohio, was impeccably bilingual in Spanish and English. He did not hear what triggered the outburst, but red-faced with anger, Castro blurted in his hoarse Spanish, "Yes, I tell you, two hundred thousand Yankee *gringos* will die if the United States sends the Marines to Cuba!"[5]

Castro's words were caught not only by Perez but also by other foreign news reporters nearby. Later, Perez told a fellow correspondent, Edwin Tetlow of the *London Daily Telegraph,* that there was no chance that he, Perez, had misunderstood the inflammatory threat.

In blaring newspaper headlines, the "two hundred thousand Yankee gringos will die" exclamation burst like a meteor over the United States. Americans were stunned—especially leaders in the Eisenhower administration. No one had given even a vague thought to invading Cuba.

Two weeks after Fidel Castro established his command post on the twenty-third floor of the Havana Hilton, he discovered the enormous communication potential of television. Soon, he became an addict. While Cuba writhed in a curious mixture of euphoria and mass confusion and sought to regain its equilibrium, the Maximum Leader began going before the television cameras to make "talkathons" that droned on for five or six hours. Limited production in the country was crippled by worker absenteeism or tardiness: Employees had stayed up until nearly dawn listening to Castro's marathon oratory.

AS THE CUBAN ship of state rocked along, seemingly rudderless, some zealous Castro supporters grew mildly disturbed. One of them was Teresa Casuso, who had recently arrived in Havana after serving a two-year term in a filthy Mexican jail for stashing Castro's weapons and ammunition in her Mexico City home. Now she was always at his side and noticed that he had grown arrogant under the avalanche of adoration.

Casuso was appalled as she watched Castro behave like what she called "an irresponsible adolescent." He carried a checkbook in the breast pocket of his green fatigue jacket. As he flitted from place to place on his daily meandering around Havana, he would write a check for some project or scheme that appealed to him when it was brought to his attention by Cubans pressing against him day and night. Hopefully, there would be enough money in the government treasury to cover the check.[6]

CASTRO SOON began attacking comrades. A member of the revolution's Old Guard, Mario Llercna, a journalist, published an article entitled, "Let's Not Deify Fidel." It was but a simple, constructive suggestion that the Maximum Leader get himself organized now that he ruled Cuba. But Castro exploded. Chomping furiously on a cigar, he rushed to the Havana television station and spent more than an hour on the air in a blistering tirade against his longtime confederate Llerena. After that verbal scalding, no Cuban newspaper would dare to publish any of Llerena's articles.[7]

Castro's bitter harangue was but another blow in his systematic destruction of a free press. He already had killed off print media and radio stations that he felt had supported Batista. Five daily newspapers had been shut down in Havana alone, a measure applauded at the time by most Cubans. But Communist-oriented newspapers, including a pair of major ones, *Revolución* and *Hoy*, were permitted to continue publication.

Hoy and *Revolución* were given permission to distribute in the provinces and allowed to use military aircraft and trucks for this purpose. Then the Maximum Leader, knowing that advertising is the lifeblood of newspapers, began economically strangling other publications by ordering all government advertising to be placed with *Revolución* and *Hoy*. Prudent commercial advertisers followed suit.

WHILE CASTRO was wiping out the last vestiges of a free press in Cuba, many newspapers around the world were creating an uproar over the bloody vengeance being wreaked by the victorious rebels. Three hundred men, quickly convicted in kangaroo courts as torturers and murderers for the Batista regime, were executed.

Castro was unruffled by this flood of foreign condemnation. He took to the television cameras and shouted, "We have given orders to shoot every last one of these murderers, and if we have to oppose world opinion to carry out justice, we are ready to do it." He threw in a crowd-pleaser: "If the Americans do not like what is happening, they can send in the Marines." Castro assured his television audience that the Cuban beaches would run red with American blood.[8]

8

The U.S. Power
Barons Disagree

O N FEBRUARY 16, 1959, five weeks after he had reached Havana from
the Sierra Maestra, Fidel Castro appointed himself premier and
designated brother Raúl as commander of the Cuban armed forces.
One of the Maximum Leader's first actions was to legalize the Partico
Socialista Popular (Communist Party), which had been outlawed by
Fulgencio Batista. Then Fidel announced that he was postponing, for
two years, the free elections he had promised the people.

Fidel Castro, a burly man who was seldom seen without a cigar
poked in his mouth, was almost constantly on the go, dashing about
his island domain in his green camouflaged fatigue uniform that designated him as a major, the highest military rank in the Cuban armed
forces under the new landlords.

All the while, the executions of Cuba's "enemies of the people"
continued unabated. In Santiago, a three-judge tribunal, appointed by
Castro, was holding a trial of nineteen pilots, ten gunners, and sixteen
mechanics of Batista's air force. They were charged with "genocide"
for bombing and strafing "open towns" in rebel-held Oriente Province.

Their fate seemed certain. Castro had already publicly condemned
the defendants as "the worst criminals of the Batista regime." The
prosecution charged that Batista bombers had killed ten and injured
from 160 to 600 civilians. But the tribunal acknowledged that the villages were legitimate military targets since "our forces were in them"
and added that it was impossible to "identify which of those on trial
were those who produced the deaths." All of the airmen were acquitted.

Castro was furious. He had Aristedes Dacosta, chief defense counsel, hauled in by rebels and flown to Havana, where he was given a
verbal blistering by the Maximum Leader. Then Castro dispatched
Defense Minister Augusto Martinez to Santiago to form a "review

court." The new verdict: Twenty years at hard labor for the pilots, lesser sentences for nonpilots. Two airmen were acquitted.

While the second Santiago trial was in progress, firing squads across the island were busy. Thirty men were shot, bringing the Castro execution total to 392.

That same week, only two months after the Maximum Leader had taken control of Cuba, he burst into a television station and rambled on for three hours and twenty-two minutes about perceived threats of counterrevolution. His enemies, he shouted, were buying arms in Miami. Then he tore into the FBI for "not doing anything about it."[1]

No doubt stung by the flood of sharp criticism he was receiving from around the world, Castro devised a new technique to demonstrate the solidarity of the Cuban people behind the wave of official killings and his verbal attacks on the United States. He called for a massive outpouring of citizens into Misiones Park, across from the Presidential Palace.

Castro henchmen made certain that the rally would be a tremendous success. Buses fanned out over central Cuba and brought in tens of thousands of bug-eyed peasants, most of whom had never been in Havana before. On the appointed day, perhaps a half million persons jammed into the park for the "spontaneous" assembly.

Over a loudspeaker, the Maximum Leader, flanked by bearded rebels of the Sierra Maestra days, harangued the crowd for more than two hours. He was his most eloquent best. The crowd shouted and roared as he declared frenziedly that "we Cubans have no need to apologize to the United States because of the executions."

The throng's frenzy reached fever pitch. It chanted relentlessly *"par-e-dón, par-e-dón!"* American journalists covering the spectacle were chilled by the *paredón* chant. They had never heard the word before, but it seemed to have an ominous implication. One reporter asked a perspiring, red-faced Cuban, "What does *paredón* mean?" His eyes ablaze, the Cuban replied excitedly, "It means send them all to the execution wall!"[2]

IN WASHINGTON, meanwhile, the sharp Herter/Dulles division of opinion continued over the aims and political philosophy of Fidel Castro, the man some of the U.S. media had dubbed the Guerrilla Prince, the George Washington of Cuba, and the Robin Hood of the Caribbean. Secretary of State Herter seemed to absolve the Cuban leader of Communist leanings or Communist influences in his government.

On the other hand, Allen Dulles, the veteran chief of the CIA, told President Eisenhower: "The Castro regime is moving toward a complete dictatorship. Communists are now operating openly in Cuba. Communists are in the armed forces, the labor unions, and other organizations."[3]

William C. Sullivan, coordinator of the FBI's Counterintelligence Program (COINTELPRO) and one of the handful of aides J. Edgar Hoover called by his first name, submitted a lengthy report to the agency boss. The document concluded that Castro and his cohorts were not Communists nor were they influenced by Communists.[4]

Back in 1956, Hoover had appointed Sullivan to supervise and orchestrate COINTELPRO, an aggressive program to destroy the Communist Party in the United States. Sullivan would later describe the plan as an application of World War II counterintelligence methods used against domestic subversive groups. "No holds were barred," Sullivan later stated. "We have used [these techniques] against enemy agents. They have used them against us."[5]

The goal of COINTELPRO as described by another FBI official was to "keep the pot boiling within CPUSA [Communist Party, United States of America]."

To achieve that objective, Bill Sullivan and his operatives hatched numerous schemes. FBI moles were planted in CPUSA to attend meetings and openly raise sensitive questions designed to divide and disillusion members. "Why did the Soviet army invade Hungary [in 1956] and its tanks kill so many innocent civilians? Why is there so much anti-Semitism in the Soviet Union?"

FBI undercover agents became so prominent in CPUSA feuds that Hoover and Sullivan seriously considered having the FBI covertly support a certain faction in a struggle to control CPUSA. That ploy was scuttled, however, because Hoover feared the Bureau might back the losing clique, thereby causing the FBI moles to be expelled from CPUSA.[6]

One of the most effective COINTELPRO schemes was the placing of a "snitch jacket" on a loyal Communist Party member. William Albertson, a hardworking and effective Communist official in New York City, became a prime target for a snitch jacket. Bureau undercover operatives planted what appeared to be an FBI informant's report in Albertson's automobile, then, by means of an anonymous telephone call to another Communist functionary, made certain the "incriminating" document was discovered. As a result, Albertson was drummed out of CPUSA and his life threatened. The Communist newspaper in New York, the *Daily Worker*, blasted him as a "stool pigeon."

The planting of stories with "friendly" media contacts also caused disruption and finger-pointing within the party. When Gus Hall, the Communist leader, bought a new car, reportedly with CPUSA money, the event was given coverage in newspapers and magazines. Other

CPUSA functionaries found themselves as the star attractions in media stories accusing them of embezzlement, fraud, and other criminal actions.

Anonymous telephone calls and unsigned letters spread derogatory information, real or created, such as planting a rumor that a Communist leader was a homosexual, an adulterer, or a sexual deviate. Persons defending themselves against these accusations had to devote so much time to the effort that they lost their effectiveness within the party.

Director Hoover was delighted with the results of these machinations and ordered Sullivan and special agents at FBI field offices to submit new and imaginative schemes for disrupting CPUSA.[7]

Based on his successes as the guiding light of COINTELPRO, Bill Sullivan became recognized as the FBI's foremost authority on Communism. So in early 1959, when he reported that the Fidel Castro regime was not Communist-oriented, his conclusion received great weight in many quarters of the Eisenhower administration, especially the State Department, which held a similar view.[8]

AT ABOUT THE SAME TIME that Bill Sullivan was submitting his Castro report to J. Edgar Hoover, a handful of U.S. publications began chipping away at the facade of adulation in which the Maximum Leader had been wrapped. Constantine Brown of the *Washington Evening Star* castigated "those in the State Department peeking at Cuba through rose-colored glasses." Secretary Herter and his key officials had chosen to overlook the A-1 intelligence concerning the Communist backgrounds of the Castro brothers, Brown declared.

"Fidel has a well established reputation as a strong Communist sympathizer who helped organize the 1948 Bogotá demonstrations against [Secretary of State] George C. Marshall," the reporter wrote. "Now all of a sudden Castro has been declared by the State Department to be lily white."[9]

An article in *U.S. News & World Report* quoted "a confidential report on Raúl Castro by a non-U.S. intelligence agency." This analysis characterized Raúl as "a dedicated Communist and the most dangerous of them all among [Cuba's new leaders]. He was married recently to Vilma Espín. She is a Communist and is known as a first-class U.S. hater. Raúl also is violently anti-U.S."[10]

THESE OMINOUS red lights that a handful of the media were flashing were dwarfed by the pro-Castro hoopla being spread across the United States. Counting on continued support from gullible Yankee print, radio, and television, Fidel was preparing to score a propaganda bonanza, not in Cuba but in Washington and New York.

9

A Safari to the
United States

STROKING HIS BEARD as was his custom when contemplating a proposal, Fidel Castro eyed his American visitor curiously. Bernard
Relling, an executive of a New York public-relations firm retained by
Castro, had come to Havana to brief the Cuban chief on how to project
a favorable image during his approaching visit to the United States.

Relling had made two radical suggestions to the Maximum Leader:
Have the rebels in his traveling entourage shave off their beards and
cut their shoulder-length hair, and select for his bodyguard only those
soldiers with university backgrounds who spoke English. Finally, Castro barked, "No!"

Castro's invitation had its origin about three months earlier in
New York City's Sardi's, a popular watering hole for the show business
crowd. In January 1959, only a week after Castro had made his triumphant entry into Havana, three editors were sipping noontime
cocktails and trying to settle on a "name" speaker for the annual convention of the American Society of Newspaper Editors (ASNE) in mid-
April. They were the current president of the ASNE, George Healy of
the *New Orleans Times-Picayune*, Alicia Patterson of New York's
Newsday, and Don Maxwell of the *Chicago Tribune*. Between martini
sips, they bounced names off one another, and then one suggested excitedly: "What about Castro?"

It was a logical choice, all agreed enthusiastically. National curiosity about the youthful revolutionary chief was rampant, so his appearance would create a flood of publicity for the convention. But first
they checked with Turner Catledge, executive editor of *The New York
Times*. "Great idea!" Catledge replied.

That same afternoon, Maxwell phoned the *Chicago Tribune's* correspondent in Havana, Jules Dubois, and told him to issue the invita-

52

tion to Castro. Dubois called back before the sun set: The rebel chief had accepted.

CLAD IN WRINKLED battle fatigues, Fidel Castro and his large entourage of shaggy-haired rebels lifted off on April 17 from Havana Airport in a turboprop Britannia. During the flight, Teresa Casuso sat silently at his side while Castro read comic books.[1]

Two hours late, the aircraft landed at Washington's National Airport, rolled to a halt, and the Maximum Leader stepped down from his winged chariot. A tumultuous roar erupted from the thousands of Americans who had turned out to welcome him. There were shouts of "Hi, Fidel!" as the throng clawed and scratched to get near, to touch him.

During his stay in Washington, Fidel was at his most charming, telling everybody what they wanted to hear. Appearing before the Senate Foreign Relations Committee, he gave assurances that he had no intention of confiscating U.S. properties in Cuba. "What is your connection with Communism?" bluntly asked Senator John Sparkman of Alabama. "None," was the terse reply.[2]

Most members of Congress were deeply impressed by Castro's views and his seeming sincerity. Declared Congressman James G. Fulton of Pennsylvania: "I think we should help him all we can."[3]

At the lavish Statler-Hilton Hotel, Acting Secretary of State Christian Herter gave a sumptuous luncheon for the Maximum Leader, attended by countless Washington bigwigs and twenty-seven top national personalities. These capital insiders, accustomed to nearly every kind of bizarre conduct, no doubt were amazed when Castro brought eight heavily armed, bearded bodyguards with him and insisted that they be seated with the guests in the dining hall.

There were awkward moments for the State Department hosts. Finally, it was agreed that the revolutionaries would stack their weapons in an adjoining room, after which they entered the dining hall and sat on the floor.

That same day, the weekly issue of *Time* magazine reported that the Castro execution toll in Cuba had reached 521.

The mood of good feeling continued when Fidel Castro appeared on NBC-TV's popular *Meet the Press* and told a nationwide audience that he strongly opposed Communism and that in any showdown with the Soviet Union, he would side with the United States. During an impromptu gathering in a Washington public park, he told students that he stood for "Cubanism," not Communism.

Back in Havana, Raúl Castro was furious. Each night, he was on the telephone to his big brother, scolding him, saying, in essence, "Fidel, are you selling out to the Yankees? That's what people are thinking back here!"[4]

In the hubbub and excitement and crush of jostling media photographers and reporters, few noticed the absence from the scene of the president of the United States. "I was more than irritated by the news of the [Castro] invitation," Dwight Eisenhower would declare.[5]

Eisenhower had rushed off from Washington to the temporary White House near the beckoning golf links at Augusta, Georgia. He was an avid, if pedestrian, golfer. The working vacation was timed so that the president would not have to play host to a bearded revolutionary who had repeatedly attacked him and the United States. That task was turned over to his forty-six-year-old vice president, Richard M. Nixon.

Nixon and Castro would meet in the vice president's seldom used office in the Capitol on a quiet Sunday afternoon when the magnificent structure would be virtually deserted. There were to be no staff members present. No photographs would be permitted. Nixon was determined that Castro would not be accorded the same reception as that given friendly visiting dignitaries.

April 19 was a rainy day, but Castro arrived for his appointment with a sunny disposition, smiling and gracious. He had good reason to be buoyant: He had just completed his appearance on *Meet the Press,* where his ratings had been, in Madison Avenue jargon, socko. Not long into routine chitchat, Nixon sized up the Cuban: intelligent, shrewd, and eloquent.

Nixon bombarded Castro with blunt questions. Why had he not scheduled free elections? Castro stroked his beard and replied, "Because the Cuban people don't want elections. Elections result in bad government." Why didn't the Cuban leader give fair trials to his foes? "The people don't want them to have fair trials; they want them shot as soon as possible." Wasn't he concerned that the Communists in his government would seize control? "I am not afraid of the Communists, I can handle them."

Later, in a detailed report to President Eisenhower on his nearly four-hour meeting, Nixon stated: "Castro is either incredibly naive about Communism or is under Communist discipline."[6]

The demand for tickets to Castro's speech before the American Society of Newspaper Editors at the Statler-Hilton Hotel in Washington had been the heaviest since General Douglas MacArthur had made his farewell appearance before the group a decade earlier. With more than one thousand news executives crammed into the room and hanging intently on every word, the bearded Cuban, clad in his olive-green revolution uniform, assured those present that he was a staunch advocate of a free press. "A free press is the first enemy of dictatorship," he exclaimed.

Castro had told these customarily suspicious journalists what they wanted to hear. They took him at face value and gave him a thunderous standing ovation.

Leaving behind the Washington hoopla and pomp and circumstance, Castro's traveling medicine show rolled on by rail toward New York City. On the way, it stopped at Princeton University, where a wealthy, liberal professor, Roland T. Ely, had urged President Robert Goheen to approve the Maximum Leader's appearance on campus.

When the train halted and Castro stepped regally from a luxury coach, his eyes were greeted by hundreds of cheering students waving Cuban flags. That night at the university's Woodrow Wilson Hall, a fascinating scenario unfolded. With the huge chamber packed with faculty and students, ten bearded Cubans with their long hair and olive-green fatigue uniforms tramped in through a rear door and swaggered down the central aisle toward the stage. Hard on their heels strode Fidel Castro, who responded to greetings from all sides as the hall erupted with booming cheers and applause.

Once the clamor had subsided, Castro spoke about the need for cooperation between the United States and the "new Cuba." He spoke for nearly two hours before leaving the stage in the escort of his bodyguards. Excited, exuberant students lifted the 210-pound Castro onto their shoulders and carried him into the night.

On Castro's arrival at Grand Central Station in New York, he and his entourage climbed into limousines for the ride to their hotel. The caravan was engulfed by humanity, a classic mob scene, as tens of thousands of delirious people struggled, shoved, clawed, and elbowed to get closer to the Maximum Leader.

At the Astor Hotel, Castro gave an encore performance of his champion-of-a-free-press spiel before a noon luncheon of the Overseas Press Club. A natural born actor, he was at his adroit best, speaking eloquently of his love for freedom and his friendship for the wonderful people of the United States. He received tumultuous applause.

A DAY AFTER Castro departed from the fairy-tale land of American adulation and returned to chaotic and problem-ridden Cuba, Christian Herter briefed President Eisenhower. Castro, Herter said, "is a most interesting individual, very much like a child in many ways, quite immature regarding problems of government, and puzzled and confused by some of the practical difficulties now facing him.

"In English he spoke with restraint and considerable personal appeal," Herter added. "However, when speaking Spanish, he became voluble, excited, and somewhat wild."[7]

Although Eisenhower had a high opinion of the integrity of the sixty-five-year-old Herter, who suffered badly from arthritis, the former governor of Massachusetts had long been identified by Washington insiders as "Ike's liberal." Part of this label had resulted from his being linked with Harvard University in the eyes of many.

Consequently, Eisenhower sought a "second opinion" from Allen Dulles, the CIA chief, on the Cuba situation. Within hours after Herter's leaving the White House, Dulles arrived in the Oval Office. Castro had stressed that Cuba would stay in the Western camp in the Cold War with the Soviet Union—"but he was unconvincing," the CIA boss stated.[8]

Dulles felt that there was a "probability that the land reform [Castro] was insisting upon may adversely affect certain [U.S.] properties in Cuba."[9] By this he meant that Castro might one day confiscate them.

"[Castro] confuses the roar of mass audiences with the rule of the majority in his concept of democracy," Dulles explained. "It would be a serious mistake to underestimate this man, however. He is clearly a strong personality and a born leader of great personal courage and conviction."[10]

Despite this alarming assessment, the CIA concluded that while "Castro remains an enigma, there still may be a possibility of developing a constructive relationship with him and his government."[11]

As Allied supreme commander in Europe in World War II, as commanding general of NATO forces, and as president, Eisenhower had personally been involved with scores of leaders of every stripe from many nations. Now, he remained dubious about the Cuban. After Dulles departed, Eisenhower scrawled on the margin of the report: "File. We will check in a year!"[12]

IN CUBA, meanwhile, the hastily appointed revolutionary administration was falling apart under the stress of trying to keep up with the whims of Fidel Castro, who was not only the premier but also a government in his own right. Castro and Manuel Urrutia, the judge Castro had impulsively appointed president, locked horns repeatedly. Urrutia objected strongly to the increasing presence of Communists in the government.

On the night of July 16, the rebel chief took to television and radio and bitterly attacked Urrutia. He declared that Urrutia had refused to sign laws (ones that Castro had created), had portrayed himself as the champion of anti-Communism, and had become a traitor to Cuba. Even while Castro was making the denunciation of Urrutia, howling mobs descended upon the Presidential Palace in a finely tuned orchestration, with shouts of, "Out with the traitor Urrutia!" The short-term president resigned before the Maximum Leader had completed his television tirade.

Castro's figurehead cabinet rubber-stamped his new choice for president, forty-year-old Osvaldo Dorticós, a former president of the Havana Bar Association who was serving as minister of Revolutionary Laws. Dorticós was considered a Communist by many of those who knew him. His devotion to the much younger Castro was unswerving.[13]

EARLY ON THE MORNING of July 29, Major Pedro Díaz Lanz, one of Castro's Old Guard and commander of the Rebel Air Force, was in bed recovering from an illness when a friend arrived and informed him that Castro was going to fire him. Many revolution veterans had been complaining over Communist infiltration of the armed forces, but Díaz Lanz had gone one step further. He had signed an order discontinuing the Communist indoctrination that was being given to his air force cadets.

Major Díaz Lanz climbed out of bed, dressed hastily, and went to see his old friend Fidel. Castro turned his back on him and stomped out of the room. The major knew that the handwriting was on the wall, but now he compounded his heresy. He issued a statement to the press stating that rumors had been circulated that he was a prisoner, but that he was returning from sick leave and had resumed his post as commander of the Rebel Air Force.

"I wish to make it clear that we revolutionists were prisoners only under the Batista dictatorship, and such a thing could not happen under a democratic regime," he stated. Then the major sealed his fate by adding: "I am against every type of dictatorship, including the most inhumane system of all, Communism."

Fidel Castro was nearly apoplectic and sent for Díaz Lanz. "How dare you talk to the press like that!" the Maximum Leader exploded.

"I only denied that I was a prisoner and am opposed to Communism," the major declared. "What is wrong with that?"

Castro ordered Díaz Lanz to go to his home and stay there. "I'll decide later what to do with you," Castro shouted.

Fully aware of the fate of those who perpetrated undefined "crimes against the revolution," Diáz Lanz escaped with his wife and brother on a small boat to Florida. He became the first high-ranking rebel to defect from Castro's revolution.[14]

IN MID-SEPTEMBER, Nikita Khrushchev, the bombastic Soviet dictator, arrived in Washington for two days of talks on banning nuclear tests. Born in 1894, he had been a Red Army political general and political commissar in World War II. When Josef Stalin died in 1953, Khrushchev was comparatively unknown. But behind an outward mask of joviality, he followed Stalin's pattern of first winning control of the Communist Party and then using that control to dominate all Soviet life. Khrushchev had seized total power on March 28, 1958.

Now in the United States, Khrushchev and Dwight Eisenhower took a helicopter to Camp David, the presidential retreat in Maryland's Catoctin Mountains. The rustic lodge had been called Shangri-La by President Franklin D. Roosevelt, but Eisenhower renamed it after his grandson, David.

During two days of talks, the Soviet dictator boasted repeatedly to the president of his country's military strength. Not only were the Russians building more powerful nuclear submarines than the Americans, but the Soviets would soon have all the missiles they needed—which, he added, were "a lot."[15]

10

"The United States Should Go It Alone!"

L ATE ON A WARM AFTERNOON in October 1959, hundreds of delegates to a convention of the American Society of Travel Agents were enjoying the cocktail hour at the Havana Hilton. The group had been wooed to Cuba by Fidel Castro's adroit salesmanship. For many months, the Maximum Leader had been trying to replenish his regime's dwindling treasury by luring back American tourists and their greenbacks.

Above the buzz of the idle conversation taking place in the Hilton's ballroom could be heard the terrific racket of antiaircraft guns firing. Rushing outside, the travel agents spotted a twin-engine World War II vintage bomber without markings roaring over the harbor. Untouched, the plane flew through the flak to the center of the city and opened bomb-bay doors. Out floated thousands of leaflets branding Castro a Communist. Then the bomber banked and flew off in the direction of Florida.

No doubt embarrassed at the impudent action of the intruding aircraft, Castro rushed to a television studio and for nearly two hours upbraided "the traitor" who he was convinced (accurately) had been at the controls of the bomber—Major Pedro Díaz Lanz, the former chief of Castro's air force and the first 26th of July Movement leader to defect and flee to refuge in Florida.

Also a target for Castro's wrath in his long television tirade was President Eisenhower and the U.S. government, whose CIA had indeed furnished Díaz Lanz's bomber, probably without the knowledge of the White House.

Now the Castro regime's propagandists went to work. *Revolución* exploded indignantly in a blaring headline: HAVANA'S PEARL HARBOR.

Sensing much favorable media mileage to be gained around the world from what Castro had branded "a cowardly bombing of innocent civilians and children," hundreds of photographs of piles of corpses (no doubt taken elsewhere at an earlier time in Cuba or some other country) were distributed. Presumably each victim had been killed by a fluttering leaflet.

A FEW DAYS LATER, Major Camilo Cienfuegos, who had lived in New York City for several years, climbed into a small airplane in Camagüey Province in central Cuba and set a course for Havana. He was making a routine visit as chief of staff of the army under Raúl Castro. Also in the plane were the pilot and a bodyguard.

Cienfuegos was one of The Apostles, the twelve Cubans who had survived the ambush by Batista forces when Fidel Castro invaded Oriente Province with eighty-one rebels in December 1956. In 1958, Cienfuegos and Raúl Castro had led two armed bands that had seized Santa Clara, the first large city to be "liberated" from Batista.

Cienfuegos was considered to be the most charismatic of the revolutionaries, and his popularity among Cubans following the overthrow of Batista had been exceeded only by that of the Maximum Leader.

Like Fidel Castro, Cienfuegos had a flair for theatrics. A long beard covered most of his face, but peeping through the foliage were twinkling black eyes and lips that curled in an almost perpetual smile. Crowning the beard and a thick thatch of long black hair was a Texas cowboy-type, wide-brimmed hat that came to be his personal trademark. His sense of humor and charm endeared him to the masses, and each time he appeared in public, he was loudly cheered and applauded.

Cienfuegos's immense popularity with the people did not go unnoticed by either Fidel or Raúl Castro or their ambitious subordinates. Humorless, colorless Raúl was known to have been especially jealous of the public worship heaped on Cienfuegos. Presumably, Fidel himself was not too enthralled by the competition for public affection presented by his longtime crony.

Now in October 1959, after taking off on its flight to Havana, Cienfuegos's plane never reached its destination. It simply vanished without a trace. The mysterious disappearance of one of Castro's top men created a buzz of conjecture and apprehension in the upper echelons of the regime. Had the Apostle followed the example of Major Díaz Lanz and defected to Florida?

Not until three days after Cienfuegos had vanished did an official statement disclose that the free-spirited army chief of staff was missing. Then swarms of volunteer searchers beat the bushes in the wild, remote areas between the Camagüey airport and Havana. Cuban pilots scoured the sea and land. No trace of the missing plane would ever be found.

What had really become of Camilo Cienfuegos? Had he actually fled to asylum in the United States, shaved his beard, and gone into hiding with the help of the Central Intelligence Agency? Would he live out his life incognito in the United States for fear that a disclosure of his defection would result in his assassination and that of his wife and brother? Had he been defecting to Florida when his plane ran out of gas and plunged into the sea? Had the aircraft crashed into a remote area of Cuba? If so, why had the wreckage never been found on the relatively small island?

Rumors were rife in Havana. One was that the unarmed Cessna had been shot down by a Cuban Air Force jet, sent on the mission by an unknown party to eliminate the popular Cienfuegos. Could the culprit have been Raúl Castro, who, as Cienfuegos's boss, would have known of his flight plan? If Fidel Castro were to be eliminated, perhaps by CIA operatives, who would succeed him in Cuba's highest office: Brother Raúl or Camilo Cienfuegos? Or so went the whispers.

No outsider would ever come up with the answers to these vexing questions.

AMONG THOSE ardently seeking clues as to the mysterious disappearance of Cienfuegos was his good friend, Major Húber Matos, another genuine hero of the revolution. A schoolteacher by profession, he had earned the deep gratitude of Fidel Castro in March 1958 by flying a planeload of arms and ammunition from Costa Rica to the rebels' Sierra Maestra stronghold, the first major shipment of weapons for the 26th of July Movement. Matos had remained in Cuba and fought with courage and distinction, rising to the highest rebel rank of major. As a reward, Castro appointed him military commander of Camagüey Province after Batista's departure.

For several months, Major Matos had been on a collision course with the Maximum Leader, beginning with a speech in which Matos denounced the influx of Communists into the armed forces and their move into leadership roles previously held by the 26th of July Movement veterans. Then Matos had written to the then President Urrutia, demanding to know why Communists were being put into key positions in provincial and town governments.

Matos tried to take his case to Castro, who was too busy to see his old comrade. Frustrated, disillusioned, and angry, Matos decided to dramatize his protest. On October 19, he sent Castro his resignation from the army. Eighteen of his Camagüey officers also resigned.

Castro's gratitude to Húber Matos was short-lived. Just before dawn on October 21, a large contingent of Castro's soldiers surrounded Agramonte Barracks, Matos's headquarters, disarmed the 1,000-man garrison, and arrested the major, who was sitting quietly with his wife in their living room.

An hour later, Castro appeared on television to denounce his old friend Matos, accusing him of treason, inciting rebellion, and conspiring with ex-President Urrutia, Batista, and General Rafael Trujillo of the Dominican Republic. "The traitor Matos is under arrest," Castro exclaimed. "I have sent loyal troops into Camagüey to put down a rebellion."

Major Matos and his eighteen resigned officers were hustled off to Havana and imprisoned in the dungeons of gloomy Morro Castle. Their treason trial was held in the theater at Camp Columbia, which had been renamed Ciudad Libertad (Liberty City). A day prior to the preordained verdict, Fidel Castro took the witness stand, and as Cuban television cameras rolled, he loosed a tirade against "the traitors" that rambled on for nearly six hours. Neither the three-judge tribunal nor the prosecutor—all appointed by the Maximum Leader—dared to interrupt the marathon burst of oratory.

"The guilt of these accused has been completely proven," the Maximum Leader declared. "If they are acquitted, history will condemn this tribunal!"[1]

On December 15, the verdict was reached: guilty of treason. But Matos would be spared the firing squad. The tribunal pointed out that his sentence had been reached "in the spirit of the revolution which applies the death penalty only when the security and stability of the nation are threatened." The Old Guard warrior of the Sierra Maestra days would be let off with a twenty-year prison term.

WHILE MAJOR MATOS was being tried by a kangaroo court, 100,000 persons from throughout the island flocked to Havana's Tropical Stadium for the National Catholic Conference. A leader of the Catholic Youth Movement, Dr. José Lasaga, told the vast throng, "We believe that the Catholic attitude toward the revolution can be summed up in this phrase: `Social justice, Yes! Communism, No!'" The crowd roared spontaneously, and for ten minutes chanted, "Social Justice, Yes! Communism, No!"[2]

DURING THIS TIME, Castro wiped out another dangerous threat to the revolution—Santa Claus. The jolly, bearded, plump man in the red suit had been imported, along with Christmas trees, into Cuba in the

1930s from the United States. Now Santa Claus was abolished as an "imperialist."

In Santa's place was introduced a grotesque figure called Don Feliciano (Mr. Happiness), who wore a *quayabera* (tropical dress suit), a straw hat, and a black beard—a typical Cuban farmer. Don Feliciano may have been happy, but none of the island's children were in that frame of mind: He gained little attention and no respect.

At the same time, Christmas trees also were banned from import or from being displayed in Cuba. But the regime launched a propaganda campaign stressing the need to celebrate and to give thanks, not to God, certainly not to Santa Claus, but to Fidel Castro.

ONE OF THE MANY HATS Fidel Castro wore was that of president of the National Tourist Institute, so on New Year's Eve, 1959, he played host to a gala reception at the Havana Hilton for nearly one thousand Cuban and foreign guests. Almost all those from the United States were black. To show the developing countries of Africa, whom he hoped eventually to woo into his revolutionary orbit, that he was a champion of black people, he had focused his invitation on prominent black sports figures, including ex-heavyweight boxing champion Joe Louis and baseball greats Roy Campanella, Willie Mays, and Jackie Robinson. Only Joe Louis showed up in Havana, and he was given a place of honor at the head table next to Fidel Castro.

After serving his country in uniform during World War II, Louis, one of the greatest of champions, had fallen on hard times. He was not only broke, but the Internal Revenue Service had been trying to collect in excess of $1 million in back taxes allegedly due. Recently, he had been picking up a few bucks working at Caesar's Palace in Las Vegas as a shill at the blackjack tables. So in December 1959, Louis needed friends, recognition, and money—and Castro provided all three commodities.

If Castro expected Louis to roundly lambast the United States, he was disappointed. The former champion told Havana reporters only that "there are few places in the world except Cuba where a Negro can go in wintertime with absolutely no discrimination."

SHORTLY BEFORE CHRISTMAS, Jorge Zayas, publisher of the daily newspaper *Avance*, became aware that he had been placed on Fidel Castro's hit list. *Avance* had been protesting in editorials that the Cuban chief was taking the country into a Communist dictatorship. In a four-hour speech before a labor union, Castro branded *Avance* a "dangerous newspaper" and Zayas a traitor to the revolution. On January 18, 1960, a group of printers from the labor union burst into Zayas's office and announced that they were taking over *Avance* "in the name of the revolution."

Castro's next target was the *Diario de la Marina*, whose publisher, José Ignacio Rivero, also had been sharply critical of Communist infiltration into government, labor unions, and the armed forces. Ignacio Rivero had been bitterly assailed on television by Castro, saw the handwriting on the wall, and was ready to close up shop. But the beleaguered publisher was presented with a letter signed by four hundred employees urging him to keep fighting.

Greatly encouraged, Ignacio Rivero sent the letter to the composing room for publication the next day. But before the presses could roll, twenty bearded men burst into the plant and, swinging sledgehammers, smashed the printing plate containing the letter. Undaunted, Ignacio Rivero ordered a new plate made and left for an appointment.

That night *Diario de la Marina* was delivered routinely to the publisher's home. But the letter from his employees had not been printed. In its place was a blaring headline calling Ignacio Rivero "a tool of Yankee imperialism." After the publisher had departed earlier that day, Castroites had strong-armed their way into the plant and taken over the newspaper. Ignacio Rivero fled to the U.S. Embassy and asked for asylum.[3]

BY THE CLOSE of 1959, Fidel Castro, politically astute and ingrained with a keen sense of public-relations techniques, had convinced tens of millions of people in Latin America that any effort by the United States to link him with Communism was just another dirty trick of accusing all sincere reformers of being Communists. Privately, leaders throughout Latin America were urging President Eisenhower to get rid of Castro, but none would speak out publicly against the Cuban chief.

Back in 1954, at a conference in Caracas, Venezuela, twenty Latin American republics and the United States formed the Organization of American States (OAS) and went on record as opposing Communist intrusion in the region. Now the formidable problem confronting Eisenhower was how to prove that Fidel Castro was actually a Communist so that the OAS would take action against him.

In a memo to the president, Secretary of State Herter stated, "Successful presentation of the problem on Cuba to the OAS calls for the careful documentation of a 'case' on the Communist issue." Cynically, Eisenhower scribbled in the margin, "This has been almost zero!"[4]

A few days later, Herter advised the president that the OAS leaders said they would not support any action to overthrow Castro unless the United States at the same time moved to oust General Rafael Trujillo, the right-wing dictator of the Dominican Republic and crony of Fulgencio Batista. Herter said that forcing out Trujillo, if it could be done, would be an unwise action because the Communists might take over the Dominican Republic in the ensuing chaos and unrest.[5]

At a meeting with Herter and other top officials in the administration, Eisenhower angrily declared: "That Castro begins to look like a madman!" He stressed that if the OAS would not help boot the Cuban from power, "then the United States should go it alone!"[6]

A frustrated Eisenhower summoned Allen Dulles, the CIA director, to the White House to discuss the Cuban situation. The president felt that Herter and his State Department bureaucrats were mainly talking; what Eisenhower wanted was action.

Dulles reached into his briefcase and pulled out a good-sized number of U-2 spy plane photographs of a large Cuban sugar refinery and presented a CIA plan to sabotage the facility. Eisenhower was not impressed, pointing out that the Cubans could put the refinery back in working order within days.

"Come back when you've got a genuine program for dealing with the Cuban problem," the president told Dulles.[7]

At CIA headquarters a week later, the Special Group, a subcommittee of the National Security Council, convened to hear a Dulles briefing on a program to meet Eisenhower's demand for action. The Special Group's function was to consider CIA action proposals and make recommendations on them to the NSC.

Listening to Dulles present details of a CIA operational plan codenamed the Cuban Project were Presidential Security Adviser Gordon Gray; Livingston Merchant of the State Department; and Admiral Arleigh "31 Knots" Burke, chief of naval operations. They gave their stamp of approval to the Cuban Project, whose goal was to "eliminate" Fidel Castro.

A short time later, a Cuban Task Force was formed. Its function was to instigate and coordinate specific clandestine actions aimed at overthrowing the Castro regime without apparent U.S. involvement. At the task force's first meeting on March 9, Colonel J. C. King, the CIA's operations chief of the Western Hemisphere Division, dropped a bombshell.

Intelligence had been obtained, King said, that Fidel Castro's top associates were clamoring for an armed attack against the U.S. Naval Base at Guantanamo. Therefore, King urged the acceleration of covert actions. Unless the Big Three—Fidel Castro, Raúl Castro, and Ché Guevara—could be "eliminated in one package," it might require intervention by the U.S. armed forces, he declared.[8]

If the intelligence was accurate and the Cubans launched a military assault against Guantanamo, war could erupt and the Soviet Union probably would leap to Castro's side, King added. A major escalation in the United States–Castro vendetta was hereby launched.

Tension over Guantanamo thickened. Castro spoke out regularly about an American base on "Cuban soil" as an example of Yankee imperialism. *Hoy* and *Revolución* took up the Yankees-get-out battle cry, and Communist newspapers around the world joined in the strident chorus.

11

"Bobby's As Hard As Nails!"

S ENATOR JACK KENNEDY was fidgety as he paced from room to room in his suite in the Capitol in Washington. Then he picked up papers, read a few seconds, put them on his desk, sat down, and moved the papers. Leaning back in his chair, he stared at the ceiling, then looked at the clock. One aide thought he was like a thoroughbred racing horse waiting at the starting gate. It was 12:15 P.M., Saturday, January 2, 1960.

Minutes later, Kennedy walked down the corridor, escorted by a bevy of confidants, and entered the caucus room that was packed with reporters, radio and television crews, and fervent supporters. Approaching the front of the huge room to a thunderous ovation, the senator stood at the podium while photographers snapped pictures. Then he started to read a prepared statement: "I am announcing today my candidacy for the presidency of the United States. . . ."

Kennedy brought with him solid liberal credentials—the political-action committee of the AFL-CIO had him voting "correctly" on fifteen of sixteen key issues during his eight years in the Senate.

JACK KENNEDY'S alter ego and the driving force behind his presidential campaign was his younger brother, Bobby, who had become a national figure in his own right after serving as chief counsel and head of an investigative staff of sixty-five for the Senate Select Committee on Improper Activities in the Labor or Management Field. Top priority had been given to the activities of the Teamsters Union, which, the government charged, was corrupt and involved with gangsters.

In nationally televised hearings in the early spring of 1957, Bobby Kennedy dueled repeatedly with Teamsters president David Beck, who took the Fifth Amendment and refused to answer questions 203 times. A year later, in March 1958, James R. "Jimmy" Hoffa, who succeeded

Beck at the helm of the union, and Kennedy were involved in a shouting match and exchange of insults before a national television audience. Kennedy accused the feisty Hoffa of "grossly misusing union funds" and "running a hoodlum empire."[1]

The younger Kennedy soon gained the moniker "Ruthless Bobby" in Washington circles. Some called him "The Pitbull."

"Bobby's a tough one, all right," his father, Joseph P. Kennedy Sr., admiringly told a syndicated columnist. To another reporter, he said proudly, "Bobby's as hard as nails!" Although he would later deny that he had said it, Kennedy Senior told yet another correspondent, "Bobby's a lot like me—he hates everybody!"[2]

One day, a highly influential political figure was meandering around campaign headquarters, jabbering away as pols are inclined to do. Irritated, Bobby loudly bawled out the big wheel: "If you're not going to do any work, don't hang around here!"[3]

SOON AFTER Jack Kennedy officially entered the presidential sweepstakes, he released a controversial piece he had written that was sympathetic to Fidel Castro and the Cuban revolution. Titled *The Strategy of Peace,* the critique described the Maximum Leader as "part of the legacy of [Simón] Bolivar," the eighteenth-century general whose victories over the Spaniards won independence for Bolivia, Colombia, Ecuador, Peru, and Venezuela. Many have called Bolivar *El Libertador* (The Liberator) and "The George Washington of South America." Kennedy wrote that Castro was "part of the frustration of that earlier revolution which won its war against Spain but left largely untouched the indigenous feudal order."

In a swipe at President Dwight Eisenhower, Kennedy's piece raised the question as to whether Castro might not have taken "a more rational course" had not the Eisenhower administration backed Fulgencio Batista "so long and so uncritically." Moreover, Kennedy stated, U.S. relations with Cuba might have been better had Eisenhower given the Maximum Leader a warmer reception on his visit to Washington in April 1959.

IN JULY 1960, Bobby Kennedy was orchestrating strategy and tactics from the main command post of the Kennedy for President campaign on the eighth floor of the Biltmore Hotel in Los Angeles. Much to the astonishment of political pundits across the land, Jack had been victorious in several primary elections and now was considered by many to be the front-runner for the Democratic nomination.

Bobby seemed to be getting almost as much media ink as his brother, much of it damning him with faint praise. Widely read columnist Jim Bishop called Bobby "an irritable and irritating little man," one who was "tactless, impatient, ruthless. . . . When he concludes a brief chat with a political leader, the man is left with a feeling that if he doesn't do exactly as [Bobby] tells him, God will strike him dead."

No-nonsense Bobby, shirtsleeves rolled up, shirt collar unbuttoned, and necktie askew, captained a taut political ship. Relentlessly, he sent some forty operatives assigned to various state delegations to constantly buttonhole the delegates and urge them to back Jack. At the same time, the candidate rushed from hotel to hotel, shaking hands, cajoling, pleading for support. In one day, he spoke passionately to nine state caucuses.

The efficient, high-octane, well-oiled Kennedy political machine steamrollered all opposition. Jack was nominated on the first ballot with 806 votes to 409 for Lyndon B. Johnson, a hulking, rough-hewn, hard-bitten senator from Texas.

Now the Kennedys faced the crucial task of selecting a vice presidential running mate for Jack. A prominent Texan like Lyndon Johnson, who up until that time had been carrying conservative credentials, would balance the ticket and be crucial to carrying the South, key Democratic politicians assured Jack. So he offered the second spot to Johnson.

At the Biltmore Hotel command post, Bobby, press secretary Pierre Salinger, Sargent Shriver, Kenneth O'Donnell, and other close aides were furious. So were liberal governors and union leaders. Consequently, an urgent powwow was convened with Jack and a decision was reached to dump Lyndon Johnson.

Johnson, who secretly detested the Kennedys, had a passion for becoming a national figure. Even though Jack was only forty-three years of age, Johnson knew that one out of four presidents had died in office. So the blunt Texan was outraged at Bobby's suggestion that he withdraw voluntarily.

Desperate to avoid a disruptive floor fight that could scuttle his presidential aspiration, Jack spread the word that "Lyndon's my boy." Later, Speaker of the House John McCormack of Massachusetts, a longtime close friend of the Kennedys, told a newspaper reporter that Joe Kennedy Sr. had telephoned the angry Johnson to smooth his ruffled feathers.[4]

A major squabble over Johnson at the convention was almost a certainty. Hundreds of liberals were angry. Consequently, the Kennedy brothers engaged in a behind-the-scenes manipulation: A motion that Johnson be nominated by acclamation was gaveled through by the convention chairman. It was a done deal, even though a chorus of boos rang out.

PRESIDENT EISENHOWER was vacationing at Newport, Rhode Island, when word reached him that Kennedy had chosen Lyndon Johnson as his vice presidential running mate. "How could Johnson, having said all those [harsh] things about Kennedy, having said over and over again that he wouldn't be a vice presidential candidate, even consider it?" William Robinson, a confidant, asked.

Eisenhower thought he had an answer. "Johnson is not a big man," the president said. "He is a small man. He hasn't got the depth of mind nor the breadth of vision to carry great responsibility. He is superficial and opportunistic."[5]

As much as Eisenhower disliked Lyndon Johnson, he detested Jack Kennedy and his clan even more. He told another close aide, Ellis Slater, that he was worried that "if the Kennedys ever get in, we will never get them out—that there will be a [political] machine bigger than Tammany Hall ever was."[6]

To a friend, Eisenhower declared, "I will do almost anything to avoid turning my chair and the country over to Kennedy."[7]

Later, the president told a scientific aide, Dr. George Kistiakowsky, that "thoughtful Democratic leaders are horrified by Lyndon Johnson's selection," and that Johnson "is the most tricky and unreliable politician in Congress."[8]

AFTER A WEEK'S VACATION, Jack Kennedy took to the campaign trail and hit hard at what he charged were the "inadequacies of the Eisenhower administration." And he spoke out bluntly at what he perceived to be a "missile gap" that "Richard Nixon and Dwight Eisenhower had permitted" to occur between the U.S. arsenal and that of the Soviet Union.

Privately, Jack took potshots at the president. "I could understand it if he played golf all the time with old army friends," he told confidants. "But no man is less loyal to his old friends than Eisenhower. He is a terribly cold man. All his golfing pals are rich men he has met since 1945."[9]

Eisenhower, noted for having a short fuse on occasion, was furious over the deluge of criticism from the Kennedy camp. When Republican Senator Styles Bridges told the president that Jack had claimed earlier in the day that "seventeen million Americans go to bed hungry every night," Eisenhower snapped, "They must all be dieting!"[10]

12

A Secret Scheme Is Born

WHILE THE KENNEDY FOR PRESIDENT caravan had been rolling across the United States, a black limousine carrying CIA Director Allen Dulles and a top aide, Richard M. Bissell Jr., drove through the massive gates of the White House in Washington. The two cloak-and-dagger men had come to brief Dwight Eisenhower on a newly created secret plan designed to deal with the Cuban situation. It was March 17, 1960.

A Yale graduate and onetime professor, the hard-driving, no-nonsense Bissell had been recruited by Dulles in 1954, and shortly afterward he won his spurs with the Agency by helping to engineer the overthrow of a Communist regime in Guatemala in Central America. Then he had developed the supersecret U-2 flights over the Soviet Union, an ingenious innovation that had paid off handsomely with a wealth of intelligence until the Russians shot down one of the sleek aircraft and captured its pilot, Gary Powers.

Tall and lanky, Bissell was known for his scholarly discourse. He was one of the handful of key CIA officials who had not cut his covert teeth with the OSS in World War II—a "flaw" in his credentials that inhibited him not one iota in his dealings with more experienced colleagues.

Now in the Oval Office, Bissell, the chief of Clandestine Services, explained his plan to accelerate the overthrow of Fidel Castro. It consisted of sabotage, guerrilla operations, covert warfare, massive propaganda throughout the hemisphere, and economic and political subversion. Twenty-five Cuban exiles would be given military training at the secret U.S. Army Jungle Warfare Center in Panama, and these men, in turn, would recruit and train seventy-five other refugees. Then the entire force would infiltrate into Cuba, organize an underground, and engage in sabotage and guerrilla warfare.

Eisenhower approved the plan, then departed for the Burning Tree Country Club for a round of golf. The old general was unaware that he had just given birth to a covert project that would balloon in the months ahead into a major military invasion of Cuba.

Six days later, a second session was held in the office of Allen Dulles at CIA headquarters. Among those present to hear Dick Bissell detail his plan for toppling the Castro regime were Dulles; his deputy director, General Charles Cabell; David Phillips, a propaganda specialist; Tracy Barnes, a Harvard Law School graduate and Bissell's number-two man; and Richard Helms (who six years later would become the CIA director).[1]

Bissell's elaborate scheme called for the creation of a Cuban exiles' air force based at secret strips in Nicaragua, a flotilla of ships hidden in U.S. and Central American ports, and a small army of Cuban refugees to be trained in secret camps in Nicaragua and Guatemala. The rulers of those two countries were friendly to the United States and could be counted on to look the other way when the covert activities were unfolding in their backyards.[2]

Although the entire scenario would be orchestrated by the CIA, the idea was to make it appear to the world that Cuban exiles themselves had conceived, planned, financed, and directed an invasion of their homeland to drive out Fidel Castro and his regime.

In no other country in the world does an intelligence service operate with as much ballyhoo and openness as does the CIA. France's Deuxième Bureau and England's MI-5, the equivalents to the CIA, are barely known to exist among the rank and file of the people. Only a handful of top officials in the two governments know the name of any officer except the directors in MI-5 and the Deuxième Bureau. By contrast, the CIA is listed in government directories, and the director is given a prominent place on protocol lists.

One secret kept by the CIA, which was established in 1947 to be official Washington's eyes and ears around the globe, is how many persons it employs. Educated guesswork at this time was that there may have been as many as thirty thousand persons on the payroll. One thing was certain: They popped up at every Washington cocktail party and said mysteriously to other guests, "I work for the government."

Unlike in France and England, journalists maintain contacts at the Agency, and some CIA officials give favored reporters briefings that include "inside dope" (which may or may not be authentic). Some Agency operatives often cannot resist the temptation to gain celebrity status by puffing up their own achievements. The CIA is the only "black service" in the world that distributes press releases about its personnel.

WHILE THE CIA was developing covert operations against Castro, the French ship *La Coubre* was tied up alongside a wharf in Havana harbor. The vessel was loaded with military weapons and ammunition that Castro had purchased in Belgium. Suddenly, large sections of the city were rocked when a mighty explosion almost disintegrated the *La Coubre* while Cuban workers were unloading the cargo. Some seventy persons were killed; scores of others were injured.

Within hours, the Maximum Leader rushed to a television studio and, instead of expressing sympathy for the dead and their loved ones from the wharfside blast, bitterly denounced Dwight Eisenhower ("a warmonger") and the United States for the "vicious and cruel act of sabotage." His newspaper, *Revolución*, chimed in with a charge that the CIA had set off the explosion as an excuse for the invasion of Cuba by U.S. armed forces.

Then Castro's sophisticated propaganda machine, refined by Soviet experts, hammered incessantly on the theme of bloody American sabotage. A horror booklet was rapidly created and circulated around the world, blaming the United States for the massacre along the wharf.

In Washington, CIA experts studying what they could learn about the explosion leaned toward the theory that Castro or his emissaries had been the instigators of the carnage. They pointed out that the *La Coubre* had been tethered at a wharf, whereas ships carrying explosives generally are anchored in the middle of a harbor and the munitions carried ashore in smaller vessels.

Whatever may have been the case, the explosion worsened relations between Cuba and the United States, which were near rock bottom before the blast.

NOW CASTRO came up with new charges against the United States: Washington's "deliberate failure" to halt the light aircraft piloted by "worms" (Cuban exiles) that were taking off from Florida and "bombing" Cuba. In these darting, hit-and-run actions, small bombs and incendiary devices were dropped on Cuban sugar fields just as the harvest was about to begin. Sugar exporting is a major portion of the island's economy.

Washington, indeed, seems to have turned a blind eye to the flights, which were little more than pinpricks. Castro himself appeared to have taken no decisive steps to halt the air incursions: His jet fighters easily could have shot down these small, slow, unarmed aircraft. Perhaps the Maximum Leader was welcoming the "bombings" to turn the Cuban people against the United States and to portray Uncle Sam to the world as a brutal aggressor.

Evidence soon surfaced that the Havana regime had arranged for some of the flights over Cuba using paid American pilots as a further step toward discrediting the United States. In April, a federal grand jury in Miami dug up information that several of Castro's secret agents in Florida had had mysterious contacts with certain freelance American pilots. The evidence was circumstantial but impressive in scope.

Then intriguing incidents involving intrusion flights erupted in Cuba. While winging above the Expaña sugar mills in Las Villas Province, an airplane exploded and its pilot, an American named Robert Ellis Frost, was killed. Three weeks later, Cuban antiaircraft guns shot down a plane carrying two Americans near Matanzas. Identified as William L. Schergales and Howard Rundquist, the men survived the crash and were hospitalized.

The U.S. vice counsul in Havana managed to visit Schergales in the hospital, where he was being held under guard, and obtained from him an amazing affidavit. Schergales claimed, the U.S. State Department would later declare, that he had been paid by the Cuban government to make the flight.

Schergales pointed a finger at Juan Orta, chief of Fidel Castro's executive office, as the official who had arranged the flight and paid him. Although the Justice Department in Washington repeatedly asked for the extradition of the two Americans to be tried in Miami for violating U.S. neutrality laws, Havana authorities stonewalled the request.[3]

IN LATE APRIL, authorities at the U.S. Naval Base at Guantanamo issued a terse announcement: A Cuban labor leader working there had been fired for inefficiency. The real reason: He had been rabble-rousing constantly to stir up a riot among the three thousand Cubans employed at the installation.

Castro seized on the episode to step up his attacks against Uncle Sam. The firing of the labor leader was protested officially to Washington, along with a demand that he be rehired. Minister of Labor Augusto Martinez was hustled on to television to declare that the "Yankee lawbreakers" at Guantanamo "should subject themselves to the laws of Cuba."[4]

FIDEL CASTRO was growing more furious at the Catholic Church, the religion into which he had been baptized (as had most Cubans). His ire apparently grew even more intense after Monsignor Enrique Pérez Serantes, the archbishop of Santiago, on May 16 issued a pastoral letter denouncing Communism. "The enemy [Communism] is at our gates!" the monsignor declared.

Within a few weeks, orchestrated violence against the Catholic Church erupted at a Mass for victims of worldwide Communism in Havana Cathedral. The stately edifice was jammed to overflowing, but when Monsignor Boza Masvidal, auxiliary bishop of Havana, began his sermon, few could hear him—someone had tampered with the loudspeaker.

At the conclusion of Mass, the congregation sang "Long Live Christ the King," and then, in a spontaneous gesture, broke out with Cuba's traditional national anthem. Outside, a mob, whose members had been shouting obscenity-laced insults all through Mass, loosed a raucous singing of the Communist "Internationale."

As the worshipers began leaving the cathedral, pushing and shoving commenced, and a full-fledged riot broke out. A contingent of soldiers, supposedly on the scene to preserve order, began making arrests. None of the thugs in the disruptive mob was taken into custody. All of those hauled off to jail had been in the cathedral congregation.[5]

A MONTH LATER, Fidel Castro turned his propaganda spotlight once again on the U.S. Naval Base at Guantanamo. Major Calixo García, military commander of Oriente Province, complained that U.S. warships based at Guantanamo were violating Cuban waters and holding gunnery practice less than 3 miles from shore. This shooting, García howled, was endangering the lives of Cuban civilians.

The U.S. State Department's reply was swift and terse: "Bunk!"[6]

"Ridiculous!" chimed in Rear Admiral Frank W. "Mike" Fenno, the base commander. "There were ships firing, but they were at least twenty miles from the Cuban shoreline."[7]

Admiral Fenno was taking no chance that this latest hullabaloo was vintage Castro bluster. Gitmo, an isolated American enclave, was put on full alert. Marines and sailors, armed to the teeth, patrolled around the clock the 10-foot-high chain-link fence that ran for 26 miles along the base perimeter. Attack-trained guard dogs accompanied them on their rounds.

Now a third party jumped into the jousting over the American presence at Guantanamo Bay. In Moscow, Nikita Khrushchev, the pudgy Soviet dictator, launched into a diatribe against the United States and boasted that he would "support Cuba with missiles" if the Caribbean island were attacked.

FOR SEVERAL MONTHS, Fidel Castro and his top lieutenants, Ché Guevara and Raúl Castro, had been orchestrating a campaign to spread their revolution across Latin America and spark an uprising against the United States. In a subtle jab at Latin American countries friendly to the United States, Castro's propaganda came from what was labeled the "Free Territory of the Americas."

In Washington, the State Department vastly underestimated, or chose to ignore, the wide scope of the Cubans' propaganda campaign. A manual written by Guevara, *The War of the Guerrillas*, was shipped by the tens of thousands to Latin American countries, where it was distributed by members of the Cuban embassies.

Guevara's how-to publication detailed the strategy for organizing and conducting a successful revolution against established governments. "In underdeveloped Latin America, the revolution must be supported by peasants and workers, and the field of the armed struggle must be in the countryside," Guevara wrote.

Dr. Ernesto "Ché" Guevara was an unlikely figure to be a revolutionary leader. Although a shy introvert and a scrawny asthmatic, he had traits that fit in well with Fidel Castro—brains and ruthlessness. Like the Maximum Leader, he came from a relatively wealthy family. He grew up in Rosario, Argentina. Although he gained a medical degree, he never set up a practice. Instead, he bummed through Chile, Panama, Bolivia, Peru, and Venezuela, eking out a Bohemian existence and reading extensively. His favorite works were by Karl Marx and Mao Tse-tung, the leader of Communist China who had seized power in 1949 after a long and bloody civil war.

The freelance Communist adventurer grew to hate the United States while still in his teens. In 1954, Guevara was working as a salesman in Argentina when the CIA orchestrated the overthrow of a Communist regime. Guevara, on learning of the strife, rushed to Guatemala to help the ousted dictatorship, but he rapidly left the country and went to Mexico. There, in 1955, he met Fidel Castro. The two men were the same age and hit it off from the beginning.

A year later, Guevara, leaving behind his Peruvian wife, boarded the *Granma* ship with the Castro brothers and a band of armed guerrillas for the ill-fated expedition to seize control in Cuba.

Along with Guevara's *The War of the Guerrillas*, tons of printed propaganda flowed steadily from Cuba into Latin America. Most of the materials were printed on the presses of the independent newspapers and magazines that had been shut down by Castro. These materials ranged from handbills and leaflets to lavish four-color magazines.

Meanwhile, Cuban embassies and consulates throughout Latin America ceased to be conventional diplomatic missions and became hotbeds of propaganda dissemination, espionage, and the stirring up of political unrest. Staff members rapidly established liaisons with journalists, college students, labor leaders, and assorted dissident groups, including the Communist Party. Soon more than fifty "fronts" and "friendship societies" had been created throughout Latin America to mask Castro's true revolutionary intent.

LATE IN MAY 1960, Castro dispatched his figurehead president, Osvaldo Dorticós Torrado, Foreign Minister Raúl Roa, and several high-ranking military officers on a "friendship tour" of Latin America. Actually, the trek was a machination to lambast the United States as an economic and military aggressor against Cuba. In a large number of news conferences, Dorticós declared that Cuba was being bombed almost daily by flights from Florida against "our sugarcane fields, our industrial plants, hospitals, and even our capital of Havana."

By comparison to the United States, Dorticós said repeatedly, Cuba was a peace-loving country, one that was free of Communism, dedicated to freedom of the press and speech, and having excellent relations with the Catholic Church, the predominant religion throughout Latin America.

CASTRO AND HIS AIDES had not set their sights solely on the vast expanse from the Rio Grande along Mexico's northern border to the tip of South America several thousand miles to the south; they also envisioned the revolution eventually reaching the United States. Cuba's propaganda apparatus printed and arranged for the distribution of thousands of leaflets aimed at the black population, especially in New York's Harlem and the southern United States. Black people were urged to rise up en masse against the U.S. government.

At the same time, Castro purchased powerful shortwave radio transmitters in Switzerland, brought them to Cuba, and beamed propaganda messages toward Latin America and the southern United States. The theme of the broadcasts was the "evil men in Washington" and "Yankee imperialism."

PERHAPS HAVING GROWN BOLDER from Nikita Khrushchev's blunt threat to defend Cuba with missiles if the U.S. armed forces invaded the island, the Maximum Leader, in June 1960, demanded that three U.S.- and British-owned refineries in Cuba process two bargeloads of Soviet crude oil that had been sent to the island. The oil giants—Shell, Texaco, and Esso—refused. Castro retaliated by seizing the refineries and other corporate properties on the island.

One property after the other belonging to the "Yankee imperialists"—$1 billion worth in all—was confiscated. Sugar mills, breweries, distilleries, soap manufacturers, milk producers, chocolate companies, rice and flour mills, bottling firms, drug and department stores, paint makers, movie houses, construction firms, and shipping companies were all taken over. By late 1960, nothing American in Cuba remained for Castro to steal.

President Eisenhower was furious and swung back: Cuba would not be allowed to send the United States the remainder of its sugar quota for 1960, an action that would cost Cuba's economy in excess of $100 million in lost sales.

13

Intrigue and
Covert Actions

U NDER THE ENERGETIC DIRECTION of Clandestine Services chief Dick
Bissell, the CIA in the early months of 1960 had been as busy as
queen bees covertly mustering a sea and air force for an invasion that
would be projected to the world as an operation carried out by zealous
Cuban patriots and financed by unidentified parties. CIA men contacted Alfredo Garcia, whose Garcia Line had offices in New York
City and Havana, and the Cuban agreed to loan his freighters to the
invasion. Garcia Line had long been hauling sugar from Cuba to Central America, so the presence of its vessels in Caribbean waters would
not arouse the curiosity of Castro's intelligence agency.

A Miami yacht broker, Charles C. Mills, agreed to covertly purchase two World War II LCIs (landing craft, infantry) from surplus
firms. A pair of ocean-going ships, the *Blagar* and *Barbara J.*, were acquired in a similar manner, berthed in Key West, and registered under
the name of a dummy corporation. The United Fruit Company, with
huge holdings in the Caribbean, was contacted secretly by the CIA
with a request that two of its freighters be borrowed to haul troops,
ammunition, and supplies between embarking ports in Guatemala and
Cuba during the invasion. The role played by United Fruit was so deep
undercover that even the firm's board of directors was not told of the
arrangement.[1]

Crews for the invasion ships were all Cuban, but soon native skippers were replaced by boat captains drafted from the U.S. Navy Military Sea Transportation Service. Planners had become concerned over
the nautical qualifications of the Cuban skippers.

Planes to be used in the invasion were already in CIA hands at
Eglin Air Force Base in Florida where there was a Special Air Warfare
Center that developed techniques for supporting clandestine opera-
tions around the globe. Twin-engine B-26 attack bombers, relics from

World War II, were chosen for the operation. They would be painted with Cuban markings. Minus manufacturers' code numbers, the B-26s would dovetail nicely with the all-Cuban illusion of the operation; so many B-26s had been bought and sold on the world's surplus market for twenty years that it would be difficult for Castro's intelligence agency to trace the aircraft to the CIA.

In the time remaining, it would be impossible to train enough Cuban exiles to fly the B-26s, so the CIA set to work recruiting pilots from the Virginia, Arkansas, and Alabama Air National Guards, whose squadrons had once flown B-26s. In Birmingham, Albert C. "Buck" Persons, who was flying for a construction corporation, was called to the airport office of Major General George R. Doster, leader of the 117th Tactical Reconnaissance Wing of the Alabama Air National Guard.

"Buck, I've got a job to recruit six experienced pilots for four-engine work, and six B-26 pilots," Doster explained. "They must have no current military connections. I want you for C-54s. About all I can tell you right now about the job is this: There will be shooting involved, and it's very much in the interest of our government."[2]

Persons grabbed the offer—even before he learned that the pay would be $2,800 per month (a hefty sum at the time) plus bonuses. The job would last "about three months," General Doster told him. It required no great astuteness for Persons to guess that the secret target was Cuba.

A short time later, Persons and other recruited American pilots were given a briefing by four men who said that they represented wealthy Cubans who were funding an operation to eliminate Castro from power. Actually, the briefers were CIA agents, as the pilots well knew. At the next briefing, the four men dropped the "representing wealthy Cubans" facade. Now the American pilots were told that the four were working for an electronics company in New England.

After careful screening in Miami (including lie-detector tests), Persons and a group of fellow American pilots were herded into a Hertz rental van one night and driven to a small airport on the outskirts. After climbing aboard an aging C-54 transport plane, Persons was puzzled: The crew was Asian. The old crate rumbled down the runway and lifted off for a flight across the Caribbean to a secret airstrip at Retalhuleu, Guatemala.

At scattered points throughout the United States, Cuban exiles who would take part in the invasion were undergoing intense instruction in their specialties. Frogmen were put through their paces at an abandoned flying-boat base on the Pasquolank River, near Elizabeth

City, North Carolina. Outside Colonial Williamsburg, Virginia, Cubans were taught covert photography, lock-picking, human and electronic surveillance, microfilming, the use of invisible inks, communications, and other fine points of "black warfare." On Viegues Island off Puerto Rico, underwater demolition teams learned their trade, and leadership instruction for the invasion commanders was conducted at the U.S. Army's Jungle Warfare Center in Panama.

In the meantime, at a jungle-shrouded hideaway in Guatemala known as Base Trax, the all-Cuban combat force that would storm ashore on Castro's island was being whipped into shape by members of the U.S. Special Forces, an elite outfit skilled in irregular warfare. Based at Fort Bragg, North Carolina, the tough Green Berets (as they were popularly known later) drove their charges unmercifully, knowing that there was but a brief period in which to mold a ragtag array of mostly civilians into an organized military force.

Heavy friction soon erupted. Most Cuban trainees, who had joined up looking forward to a romantic adventure, grew to hate their harsh and demanding Green Beret instructors. Another target of the Cubans' wrath was the hard-bitten U.S. Army lieutenant colonel who commanded the camp under the *nom de guerre* (war name) Colonel Frank.

Sandy-haired, aggressive, and resolute, Colonel Frank cared nothing of what his Cuban charges thought of him or his Hawks, as the Green Beret instructors were called. He had a job to do—and he intended to succeed.

ALL THE WHILE, the CIA headquarters in Washington was concocting plots to discredit Fidel Castro. Joseph Scheider, a chemist in Technical Services, was credited with the idea of spraying the inside of Castro's Havana television studio with a substance that induced hallucinations. The theory was that the Maximum Leader would appear on television as being either highly intoxicated or mentally unbalanced. The obstacle was how to get the substance into the studio just before Castro arrived.

Another scheme was to dust Castro's shoes, presuming he would leave them outside his hotel room door to be shined, with thallium salts. Theoretically, this would cause his beard to fall out. It was never quite figured out at what hotel he might leave his shoes at any given time.

The CIA also concocted more lethal plots, one of which had a beautiful, black-haired German woman, Marie "Marita" Lorenz, as the centerpiece. In February 1959, only six weeks after Castro had seized power, the German cruise ship *Berlin* sailed into Havana Harbor. Skipper of the vessel was Heinrich Lorenz, who had brought along his voluptuous nineteen-year-old daughter Marita.

Always with an eye on favorable public relations for himself and the "new Cuba," Castro accepted an invitation to come aboard to meet the German tourists and have a dinner in his honor. Seated next to Marita, the Maximum Leader was apparently smitten with her beauty and charm. Later that night, Castro invited her to stay in Havana and work for him as his "confidential secretary."

Marita declined and the *Berlin* sailed northward the next day. Two weeks later, Castro dispatched two of his men to New York, and when the vessel arrived, the emissaries went aboard with an urgent message from Castro. He pleaded with her to reconsider, saying that he was in desperate need of a German interpreter.

Marita changed her mind and Castro sent a plane to bring her back to Havana. There she lived in an ornate suite in the Havana Libre, just a few doors from the Maximum Leader's own living quarters (which he used only occasionally).

Within a short time, Marita had had her fill of the "new Cuba"—and Fidel Castro. In some manner, she made contact with a CIA operative, who smuggled her out of the country. Several months later, presumably while under the control of the CIA, she slipped back into Havana disguised as a tourist. Waiting until Castro was out of the city, she donned the olive-green rebel uniform that the Maximum Leader had given her and, using the key she had retained, stole into his Havana Libre suite. She reportedly pilfered all the documents and maps she was able to stuff into the pockets of her jackets, then flew to Miami to hand the materials over to her CIA contact.[3]

One of the CIA spooks involved with Marita was Frank Fiorini, later known as Frank Sturgis, a soldier of fortune who had fought at Castro's side in the Sierra Maestra, then had turned against him and taken refuge in the United States. It was Sturgis who apparently asked Marita to murder the Maximum Leader, promising her a hefty sum of money for the hit job. She agreed to the mission and was given two poison capsules, which she secreted in a jar of cold cream.[4]

Lorenz made her way to Havana, got in contact with Castro, and the pair rendezvoused in a bedroom. He took the phone off the hook, made love, ordered food, and then fell asleep with a cigar in his mouth. Now was her chance. She slipped into the bathroom and opened the jar of cold cream. The capsules were not there; they had melted. It seemed to be an omen. Lorenz said to herself, "To hell with it!" and slipped out of the room.[5]

The CIA also revived a project its scientists had been working on for several years: Can an individual be made to perform an act of attempted assassination involuntarily under the influence of Artichoke? That was the code name for a mind-control experiment in which it was theorized that an individual who had access to or was in the locale of the target could have his mind "bent" to carry out a murder, although mayhem of any type may not have been in his nature. Presumably, the kinks had not been worked out of Artichoke for it to be applied to Fidel Castro.

IN EARLY JULY 1960, E. Howard Hunt, an enigmatic figure who would serve as the CIA political-action officer for the invasion of Cuba, slipped into the Caribbean island posing as a carefree tourist. The Agency's cover staff had provided him with documentation that would support his operational alias in the event he was arrested.

Lean, blue-eyed, and astute, Hunt had been sent on the covert mission to assess firsthand if Cuba was ripe for a mass revolt after the invasion force landed. It was a hazardous task: Castro's secret police and civilian informers were everywhere, especially in Havana.

After checking in at the Hotel Vedado, Hunt began strolling leisurely through the crowded streets, resisting urgent impulses to glance back over his shoulder to see if he was being tailed. He was struck by the atmosphere of repression. Newsstands that once held *Life, Time, Look,* and *Newsweek* in his numerous visits in the pre-Castro era now displayed imports from Communist China and the Soviet Union.

One night, Hunt stopped in a downtown park to listen as José Pardo Llada, a Castro propagandist, preached class hatred and malice for the *Yanquis* over a loudspeaker to a crowd of hundreds. So emotional and angry did the throng become that they chased, screaming and yelling obscenities, after five better-dressed Cubans who were running for their lives and finally vanished into the darkness.

On his return to Quarters Eye, Hunt reported to his immediate boss, Tracy Barnes, that most Cubans were solidly behind Fidel Castro and that it would be foolhardy to count on a popular uprising in support of the exiles' invasion.

Hunt submitted four recommendations. Number one on the list was Castro's murder. A blunt man, Hunt always refused to use the term "eliminate," which had been bandied about in the CIA and interpreted in different ways by various operatives involved in the Cuban Project.

In the days ahead, Hunt, impatient and action-oriented, repeatedly collared Tracy Barnes and demanded to know what progress was being made on his proposal to murder Castro. Each time, Barnes replied, "It's with the Special Group."[6]

WHILE CIA invasion plans were being developed, the National Security Council convened on July 7 to discuss the Cuban situation. Defense Secretary Thomas S. Gates laid out a wide range of possible moves against Castro, all the way from evacuating U.S. citizens from the island to an invasion and occupation by American armed forces.

Treasury Secretary Robert Anderson was hawkish, giving a "long, fairly bloodthirsty speech" about the need to declare a national emergency. "What Castro is doing in Cuba represents an aggressive action [against the United States] by the Soviets," he declared.[7]

AT THE SAME TIME, Secretary of State Christian Herter opened a second front, hoping to rally Latin American countries into a solid bloc against Castro. After calling a meeting in Costa Rica, Herter manipulated the desired statement from the group: a condemnation of "intervention or the threat of intervention" by the Soviet Union in Latin America.[8]

14

Exercises in "Health Alterations"

A T ABOUT 9:00 P.M. on July 20, 1960, a cable from the CIA station in Havana arrived at Quarters Eye. A Cuban, who had grown disenchanted with the revolution, would soon be in personal contact with Raúl Castro, the cable stated. What intelligence should the spy try to obtain?

The Quarters Eye duty officer promptly contacted Colonel J. C. King and Tracy Barnes, Dick Bissell's deputy in Clandestine Services. Barnes, a Harvard Law School graduate who had served in the OSS in World War II and had been decorated for parachuting into German-occupied France, was long steeped in how to play hardball in the deadly world of international intrigue.

Six hours after the coded cable reached Quarters Eye, a reply was dispatched to Havana: "Possible removal top three leaders receiving consideration at HQ." (The Big Three were Fidel Castro, Raúl Castro, and Ché Guevara.) Could the Cuban spy "arrange an accident" for Raúl Castro? the cable asked.[1] He would receive $10,000—payable on successful completion of the task. No money would be paid in advance for fear the spy might be a Castro double agent.[2]

The Havana case officer blanched. This would be his first involvement in violent covert actions. But he called in his new spy and was careful not to use the words "kill" or "assassinate," stressing instead the arrangement of an accident to "minimize Raúl Castro's influence." Reluctant at first, the Cuban finally agreed to the proposal, but only after the case officer had assured him that in the event of his death, his two sons would be provided college educations, courtesy of the U.S. government.[3]

Early the next morning, the case officer received a second cable from Quarters Eye: "Do not pursue ref. Would like to drop matter." The case officer was alarmed; his Cuban spy had already departed to

85

keep his appointment with Raúl Castro. Two days later, the Cuban returned, and the case officer breathed a sigh of relief: The hit man had been unable to find a method for "arranging an accident."[4]

A WEEK BEFORE the Democratic Convention to select a presidential nominee in early August 1960, five anti-Castro Cubans were sneaking into an out-of-the-way room in the Senate Office Building in Washington. They were the leaders of the Miami-based *Frente Revolucionario Democrático* (Democratic Revolutionary Front), a coalition of scores of Cuban exile groups. They had been brought in to be introduced to Senator Jack Kennedy.

The secret session had been arranged by the CIA, probably through Dick Bissell, the Clandestine Services chief, who reputedly headed an enthusiastic Kennedy faction within the Agency. Bissell was covering all bets. Richard Nixon, the Republican nominee, had long been kept current on CIA plans for Cuba in his role as vice president. Now, with Kennedy clued in, the CIA hoped for strong support for its actions against Cuba, no matter which nominee would occupy the Oval Office of the White House.

Beaming and going through the fidgets with his tie that would become a trademark, Kennedy pumped the hands of the five Cubans. Among them was Manuel Antonio "Tony" Varona, a squat, balding man who had been prime minister in the Carlos Prío administration. Prío and most of those close to him had been discredited by his regime's corruption, massive even by Cuba's standards, but Varona was known to be scrupulously honest, so much so that exiles in Florida joked that he had to be stupid not to have cashed in handsomely.

Another member of the Frente was twenty-eight-year-old Dr. Manuel Artime, who had developed and directed an underground network in Cuba from his Florida base. Artime would be chosen as the political leader for the planned invasion of Cuba.

TWO MONTHS LATER, in September 1960, Fidel Castro, along with an entourage of fifty people, lifted off in an airplane from Havana, bound for New York where he would join Soviet leader Nikita Khrushchev for an appearance before the United Nations General Assembly. Minutes after becoming airborne, Castro asked his security chief, Ramiro Valdés, if a Cuban Air Force plane would escort the group.

Embarrassed, Valdés replied haltingly that there would be no escort plane. Castro pierced his aide with steely eyes and grumbled, "We're in danger. If I were running the CIA, I'd shoot down this plane over water, then report it was an accident!"

When the Cuban aircraft neared the United States, those on board peered nervously out of windows and saw four jet fighter planes winging toward them. Perhaps the CIA had concocted the plot that Castro had suggested. However, the aircraft had the markings of the U.S. Air Force and had been sent to escort the Maximum Leader to New York.

After a short limousine ride from Idlewild (later John F. Kennedy) Airport, where the Cubans were confined until they agreed to store their arsenal of weapons, Castro and his ragtag, bobtail, bearded Cubans barged into the lobby of the Shelburne Hotel in midtown Manhattan. What the Maximum Leader did not know was that none of the hotels near the United Nations Building wanted them. Consequently, the U.S. State Department had pleaded with Edward Spatz, the manager of the Shelburne, to accept the Cubans. Spatz agreed reluctantly and even went along with the State Department request to give the Cuban retinue a cheap room rate of $20 daily.

Within moments of reaching the Shelburne lobby, Fidel Castro began shouting at Spatz. An American flag flew over the entrance to the hotel, and the Maximum Leader demanded that he be allowed to put out the Cuban revolutionary flag also. Spatz refused. Then Castro bellowed that the hotel was trying to cheat the Cubans by demanding a $10,000 deposit in advance for the rooms.

Castro's histrionics launched the opening act of a painstakingly conceived "theater" designed to favorably impress the developing nations, especially those in black Africa, that he was trying to woo into his revolutionary global orbit.

For twenty-four hours, the Cubans holed up in their rooms. Then, on cue, Castro and the entire party stormed out of the hotel and into a horde of media reporters and television crews. Posing regally for the photographers, the Maximum Leader declared, "I'm not ready to let myself be robbed!"

Castro and his entourage climbed into waiting limousines and sped off in a caravan for the seedy Theresa Hotel in Harlem. Some of the hotel's toilets wouldn't flush. The elevator broke down. This act in the scenario was intended to dramatize that the Cubans had turned their backs on the "capitalists" in midtown New York to be with the people of Harlem. Never mind that the Theresa management charged Castro double what the Shelburne had been asking. He would cheerfully pay it in return for the global publicity the skit had generated.

Castro told reporters, "I belong to the poor, humble people of Harlem." Then he invited twelve black employees of the Theresa to eat steaks with him at the coffee shop downstairs. American television cameras whirred. As soon as the television crews departed, Castro got up and left.

At two o'clock on the afternoon Castro was to speak before the UN General Assembly, the galleries were packed, and more than four hundred reporters elbowed their way into the press section. It was as though one of the momentous events of the twentieth century were about to enfold.

Until now, sessions of the General Assembly had been conducted with a reasonable amount of decorum. Language and demeanor usually was diplomatic. So far during the current sessions, British journalist Edwin Tetlow had watched with distaste the antics of Castro and Khrushchev. They seemed to Tetlow to be imitators of the Hollywood slapstick comedians Laurel and Hardy, especially when Castro applauded wildly as his Soviet mentor tried to shout down British Foreign Minister Anthony Macmillan as he called for "understanding between East and West."

Clad in an olive-green revolution uniform, Castro took to the podium at 4:00 P.M. and talked . . . and talked . . . and talked. He came down directly on the side of the Soviet Union and warmly praised Khrushchev for his efforts to "gain world peace through disarmament proposals." With a beaming Khrushchev, pudgy hands held high overhead, cuing the applause, the Maximum Leader railed that the U.S. "monopolists and exploiters" had tried to turn Cuba into a colony.

Frederick Boland of Ireland, the Assembly president, used his gavel to reprimand Castro for saying that Dick Nixon and Jack Kennedy, the presidential candidates, "lack brains" and that Kennedy was an "illiterate and ignorant millionaire." Both Americans were trying to promote armed revolt in Cuba, Castro declared.[5]

Castro rambled on for four hours and twenty-six minutes—the longest single speech ever recorded at a forum noted for long-winded orations. When he concluded, most of the audience still awake gave him a thunderous ovation.

One hour later, the Maximum Leader hurried to the UN office suite of the Czechs, principal arms dealers of the Soviet bloc, and stayed for more than three hours.

FOR SEVERAL WEEKS, a unit of the CIA's Technical Services Division, known as the Health Alteration Committee, had been conducting experiments in mind-bending drugs and poisons that would kill without a trace. However, some in the CIA felt that the most effective way to deal with Castro would be to destroy the macho image he had long cultivated.[6]

Toward this end, it was proposed that a box of Castro's favorite cigars be impregnated with a depilatory that would cause his hair to fall out, thus stripping him of his trademark beard. These doctored cigars, it was planned, would be made available to the Maximum Leader when he appeared on the popular David Susskind television talk show during the Cuban's visit to the United Nations.

CIA operative David Phillips, who was alternately billed as a propaganda specialist and the Agency's resident psychological expert, was asked if Castro's image would suffer if his beard fell out. "Yes, it would," Phillips replied. Then he posed the burning question: How could the impregnated cigars be given to Castro without running the risk that someone else, perhaps David Susskind, would smoke one and soon go bald?[7]

TWO DAYS AFTER his UN speech, which was carried live via the over-the-horizon transmission link by Havana television, Castro prepared to leave for home. A suspicious package addressed to him was delivered to his hotel. Security guards whisked away the box for opening by the New York City bomb and arson squad. It contained 10 pounds of flea powder, presumably for the beards and shaggy manes of the Maximum Leader and his entourage.

Castro's henchmen shouldered the special purchases he had made in New York, including a refrigerator, two cages of white mice, and a collection of large stuffed toys, and prepared for a Caesar-like return to Havana.

Even the departure from New York turned into a Communist rally. Castro learned that his Cuban Airlines Britannia had been impounded by a U.S. Federal Court order. A Miami agency, trying to collect an alleged unpaid $285,000 bill for tourist advertising, had asked for the writ. Grounded in the enemy's lair, Castro asked old pal Khrushchev for the loan of a plane to get the Cuban leader home. The Soviet boss was happy to comply. But first, why not gain a propaganda boost from the episode?

The Maximum Leader gathered a swarm of news reporters around him at the airport and, with television cameras rolling and flashbulbs popping, exclaimed, "The United States takes away our plane and the Soviet Union gives us a plane. The Soviets are our friends."

The carefully conceived lines were intended to portray Uncle Sam as a heartless bullyboy. But one newsman asked: "Is your government Communist?"

Castro's face flushed with anger and he snapped: "You've got Communism on your mind! Why don't you ask the CIA?"[8]

Reaching Havana in Khrushchev's Il-18 turboprop, the Maximum Leader rushed to the Presidential Palace where his minions had drummed up a crowd in excess of thirty thousand people. Speaking from the balcony over radio and television, Castro branded the United States as cold and hostile. During his ten days in New York, he asserted, hundreds of Cubans—men, women, and children—had been beaten up and brutalized by "government henchmen."

Blacks were being persecuted and farmers defrauded by the great monopolies, Castro declared. The media was an "imperialistic monster," and editors lied, duping the people constantly. Newspapers that told the truth could not exist for long. "How different in a fortunate country such as Cuba, where people are well oriented, where they recognize the truth!"[9]

15

Spooks and a "Tweeping" Plot

BY SEPTEMBER 1960, Miami had taken on the appearance of Havana. Scores of Cuban refugees were arriving daily. Some came by rafts, leaky boats, and even oil drums. Spanish-worded signs were everywhere, and at night, destitute, bewildered Cubans aimlessly wandered the streets.

In the Miami area alone, there were more than a hundred Cuban exile groups and organizations, ranging in size from a man-and-wife team to the thousands belonging to the Frente Revolucionario Democrático, headed by Antonio Varona, the former president of the Cuban Senate, who had held the secret meeting with Jack Kennedy in Washington two months earlier.

Mixed in with the dazed refugees milling about were an estimated two hundred agents of Fidel Castro's intelligence service, whose mission was to infiltrate the exile groups and obtain information on the CIA role. In the Miami mix was an unknown number of FBI operatives whose function was to spy on the Castro Cubans who were spying on the anti-Castro elements.[1]

Meanwhile, Varona's executive committee designated Colonel Martin Elena, who was regarded as being far from astute, as head of military affairs. His appointment was greeted with a total lack of enthusiasm by most of those in the exile leadership. So Howard Hunt, the CIA political-action leader for the planned invasion of Cuba, informed Elena that his most important task would be to develop a military plan for the operation in a Miami hideout.

Elena was delighted, unaware that he was a figurehead. His plans would never be used on I-Day (Invasion Day) or even considered. The actual invasion design was being drafted in Washington by the CIA and the Pentagon. However, there was one advantage to Elena's harmless exercise: Perhaps his invasion plan might be stolen by Castro's spies and serve as a prime deception from the actual operation.

One day, a vacationing female stenographer, whose brother worked for the FBI, was in a motel room near the Miami airport. Her room had a connecting door of lightweight wood, and the lower edge left about a 2-inch clearance. Suddenly, she became aware that two heavily accented voices were holding a discussion next door. She took down the conversation in shorthand, then turned it over to the FBI, confident that she had overheard two Castro conspirators. An investigation was launched. One of the "plotters" turned out to be Frank Bender, CIA headquarters chief of political action for the Cuban Project.

Bender's real last name was Drucher, and he was a German refugee. Much to the annoyance of Howard Hunt, the on-site political-action coordinator, Bender had been visiting Miami so frequently as to cause confusion among exiles and American operatives alike concerning his true role. Bender was authorized to operate only in New York and Washington at his own discretion.

When the stenographer heard the two "conspirators" next door, Bender had been holding a conference with one of the Cuban exile leaders, unbeknownst to Howard Hunt or other CIA operatives in Miami. After the FBI delivered the findings of its investigation to CIA security officers in Washington, Frank Bender was given a reprimand for his carelessness.

Operational security was an ongoing problem. Hunt was receiving so many visitors in his one-room Miami apartment that neighbors called police. In the guise of a credit investigator, a detective questioned the landlady, who told her that she believed Hunt was a bookie.

This "criminal investigation" caused Hunt to find other, larger quarters where the parade of "guests" would not be so noticeable to neighbors. He finally settled on a sizeable house overlooking the bay in suburban Coral Gables. But when the owner telephoned the credit reference Hunt provided, the contact apparently tried to keep the CIA man's cover, so he told the caller that he had never heard of Howard Hunt.

The owner was convinced that Hunt was a shady character, probably a gangster from New York or Chicago. So negotiations were broken off and Hunt finally rented a two-bedroom house in suburban Coconut Grove. He figured the place was ideal for clandestine activity: Plants and trees concealed much of the house and partially screened the entrance to the large yard. For his cover, he told his nearest neighbor, a friendly, middle-aged widow, that he had taken the hideaway to recover from the deep emotional stress of a nasty divorce. (Actually, Hunt was happily married.)

One day, the petite widow, in casual conversation, asked why so many "foreign-looking" men were traipsing in and out of Hunt's house. He told her that he owned a piece of a Cuban professional boxer of considerable promise, and those calling at the house were his partners in the investment deal.

The widow had a beautiful blonde daughter who did television-commercial modeling in New York and periodically flew down to spend the weekend with her mother. Later, the widow confided to Hunt that because of the stream of male visitors, she and her daughter had decided the CIA operative was a homosexual.[2]

ON OCTOBER 18, 1960, less than a month before the presidential election, FBI Director J. Edgar Hoover informed Allen Dulles of the CIA that Sam "Moo Moo" Giancana, a big shot in the Chicago underworld, was involved in a Mob conspiracy to kill Fidel Castro. Giancana's telephone had been tapped by the FBI for many weeks in a covert operation to disclose the inner workings of organized crime.[3]

Hoover's disclosure came as no surprise to some in the CIA. The murder plot was in fact an elaborate CIA-orchestrated scheme that Dick Bissell had hatched two months earlier. Bissell reasoned that members of the Mob, who had been deprived of millions of dollars in profits from gambling, booze, and prostitution when they had to scurry out of Cuba ahead of Castro's arrival in Havana, might have an incentive to get rid of the Maximum Leader and return their highly lucrative operations to the island.[4]

Bissell had called in an expert on covert activities, Robert A. Maheu, a former FBI agent and now on a monthly retainer by the FBI. Maheu was to contact certain Mob honchos and inform them that he was representing a consortium of Wall Street financiers and international corporations that had put up funds to "tweep" (CIA jargon for "terminate with prejudice") Fidel Castro. Great pains were to be taken to keep from connecting the CIA to the plot.

Maheu met with Johnny Roselli, the Mob's representative in Los Angeles and Las Vegas, in Hollywood's Brown Derby restaurant, a favorite hangout for the celebrity crowd. Roselli was enthusiastic and suggested that two other Mob bigshots who had to flee from Cuba, Moo Moo Giancana and Santo "Sam" Trafficante, be brought into the scheme.

Soon, Maheu's "big business" facade was dropped. Roselli sensed that Maheu was a CIA operative. Some would say that Roselli had viewed the mission as his patriotic duty. But years earlier, he had entered the country illegally under his true name and may have regarded "patriotic duty" as insurance against deportation.

Sam Giancana was contacted and he, too, was excited over the prospect of wiping out Castro. Both he and Roselli refused to accept the $150,000 "fee" the CIA had authorized for their help. Presumably, they envisioned far greater financial rewards in the future from the international investigative branch of the U.S. government being indebted to the two mobsters.

Giancana, a World War II draft dodger, was the undisputed crime boss in Chicago. His credentials included a record of sixty arrests (three for murder while a teenager) and a place of honor as one of the FBI's Ten Most Wanted Criminals. He had numerous friends among the Hollywood elite, including superstar Frank Sinatra, and his girlfriend was attractive Phyllis McGuire of the popular vocal trio the McGuire Sisters, who was more than twenty-five years Giancana's junior.

Robert Maheu, tough, astute, dynamic, was the perfect professional to implement the CIA scheme to tweep Fidel Castro. A native of Maine, he graduated from the College of the Holy Cross, and after attending Georgetown Law School, he became a special agent in the FBI soon after the eruption of World War II. During his six years with the Bureau, Maheu performed with distinction and was said to have been a favorite of J. Edgar Hoover. In 1947, at age thirty, he precipitously left the Bureau.

His spy-for-hire career began in 1954, when he formed Robert A. Maheu Associates in Washington. In the capital's lingo, he was "super connected," meaning he had high-level contacts in the government, law enforcement, covert agencies, big business, and the underworld. No doubt his most influential connection was with the CIA, which paid him a monthly retainer to perform "impossible missions" (Maheu's term) and provide cover for Agency operations.[5]

Maheu was the consummate spook, a term used in the gray, ambiguous world of covert operations. Spook not only connotes skill in the intelligence trade but also suggests an elusive mixture of force, deception, and dirty tricks.

By 1956, Maheu had become the chief spook for the eccentric billionaire Howard Hughes, who was described as being "extremely shy" (translation: paranoiac). Twice a month, Maheu flew from Washington to meet with Hughes at his palatial Los Angeles home. He conducted surveillances and investigations of the billionaire's own executives, siphoned Hughes's millions into political contributions (mainly to conservative Republicans), introduced ciphering to the vast Hughes financial and properties empire to keep his executives and outsiders from learning his true worth and business deals, and rounded up Hughes look-alikes to stand in for him at certain public events.

One of Maheu's assignments for Hughes was to find out if a man named Stuart Cramer III, ostensibly an executive of Lockheed in southern California, was also a CIA undercover agent. Cramer had been courting Jean Peters, a beautiful Hollywood film star with whom Hughes was enchanted.

Maheu got in touch with a few Washington contacts and told Hughes that Cramer was indeed a CIA operative. A few months later, Peters and Cramer got married, and they separated a short time later. In December 1956, Mrs. Cramer got a divorce, and she and Howard Hughes were married in the spring of 1957.

Now, in September 1960, after the Brown Derby meeting in Hollywood, Maheu and Johnny Roselli flew to New York, registered at the posh Plaza Hotel, and were joined by CIA case officer Jim O'Connell. Then the three conspirators winged to Miami and checked in at the elegant Fontainbleau, where they were joined by Moo Moo Giancana and Sam Trafficante. Three of the conferees used aliases: Giancana was Sam Gold, O'Connell was Jim Olds, and Trafficante was Joe.

Trafficante, the boss of organized crime in Florida, had a long record as a suspect in several gangland killings in New York and elsewhere. When Meyer Lansky and other Mob kingpins left Cuba with Fulgencio Batista on New Year's Eve 1958, Trafficante was the only gambling syndicate honcho to remain behind.

Fidel Castro promptly put Trafficante in prison. Although an "enemy of the people," the American lived behind bars in relative comfort, leading some in the Mob to feel that he might have cut some kind of deal with the Maximum Leader for future implementation. Pals from the United States often called on Trafficante, one visitor being a small-time hood from Dallas named Jack Ruby. (Four years later, Ruby would gain notoriety for shooting to death Lee Harvey Oswald, the prime suspect in the assassination of President John Kennedy.)

On being released in September 1959, Trafficante went back to Florida and reputedly continued illegal operations in Tampa and Miami. Left behind in Cuba was part of his gang.

Trafficante's release stirred up much conjecture in the Cuban exile community in Miami. Why had Castro let the mobster go? Rumors were that Trafficante was kept in a Cuban jail to make it appear that Castro had a strong dislike for the American, when in fact, Trafficante had long before agreed to become a double agent for the Maximum Leader when he went back to Florida.[6]

Filling his role in the Castro assassination scheme, Sam Traffi-cante recruited a Cuban exile who agreed to take part and was paid $10,000 in CIA funds. Tweeping Fidel would be achieved with poison pills, the Cuban said. He knew a woman who worked in Castro's favorite restaurant in Havana, and she would put botulism in his food. It would take two days for the Maximum Leader to become sick and die, and an autopsy would rule the death the result of natural causes, the exile explained.

Plans were moving ahead when, suddenly, Moo Moo Giancana was stricken with a fit of jealousy. He suspected that his love interest, beautiful Phyllis McGuire, was involved in a romantic liaison in Las Vegas with Dan Rowan, the television comedian. Bob Maheu, to keep Giancana from bolting to Las Vegas to personally take care of the matter, arranged to have a bug put in Rowan's Las Vegas hotel room.

Using CIA funds, Maheu paid a contact $1,000 to do the job. The contact turned the installation over to an associate, who bungled the job. Discovered by a hotel maid who walked into the room, he was arrested by the local sheriff's deputies.

Now the CIA's role in the Castro hit was in danger of being exposed. Maheu had to ask the Agency to intervene with Las Vegas authorities. Embarrassed over the comedy show in Dan Rowan's hotel room, the CIA told the Justice Department that national security was involved, and the charges against the bungler were eventually dropped.

As it developed, the plot to kill Castro came unstuck. Apparently the woman in his favorite restaurant had received the poison pills and was prepared to carry out her task. Then Castro ceased eating at that dining location and never returned. It appeared to Robert Maheu and CIA men involved in the enterprise that the Maximum Leader had been tipped off by a mole in the project's planning group in Miami. Sam Trafficante was the prime suspect.

BY MID-OCTOBER at the secret Base Trax in Guatemala, a wide variety of modern weapons in unmarked crates had been flown in by unmarked planes and unidentified pilots (probably those recruited from the U.S. Air National Guard). Under the energetic Colonel Frank, the motley band of Cuban trainees was formed into a combat force, whose men adopted the designation Brigade 2506. They took the name in honor of Carlos Santana, serial number 2506, who had been the first recruit to die, the victim of a training accident.

Appointed brigade commander was twenty-nine-year-old José Pérez San Román, a former Cuban army officer who had served under a democratic regime, a dictatorship, and briefly under Fidel Castro.

Tall, slender, and reserved, "Pepe" San Román had been among those freed from a Batista prison when the Cuban Messiah came down from the mountains in early 1959. Later that year, San Román fell out with Castro and was imprisoned, but he managed to escape and flee to Miami. As one of the handful of Cuban officers who had undergone training at Fort Benning, Georgia, and Fort Belvoir, Virginia, San Román was a natural choice to lead Brigade 2506.

Colonel Frank formed the brigade into four battalions, but Pepe chose their commanders. He named Alejandro del Valle to lead the First Battalion (paratroopers); Hugo Sueiro to command the Second Battalion (infantry); Erneido Olivo to lead the Armored Battalion; and Roberto San Román, Pepe's brother, to take charge of the Heavy Gun Battalion.

Also known to Cuban exiles as the Army of Liberation, Brigade 2506 was but a skeleton force. Colonel Frank explained that once the invaders were ashore, their ranks would be rapidly swollen by thousands of Cubans deserting Castroism and rushing to the brigade's colors. At least, that was what the colonel had been assured by CIA analysts in Washington. So the battalions initially would be the size of companies, and the companies actually platoons.

Operation Pluto, as the invasion had been code-named in the Pentagon, was planned in Washington by U.S. Marine Colonel Jack Hawkins and a CIA official, Jacob Esterline.[7] Hawkins (code name Colonel Alcott) had been loaned to the CIA at the request of Allen Dulles. The Marine had gained heavy experience in World War II conducting guerrilla operations behind Japanese lines on the island of Mindanao during the Philippine conflict.

In the last week in October, CIA operatives involved in Pluto received a jolt. *La Hora*, a Guatemala city newspaper, splashed a story across the front page saying that an invasion of Cuba was being prepared and hinting of U.S. collusion.

16

"Beardless, Ignorant Kids"

I N THE FALL OF 1960, the two presidential candidates described by Fidel Castro as "beardless, ignorant kids," Republican Dick Nixon and Democrat Jack Kennedy, were butting heads in one of the most heated campaigns in decades. It was a classic conservative versus liberal confrontation. Nixon, intelligent, dour, and largely humorless, was branded a rabid hawk on Cuba and a Communist baiter; Kennedy, debonair and witty, was labeled an enlightened dove on these crucial topics.

Castro and Cuba soon became the overriding issue; Americans had grown alarmed over a Communist beachhead only 90 miles from their shore. So each candidate implied repeatedly that the other was "soft on Communism." Kennedy blamed the "Nixon-Eisenhower" administration for losing Cuba to Fidel Castro.

Nearly all members of the Kennedy clan were highly active in the campaign. However, Joe Kennedy Sr., who was known to hold conservative views and had been attacked in partisan newspaper advertisements as being anti-Semitic (he had indicated in 1940 that Nazi Germany would win the war in Europe), kept a low profile. Republican leaders quipped that twenty-eight-year-old Teddy Kennedy was "in charge of hiding Joe."

Sister Eunice and Ethel (Mrs. Robert F. Kennedy) swept through Texas, assuring countless media reporters that their candidate was going to win. Seventy-year-old Mother Rose trekked to fourteen states and made more than fifty appearances at various functions. Twelve-hour workdays were her norm. Teddy Kennedy traveled up and down California, passing out PT-109 tie clasps, shaking thousands of hands at factory gates, giving hundreds of speeches from the stump.

Jacqueline Kennedy, the candidate's glamorous wife, who was pregnant and due to give birth in early December, could not travel with

Jack. But she granted scores of television interviews, hosted teas, loaned her name to a program to collect women's views on campaign issues, and rode with Jack in a New York City parade.

Bobby Kennedy was the driving force for the campaign, and he often plunged into the eye of the political hurricane. On one occasion, he publicly castigated a few Southern members of Congress for blocking legislation Jack favored. Later, Bobby even lambasted Jackie Robinson, the baseball star who broke the major league's unspoken color barrier, for having the audacity to question Jack's commitment to civil rights.

As Bobby dashed madly about the country, he bawled out already exhausted volunteers and knocked the heads of Democratic leaders he felt were only lukewarm about Jack's candidacy. These party kingpins began to warn one another: "Be careful, Little Brother is watching you!"

Arthur S. Schlesinger Jr., a Harvard professor brought into the Kennedy campaign to appease liberal supporters, later would state: "John Kennedy recognized that a campaign required a son of a bitch—and that it could not be the candidate. Robert [did] what the candidate should not have done."[1]

As the campaign heated up, Kennedy strategists grew increasingly concerned that the CIA-produced invasion of Cuba would strike before the November voting, resulting in Nixon gaining credit for eliminating the Castro regime. Just as avidly, the Nixon camp was rooting for the invasion to hit prior to the election, in which case its man "would be a cinch to win."[2]

Kennedy, therefore, adopted a new campaign tactic. Wrapping himself in hawk's feathers, he began lambasting Nixon for "doing nothing about the Communist menace that had been permitted to arise under our very noses."

"The forces fighting for freedom in exile and in the mountains of Cuba should be sustained and assisted," Kennedy declared in a speech. A week later, he called for "encouraging these liberty-loving Cubans who are leading the resistance to Castro." He claimed that the "Nixon-Eisenhower" administration had done nothing to help overthrow the Communist dictator.

Nixon, a political street fighter from the old school, was furious, ranting to aides that Kennedy was taking cheap shots at him. Kennedy, he was convinced, knew of the secret camps in Florida and Guatemala and of the developing plan to invade Cuba, as indeed Kennedy did.

Kennedy's sudden emergence as a hawk and vocal anti-Communist, Nixon held, was a campaign tactic designed to give the voters the impression that should the invasion strike before the election, the Eisenhower-Nixon administration had been goaded into taking action by Kennedy's verbal haymakers.

Nixon had to bite his tongue; the covert operation had to be protected. Nixon could not even imply that the U.S. government had been giving aid to exile forces in and out of Cuba. So Nixon flip-flopped to the other extreme and became a crusading dove. He attacked Kennedy's proposals as "reckless and irresponsible" and branded his opponent's help-the-exiles call as "fantastic." Kennedy, Nixon exclaimed, was risking World War III by his harping for an invasion of Cuba.

Privately, Dick Nixon cursed, brooded, and fidgeted.

IN HAVANA, Fidel Castro had been closely monitoring the U.S. election campaign, and his ego apparently had been bruised by the almost daily verbal assaults made on him or his regime. Consequently, he and the Cuban media steadily got in their retaliatory licks against the "imperialistic leaders" in the north. Castro hurled epithets at Dwight Eisenhower and the two presidential candidates, then his print and broadcast mouthpieces amplified the lurid descriptions.

Jack Kennedy, Radio Mambí declared, was an "imbecile and a cowardly, despicable, and miserable dog," who was trotting around the United States telling "slimy lies" about Castro and his regime. "Melonhead" Eisenhower was a "decrepit and stupid old man." Christian Herter had the "brain of a mosquito." And the United States was ruled by the "worst gang of murderous thieves in history."

IN MID-SEPTEMBER, America's eyes were on Chicago, where the two presidential hopefuls were preparing to tangle in a television spectacular being hyped as the Great Debate. Jack Kennedy was coolly confident—perhaps because he had nothing to lose. Polls had Nixon at 48 percent, Kennedy at 42 percent, and 10 percent undecided.

"This is my chance to catch him," Kennedy told Dave Powers, his confidant. Around the Kennedy camp, Nixon was always referred to as "him."

After long hours of often heated wrangling, handlers for the two contenders settled on Howard K. Smith, the CBS White House correspondent, to be the moderator.

Four televised Nixon-Kennedy debates—all of them live—were scheduled. But the first one, set for September 26, would be crucial. People would make up their minds on this night and then later watch the other three debates for entertainment and to confirm that they had reached the right decision.

"I feel like a prize fighter going out into Madison Square Garden," Kennedy mused to Dave Powers minutes before departing his hotel for the "boxing ring," the studio of WBBM, the CBS-owned station in Chicago.

No doubt CBS's Don Hewitt, the agreed-upon director of the first debate, felt that he was the referee for the verbal slugfest. When Dick Nixon entered from one side and Jack Kennedy from the other to take their places, Hewitt quipped: "I assume you two gentlemen know each other."

Now a hush of expectancy hovered over the studio audience. Lights. Camera. Action! After the mandatory handshake, Nixon and Kennedy took their places at podiums and went through the ritual of questions and answers. Millions of home viewers paid scant attention to what was being said: They were concentrating on how Kennedy and Nixon looked and acted.

Nixon had been ill for several days and had lost weight. Numerous times a camera's cold, unblinking gaze caught him with eyes darting about, licking his lips and wiping perspiration that was streaking the Lazy-Shave on his pale and haggard face. Jack Kennedy, wearing a healthy-looking California suntan, by contrast, came across as cool, calm, and collected, exuding an air of supreme confidence and vigor.

ON OCTOBER 20, Dick Nixon was in New York City getting ready for another television debate when he was handed a press release from the Kennedy camp: "We must attempt to strengthen the non-Batista democratic anti-Castro forces in exile, and in Cuba itself, who offer eventual hope of overthrowing Castro." The words were Kennedy's.

Red-faced with anger, Nixon nearly shouted to Interior Secretary Fred Seaton, who was with him in the hotel suite, "Goddamn it, Fred, call the White House. Find out if Dulles had briefed Kennedy on the CIA training exiles for the purpose of invading Cuba."

Over the security line, Seaton talked with Brigadier General Andrew J. Goodpaster, President Eisenhower's contact with the CIA. "I'll get right back to you," Goodpaster said. Thirty minutes later, he telephoned a reply: "Kennedy had been briefed on this operation [the looming invasion]."[3]

At the final nationally televised debate between the two candidates, a self-assured and confident Jack Kennedy promised to give U.S. support to those seeking to overthrow Castro. Nixon came across as vague and indecisive about Cuba. He could not betray to Castro that an invasion was in the works.

Almost without exception, the thousands of Cuban exiles in Florida and anti-Castro forces training in Guatemala and Nicaragua began rooting for the perceived hawk Kennedy over the perceived dove Nixon.

IN NOVEMBER, 69 million Americans went to the polls to pick a new President. Kennedy had closed the gap. Pollsters predicted the margin of victory for either candidate would be razor-thin. When the final tally was announced, Kennedy had won by 112,803 votes, the thinnest margin of the twentieth century.

FBI Director J. Edgar Hoover learned later that returns in Illinois, where Chicago boss Richard Daley's powerful machine held sway, were "creatively falsified" to swing the crucial state into the Kennedy column. FBI electronic eavesdroppers had been listening over the telephones as the vote counters in working-class Chicago precincts put together a counterfeit victory.[4]

However, Kennedy did not require the Illinois electoral vote. He would have won anyhow with the results in Texas, the home state of his running mate, Lyndon Johnson, where the Democratic standard-bearers crossed the finish line first by only some 48,000 votes. Johnson long had been a legend in the Lone Star state for pulling in votes in his past elections, including the prowess to raise the dead. Years earlier, a last-minute avalanche from the grave had elected him to the Senate by a tiny margin that earned him the moniker Landslide Lyndon.

When the returns were announced on election night, Miami's Little Havana erupted in tumultuous celebrations. Based on Kennedy's campaign oratory, the Cubans in Miami were convinced the president-elect would lead them to the promised land, that is, back to a Cuba without Fidel Castro and his cohorts.

About one hundred miles from Miami, José Jiminez, the figurehead president of Cuba, appeared on Havana television and said the election results would make no difference in Washington's hostile view of the Castro regime. Kennedy, he felt, would be compelled to show his muscle and demonstrate Uncle Sam's power by invading Cuba with the U.S. Marines.[5]

Radio Mambí in Havana charged that imperialist monopolies in the United States had made possible the election of a "new Caesar and Atilla [the Hun]." Radio Union declared that the "ignorant millionaire and monopolist Kennedy" had defeated "the gangster Nixon."

At the same time, Fidel Castro announced that his intelligence service had uncovered a "sinister plot" by the "Yankee imperialists," and he put Cuba's armed forces and militia on full alert to meet a surprise attack by the United States. If the Americans invaded the island, he asserted to a group of schoolteachers, they would suffer heavier casualties than the U.S. forces that had landed in Normandy or Okinawa, two bloody battles in World War II.[6] In the wake of Kennedy's victory, a rash of studies erupted to analyze how the television coverage of the Great Debate had influenced the outcome of the race. Researchers concluded that the visual impact of television had been gargantuan. A majority of those who had only *listened* on radio leaned toward Dick Nixon, while most of those who had *watched* on television had been in favor of Jack Kennedy.

Clearly, a new age in presidential politicking had burst forth in America. Substance was secondary. What counted now were suit colors, necktie patterns, makeup, backdrops, lighting, suntans, and camera angles. No doubt Abraham Lincoln and Stephen A. Douglas, who had engaged in the last Great Debate 102 years earlier, were whirling in their graves.

Television had become the opium of the people—the more they watched, the more they wanted, or needed. Television was a massage, a "there, there," a need, a psychic fortress, a friend. Viewers ogled the screen until midnight when the stations played the *Star-Spangled Banner* and went off the air, then remained to watch the little white ball of light slowly disintegrate.

Newly elected President Kennedy grasped these curious workings of the human psyche. The widely ballyhooed Great Debate had barely won for him the highest office in America, so he told confidant Dave Powers, "I will use the [televised] news conference so the next one [his reelection bid in 1964] won't even be close." In Washington, lame-duck President Dwight Eisenhower was getting fed up with what he called "the press." The Old Warrior's feelings already had been hurt. Despite the assurances of friends and aides to the contrary, he took the election results as a repudiation by the American people of his eight years in the White House.

Eisenhower's tail feathers were ruffled even more by the manner in which the media was casting Jack Kennedy as almost a savior, even though the United States had enjoyed peace and prosperity during Eisenhower's two terms. Television and print reporters launched a feeding frenzy in which they tried to outdo one another in extolling the brilliance, vision, and Christlike virtues of the president-elect.

In a bitter letter to a friend, Eisenhower blasted a prominent journalist, Ralph McGill, about whose writing the president had a high regard. "Now it seems to me that [McGill] has sold himself on a naive belief that we have a new genius in our midst who is incapable of making any mistakes and therefore deserving of no criticism whatsoever," Eisenhower stated.[7]

17

An "Evil Nest of Yankee Spies"

IT HAD TAKEN JACK KENNEDY only fourteen years to climb up the totem pole of power from the muck of ward-heeling Boston politics to president of the United States. His euphoria was tempered by the vote-fraud charges in the media, but Dick Nixon assured the victor that he did not plan to contest the outcome legally.

There was much work to be done. A new administration had to be put together, a task similar to dismantling the General Motors industrial empire then replacing it almost overnight with new faces and new ideas.

Kennedy's inner circle of mostly Ivy League graduates in their late thirties and early forties were in favor of replacing sixty-six-year-old FBI Director J. Edgar Hoover with a much younger man more attuned to the liberal goals of the New Frontier, as Kennedy called his agenda. But Kennedy explained to his confidants: "You don't fire God!"

At his first formal press conference on November 10, the president-elect announced the reappointment of Hoover, who may not have been God to tens of millions of Americans but certainly was a hero to them. Among the top G-Man's boosters was Joe Kennedy Sr.

Soon after the press conference to announce Hoover's reappointment, Jack Kennedy flew to his father's home in Palm Beach, Florida, for a brief respite from the rigors of exhaustive campaigning. On November 17, he was visited by CIA Director Allen Dulles, whom the president-elect had also reappointed over the protests of the Kennedy inner circle. With Dulles was Dick Bissell, the CIA's chief of Clandestine Services and the architect of the Cuban invasion project.

Bissell briefed Kennedy on the combined military and psychological aspects of the operation. Sixteen of the exiles' B-26s were to launch the invasion by a Pearl Harbor–like sneak attack to wipe out Fidel Castro's air force on the ground. Then the 2506 Brigade, which would sail from Guatemala, would storm ashore on the southern coast of Cuba and hack out a beachhead. Then the bombers would return and destroy the entire transportation and communications network, a task that could be accomplished because Cuba's telephone system, railroad patterns, and radio and television facilities relied on microwave relay stations that could be blown up by a few accurately dropped bombs.

Kennedy was skeptical. How could an invasion force of fourteen hundred men hope to defeat the estimated two hundred thousand members of Castro's regular army and militia? Castro, isolated in Havana without communications, would be confronted by a military threat of undetermined proportions, Bissell explained. Aided by exile "disinformation" reports over the CIA radio station on Swan Island, wild rumors of new landings and armed uprisings would cause Castro to grow bewildered and panicky.

Then, according to Bissell's scenario, the CIA-created Cuban government-in-exile would be flown from Florida into the beachhead established by the 2506 Brigade, proclaim itself the legally constituted regime, and call on Cubans to rally to its colors. The United States would formally recognize the new government, and this action would be quickly followed by "international diplomatic intervention." At this point, Bissell stated, a cease-fire might be negotiated with a confused Castro, followed by free elections in Cuba.

Puffing thoughtfully on a cigar, Kennedy mulled over the invasion plan, then gave a green light for preparations to continue. Due to his repeated campaign promises to aid the exiles in overthrowing Castro, the president-elect, for better or worse, had painted himself into a corner. However, there was still plenty of time to cancel the operation.

BY EARLY DECEMBER, the looming invasion of Cuba had become an open secret in the United States and in Latin America. Neither panicky nor bewildered, Fidel Castro took to the air to blast the Cuban "worms" and "traitors" who were "conspiring with the imbeciles of the CIA" to overthrow his government.

Castro's spies were embedded in Miami, in Washington, and perhaps in the secret camps in Guatemala and Nicaragua; his *Dirección Generale de Intelligencia* (intelligence agency) knew of the invasion plan in broad form and in many details. *The New York Times* and other U.S. publications ran stories on the Guatemala exile training camps, as did the press in Latin America. *Time* magazine even published the code names used by some CIA men in the operation.

ON DECEMBER 6, Jack Kennedy was in Washington and met with Dwight Eisenhower in the White House. Although at his affable best, the outgoing president was especially angry over Jack's campaign charges about the Eisenhower administration ignoring the Castro regime when, in fact, the Democratic challenger had been briefed on the planned invasion of the island by Cuban exiles.

In the privacy of the Oval Office, Eisenhower referred to Jack as "Little Boy Blue," called Bobby "that little shit," and dismissed Teddy as the "Bonus Baby." Moreover, Ike never liked Jack's liberal voting record in Congress and was convinced that the Democrat had beaten Dick Nixon because of Kennedy Senior's money.[1]

The contempt Eisenhower felt was mutual. After the two men conferred for more than an hour, Jack came away regarding the Old Warrior, twenty-seven years his senior, as shallow.[2]

PRESIDENT-ELECT KENNEDY continued to spend much of his time sifting through recommendations from close friends for cabinet posts. He paid special attention to the views of Robert A. Lovett, a conservative Republican and former secretary of defense, and his father, Joe Kennedy Sr. For three years, it had been known in the family that his father's goal was to see Jack in the White House, Bobby as attorney general, and Teddy in the Senate.[3]

Since Jack announced for the presidency a year earlier, the Kennedy clan had been joking good-naturedly about the new president's administration lineup. At a family dinner, Eunice, the sister, had quipped: "Bobby we'll make attorney general so he can throw all the people Dad doesn't like in jail! Of course, they'll have to build a lot of new jails!"[4]

After his election, Jack sent Clark Clifford, a veteran Washington wheeler and dealer and head of Kennedy's transition team, to try to talk Joe out of his insistence that Bobby be named to the important and prestigious post. Clifford himself had "very serious reservations" about the choice of Bobby to head the Justice Department with its thirty thousand employees. So no doubt he was disappointed that Kennedy Senior wouldn't budge. It had to be thirty-four-year-old Bobby.[5]

After the appointment was announced at a media conference outside the president-elect's home in the wealthy Georgetown section of Washington, reaction was prompt. "If Robert Kennedy was one of the outstanding lawyers of the country, a preeminent legal philosopher, a noted prosecutor or legal officer at federal or state level, the situation would have been different," stated *The New York Times*, which had supported candidate Jack Kennedy. "But his experience is surely insufficient to warrant his present appointment."[6]

Robert Novak, writing in the *Wall Street Journal*, was brutally blunt. Bobby Kennedy, he stated, might well be an "unqualified disaster."[7]

Vice President–elect Lyndon Johnson, who intensely disliked Bobby, told an aide that conservative Senator Richard Russell was "absolutely shittin' a squealin' worm. He thinks it's a disgrace for a kid who's never practiced law to be appointed. I agree with him. But I don't think Jack Kennedy's gonna let a little fart like Bobby lead him around by the nose."[8]

AT QUARTERS EYE, meanwhile, those involved in the Pluto operation received a heavy jolt. Two CIA spooks, code-named Sam and Jeff, had met in a safe house in Mexico City to peruse secret documents pertaining to the invasion. Then the papers were put into a briefcase and Sam drove to his office, parked the car, and locked it with the briefcase lying on the front seat. When he returned to the vehicle an hour later, the lock on the door was broken and the briefcase was gone.

The episode could bode disaster for the invasion and result in the underground in Cuba being wiped out. Along with CIA codes, the missing documents included the names of secret agents in Cuba and the names of CIA undercover operatives throughout the Western Hemisphere.

Lying about the true contents of the briefcase, the CIA station chief in Mexico City asked the federal police to check their underworld contacts for the container. A massive search was launched—to no avail. The briefcase was never found.

After soul-searching discussions in Quarters Eye, it was concluded that Castro's spies had not pilfered the briefcase, rather that thieves had broken into the car by happenstance and pitched away the container and the seemingly useless documents.

There were other maddening problems. Because of the limited fuel capacity of the B-26 bombers, CIA operatives tried to arrange for a refueling stop at some isolated landing strip between Central America and Cuba. The president of Mexico, who was in on the secret, suggested that the official in charge of the airstrip on remote Cozumel Island be approached.

The CIA station chief in Mexico City hurried to Cozumel and contacted the Mexican Air Force officer in charge. Could Cozumel be stocked with a few hundred drums of high-test aviation gasoline to refuel the B-26s on their way to an undisclosed destination? Most certainly, the Mexican responded—for a fee. And what was that fee? Four new air-conditioned Thunderbird convertibles.

Strident haggling ensued. The CIA man even offered the equivalent to four Thunderbirds in cash. No, it had to be the sleek automobiles or nothing. Exasperated, the American departed, his mission a failure.[9]

FANNED BY FIDEL CASTRO'S inflammatory television speeches and screaming headlines in *Hoy* and *Revolución*, an epidemic of "Yankee invasion fever" broke out on the island. Patriotic tunes and rebel anthems blaring over hundreds of loudspeakers flooded Havana day and night. Television, radio, and newspapers kept up a drumfire barrage of hate-America propaganda. Leaflets and posters screamed a Castro exhortation paraphrased from a famous Winston Churchill speech: "We will defend every house from the rooftop to cellar, and where there is nothing else left we shall defend the ruins!"

Castro exulted over television: "We have acquired arms, much arms [from the Soviet bloc], much more of them than the Yankee imperialists have imagined."

Indeed, Castro had acquired a substantial arsenal. On January 2, 1961, with the Maximum Leader looking on from the reviewing stand, a full range of modern weapons rolled past in a huge Havana parade—heavy tanks, 105-millimeter artillery, rocket launchers, mortars, antitank guns, machine guns, and antiaircraft weapons.

A day later, Fidel Castro delivered one of his marathon speeches on Havana television and charged that the U.S. Embassy in Cuba was "an evil nest of Yankee spies and rabble-rousers." He demanded that the embassy staff of some three hundred persons be reduced to a skeleton crew of eight—within twenty-four hours. The Maximum Leader's anger had been raised after Eisenhower, hoping to tighten the economic squeeze on Castro, had banned all exports to Cuba except food and medicine.

Eighteen hours after Castro's television harangue, Eisenhower called in his key advisers. Clearly angry, he declared that "the United States won't tolerate being kicked around [by Castro]." Most of Eisenhower's aides were hawkish. Treasury Secretary Robert Anderson spoke out in favor of "[military] action now to get rid of Castro."[10]

Secretary of State Christian Herter, who long had advocated moderation in dealing with Castro, no doubt shocked the conferees with a radical proposal. "We should stage a [phony] attack" on the U.S. Naval

Base at Guantanamo, "using the same scheme that Adolf Hitler employed on the German-Polish border" in the fall of 1939, Herter suggested.[11]

Hitler had created a fake provocation as an excuse for sending his powerful *Wehrmacht* (armed forces) against militarily weak Poland. The idea was to convince the world that Poland was the aggressor and that he was sending his panzers plunging over the border to protect Germany.

Twelve German criminals had been taken from prison, dressed in stolen Polish uniforms, and taken to Gleiwitz, a small German town near the frontier. At night, the guinea pigs were given drug injections that rendered them semiconscious, taken to a radio station outside Gleiwitz, placed about the grounds, and shot to death. Then several German soldiers dashed into the station, fired shots into the ceiling, and a Polish-speaking German shouted threats against Adolf Hitler into the radio transmitter.

After dawn, German newspaper photographers and reporters were rushed to Gleiwitz to view the "Polish atrocity." Soon publications throughout the world carried gruesome pictures of the "Polish soldiers killed by German troops heroically defending the radio station."[12]

Twenty-four hours later, thousands of waiting German tanks, supported by swarms of Stuka dive bombers, charged across the border into nearly defenseless Poland.

It was doubtful if Christian Herter had such an elaborate *ruse de guerre* in mind. Perhaps selected Marines could sneak out of the U.S. Naval Base into Cuban territory under cover of night and pour a few bursts of small-arms fire into the 10-foot-high chain-link fence in an isolated region where no one would be hit. President Eisenhower could loudly denounce the attack. Then U.S. armed forces could invade Cuba in response to Castro's "warlike provocation" to protect American lives and property.

A day after the grim White House conference, Herter announced that diplomatic relations with Cuba had been broken off. The large, graceful, white embassy building off the Malecón was boarded up and left empty, except for two Swiss officials who had agreed to keep an eye on the structure. Switzerland would represent the United States in dealings with Communist Cuba—if any.

FIVE WEEKS after Kennedy's election, Mikhail Menshikov, the Soviet ambassador to the United States, invited Bobby Kennedy to lunch. "Comrade [Nikita] Khrushchev greatly admires [your brother's] intelligence and vigor," Menshikov said amiably. "[He] believes it is now possible to have a clear and friendly understanding between the Soviet Union and the United States."[13]

Jack and Bobby were encouraged by this signal of lessening hostility. Then, a month later on January 6, 1961, Nikita Khrushchev delivered a fire-and-brimstone, podium-pounding speech in Moscow. His theme was the irresistible triumph of worldwide Communism.

"This inevitable victory will come through national liberation wars," he declared, the only method for "bringing imperialism to heel." Cuba was cited as an "awakening nation" where the "revolutionary struggle will bring victory over capitalist exploiters."[14]

ON JANUARY 19, Eisenhower and Kennedy met again in the White House. The president-elect asked about the United States supporting anti-Castro guerrillas. Eisenhower strongly endorsed the activities at Base Trax in Guatemala and added forcefully, "We cannot let the present government [in Cuba] go on." He suggested that Kennedy continue the search for a leader who was both anti-Batista and anti-Castro to head a Cuban government-in-exile.

"When the invasion [of Cuba] hits, it would have the appearance of a more legitimate operation," Eisenhower stressed.[15]

NEAR NOON on January 20, Jack Kennedy arrived at the Capitol for the inaugural ceremonies, a changing of the guard. It was bitterly cold, but he did not wear a hat or an overcoat (although he was clad in long thermal underwear), a ploy no doubt to enhance his image of toughness in dealing with a dangerous and volatile world.

At 12:51 P.M., Kennedy was sworn in as the thirty-fifth president of the United States by Supreme Court Chief Justice Earl Warren. Then Jack delivered the inaugural address he had rehearsed many times. It dwelt almost exclusively with foreign affairs, and millions of viewers in the United States and abroad were thrilled by the forcefulness of his rhetoric: "We shall pay any price, bear any burden, meet any hardship, support any friend, oppose any foe to assure the survival and the success of liberty."

Ten days later, on January 30, President Kennedy arrived early at the Oval Office. This was a big day. At noon, he would deliver his first State of the Union address before a joint session of Congress. At 11:00 A.M., he telephoned his father in Palm Beach to tell him to be sure to watch him on television. Kennedy Senior had attended the inauguration but returned to Palm Beach immediately.[16]

One passage in the president's speech seemed to strike an especially responsive chord with the members of Congress: "Life in 1961 will not be easy. There will be further setbacks before the [Communist] tide is turned. But turn it we must. The hopes of all mankind—the exile in Cuba and the peasant in Laos—rest upon us."[17]

AMONG THE MILLIONS tuned to the televised address was Fidel Castro in Havana. Now there was no doubt in his mind that President Kennedy planned to vigorously pursue the overthrow of the Cuban government and its Maximum Leader. A day after the State of the Union speech, Radio Havana stated, "President Kennedy has taken off the mask. This is a new attack on Cuba by the United States."[18]

Other media throughout Cuba and in some Latin American countries launched a propaganda blitz against the United States and warned of "looming invasions by Yankee imperialists." Castro was confident, even cocky, daring the Cuban exile force in Guatemala to land on his island. "You will be utterly destroyed," he declared.

18

Showdown on Guantanamo Bay

PERHAPS TO TEST THE METTLE of the new president of the United States, Fidel Castro began agitating again for the "Yankee exploiters" to get out of Guantanamo, the naval base he considered to be a "dagger pointed at the heart of Cuba." Castro's confidence, no doubt, was bolstered by Nikita Khrushchev's blunt threat: "If need be, Soviet artillerymen will support the Cuban people!"[1]

Castro-controlled television, radio, and newspapers in Cuba loosed a withering barrage of charges about Guantanamo, an attack designed to instill hatred for the United States in the Cuban people. Most of the charges were outright lies. A graphic (and phony) account by (nonexistent) eyewitnesses told how "bloodthirsty Marines" at the naval base had beaten and tortured an elderly Cuban civilian. Another canard told how a "gang of Marines" had raped a twelve-year-old Cuban girl whose parents worked on the base.

Castro denounced the 1903 Guantanamo treaty between Cuba and the United States as illegal and invalid, claiming that Cuban authorities had signed the document at the point of Yankee rifles. Terms of the treaty permitted commercial vessels to transit in peacetime between the Caribbean Sea northward through the Water Gate, a narrow bottleneck that separates the upper and lower bay at the northern boundary of the naval base. This access route cuts directly through lower Guantanamo Bay, which had been part of the naval base for nearly six decades.

Cuban fishing boats, which could be floating spy platforms loaded with electronic surveillance equipment, were barred from the lower bay by U.S. authorities. Periodically, Castro challenged the U.S. right to ban his vessels.

A Cuban speedboat, labeled the *Candy Stripe* by Americans because of its garish red and white hull, would periodically taunt Gitmo's har-

112

bor police, who patrolled the lower bay. The *Candy Stripe* would suddenly bolt southward through Water Gate at full throttle and race into the lower bay. As the harbor police gave chase, the Cuban boat would reverse course and dash for the Water Gate, its jeering crew thumbing their noses and making obscene gestures at the U.S. Navy men futilely trying to catch the intruder.

Castro looked on lower Guantanamo Bay as Cuban waters, and the barring of Cuban fishing boats rankled him. So he decided to test Yankee resolve. Sixty fishing boats were rounded up and berthed at Boquerón and Caimanera north of the Water Gate. One morning, all of the craft, with armed Cuban soldiers aboard some of them, poured through Water Gate and invaded lower Guantanamo Bay en masse.

Word of the fishing fleet invasion was flashed to Admiral Mike Fenno, base commander, who had earned three Navy Crosses as a submarine commander in the Pacific during World War II.[2] Reacting quickly, Fenno sent a Marine major, a hard-nosed veteran of bloody Pacific fighting, racing in a speedboat to give a message to the leader of the fishing-boat flotilla.

The Marine minced no words with the Cuban in charge. "I have a message for you from the admiral," he declared. "Get the hell out of our waters *mucho pronto*—or we'll blow you to hell out of here!"

Glancing around the bay, the Cuban saw that U.S. warships had guns trained on the intruding vessels. The fishing fleet scurried out of the naval-base waters and back northward through the Water Gate.

Castro's bold challenge to the Guantanamo naval base treaty, and the worldwide propaganda bonanza he had hoped to reap by defying the *Yanquis*, collapsed like a punctured balloon. However, the Maximum Leader's efforts to drive the United States out of Guantanamo had only begun.

MEANWHILE, at Howard Hunt's safe house in suburban Miami one night, Frank Bender, CIA headquarters chief of political action for the Cuban Project, was present when a handsome young man was ushered in and introduced as "Eduardo." Haggard and wearing a flight jacket and torn trousers, he was Major Pedro Díaz Lanz, the former head of Castro's air force.

Díaz told Hunt and Bender that he had been ill, owed money for hospital bills, and was broke. The couple did not even have money to buy a crib for their new baby. However, he pleaded to be given a role in eliminating Fidel Castro, his old comrade from the Sierra Maestra days.

After arriving in Florida in early 1959, Díaz had scraped up enough money for a modest down payment on an old World War II B-25 bomber. Friends had kicked in some cash for its overhaul, but now the airplane was under a sheriff's lien at a Miami airport.

Bender and Hunt were aware of Díaz's proven courage and leadership. "I guess we can always use another plane, not to mention an experienced pilot," Hunt said to Bender. They had just the job for him: dropping propaganda leaflets "on Castro's head."[3]

The two CIA men told the Cuban that they would arrange to pay his hospital bills, provide for medical services for his family (his wife and a son were sick), and put some Yankee dollars in his pocket. Díaz, a proud and strong man, broke into tears of gratitude.

On the following morning, Hunt telephoned the CIA chief of propaganda for the Cuban Project at Quarters Eye, a spook who went by the code name Knight, and told him that he could have an ace leaflet-dropper by merely coughing up $3,000 to get Díaz's plane out of hock. Knight, a gung-ho type always digging for a way to get propaganda on the tightly guarded island, was delighted.

Soon Díaz's flying relic was ready to take off for Cuban skies with a large batch of propaganda leaflets. At almost the last minute, Knight telephoned the Miami airport and canceled the mission. A bureaucrat in the State Department had disapproved of the venture.

Díaz was deemed a dangerous figure by the Immigration and Naturalization Service (INS), which put a watch on his B-25 to make certain that he did not take off on some endeavor to strike a blow at Fidel Castro and his regime. At a time the exiles' invasion team needed the finest players it could muster, Pedro Díaz was benched by bureaucrats in Washington.

WHEN ATTORNEY GENERAL Bobby Kennedy moved into his ornate office suite on the fifth floor of the Justice Building early in February 1961, much of the Washington crowd—media pundits, politicians, consultants, office holders, and straphangers—waited in eager anticipation for his inevitable clash with J. Edgar Hoover. Bobby, a liberal blue blood, was born to wealth and privilege, and the legendary FBI director was a staunch conservative who came from a middle-class family and reportedly had supported Dick Nixon in the presidential race.

Privately, Hoover seethed at the thought of having Bobby as his superior. There was the age factor: Hoover had become FBI director two years before Bobby was born. Hoover had disliked the younger man for years, considering him an arrogant upstart. Dick Nixon would later state that the chief G-Man had once referred to his new boss as "that sneaky little son of a bitch."[4]

As Washington insiders had predicted, friction and sniping soon erupted between the attorney general's camp and that of the FBI director. No doubt a contributing cause of the clash was the yawning gulf between the styles and beliefs of Kennedy's young eager beavers from the Ivy League universities and Hoover's older loyalists.

Machinations on both sides were subtle and ongoing. Guides who escorted large groups of visitors on the official tour through FBI headquarters were instructed to insert this passage: "Mr. Hoover became director of the FBI in 1924, two years before [his current boss,] the attorney general, was born."[5]

When Bobby Kennedy heard about the comment, which he apparently felt had been a deliberate FBI trick to dramatize his own youth, he had the sentence deleted. Hoover's camp was furious.

There were other instances of friction. Hoover's inner circle learned that Kennedy was bringing his beloved pet dog, Brumus, to his office in the Justice Building, and that the animal on one occasion had displayed non–Ivy League manners by urinating on an expensive rug in the attorney general's personal office.

Brumus's indiscretion was one of the topics discussed at a meeting of the FBI's executive conference, consisting of twelve officials (Hoover never attended the sessions). Their function was to oversee the enforcement of scores of different kinds of crimes. It was decided that Brumus was in violation of Section 201, Chapter 8, Title 2, of the Rules and Regulations for public buildings: "Dogs shall not be brought upon the property."

Reportedly, there were discussions over the violation of Section 201, including issuing charges for the destruction of public property, but the matter was finally dropped. Brumus had been given a reprieve.

Two weeks after he had taken over at Justice, Bobby Kennedy, a physical fitness advocate, discovered that the FBI had a gymnasium in the basement of the Justice Building where the investigative agency also was headquartered. Hoover's men had anticipated that the new attorney general would want to use the facility. When he arrived one day to work out, a guard posted at the door refused him entry, explaining that no one was to be allowed inside without FBI credentials.

The episode triggered two versions. The FBI story was that Bobby, after being barred, was red-faced with anger, but he didn't try again. Not so, the attorney general's camp would declare: Bobby ordered the gymnasium to be opened to all Justice Department personnel.

In another instance of one-upmanship, an FBI assistant director who welcomed the new-agent classes at nearby Quantico, Virginia, had a standard line. He praised the young men because more than 36 million others had applied for the FBI and failed, including former Vice President Dick Nixon and Attorney General Bobby Kennedy. Nixon was "not aggressive enough," and Kennedy had been rejected for being "too cocky."[6]

In essence, the subtle guerrilla skirmishing involving Hoover and Bobby Kennedy was the age-old struggle between the Old Bull and the Young Bull for dominance over the herd. Perhaps that was the reason that Kennedy's relaxed style was a source of so much irritation to the far more disciplined FBI chief, although Hoover and Kennedy tried to keep their personal relations civil.

During the workday, the attorney general and his cohorts usually took off their suit coats, rolled up their sleeves, loosened their ties, and often held discussions propped back in swivel chairs with their feet on the desk. Hoover, who had always had a strict dress code for FBI personnel since he took over in 1924, reportedly was aghast.

Style was not the only disparity between the Old Bull and the Young Bull. On one occasion, Hoover and his number-two man and confidant, Clyde A. Tolson, were escorted into the attorney general's office for a conference. Kennedy hardly took note of their arrival; shirt-sleeves rolled up to the elbows, he was engaged in an English pub game, throwing darts at a bull's-eye target pinned on the wall.

As Hoover presented his briefing, Bobby kept throwing darts. The FBI chief was angry but maintained his composure. On returning to his own office, Hoover barked, "It was pure desecration of public property!" Kennedy's darts had gone astray on occasion and chipped pieces from the expensive walnut paneling to which the target was attached.[7]

WHILE THE INTRAMURAL machinations were evolving in the Justice Department, Operation Pluto, the invasion of Cuba, was continuing to develop. Under cover of darkness on February 11, a powerboat skippered by Enrique "Kikío" Llansó, a Cuban exile, slipped out of a Florida Key and set course for Cuba. For a year, Llansó had been departing from this same port to sneak arms and ammunition to anti-Castro groups in Cuba. On board was an espionage team of five men of the 2506 Brigade. Llansó's task was to land the team at a remote beach in Matanzas Province, where they were to be met by guides and infiltrated into the island.

The Brigade espionage and sabotage teams, trained by the CIA, were mostly young, eager students who had been among the first to join up for the invasion. Their job was to go deep undercover in the cities and countryside and pave the way for the invasion by creating turmoil and inciting uprisings.

When Llansó's craft edged up to the black coast of Cuba that night, the vessel was swamped by high seas and capsized. Nearly naked, those on board swam ashore—without weapons, money, or radio communications equipment—and went into hiding. Pluto had been launched on a disastrous note.

LESS THAN A MONTH LATER, in early March, the CIA set in motion a plan in which a number of Castro's swift torpedo boats, built in Eastern Germany, would escape from the naval base of Baracoa in Oriente Province and make a dash to southern Florida. Anti-Castro officers in the Cuban Navy had advised the CIA that the scheme would work only if the torpedo boats could be refueled on the sea after leaving their base. Because the crews' loyalty to the Castro regime was considered to be questionable, the boats were kept on short gasoline rations, much less than would be needed to reach Florida.

As a means for helping the torpedo boats escape, a privately owned undersea-cable repair ship, the *Western Union*, was sent by the CIA to the U.S. Naval Base at Guantanamo with orders to load on her deck several thousand drums of high-octane gasoline.

A few days later, the *Western Union* slipped out of Guantanamo Bay, heading to a rendezvous point with the Cuban torpedo boats off Baracoa, when she was halted by a Cuban warship. An urgent request for help was radioed to Gitmo, and minutes later, U.S. fighter planes were circling the *Western Union* and the Cuban warship. Soon, a U.S. warship arrived on the scene.

For an hour, the Cuban skipper and the captain of the *Western Union* conducted a stare-down. Then the Castro vessel sailed away from a confrontation that could have had serious consequences.

However, the mission of the *Western Union* had been unmasked, and in keeping with the scenario that the United States was not involved in efforts to overthrow Castro, the cable ship set a course for Key West, Florida. There, men identified as "federal agents" kept the skipper and his crew from speaking with news reporters, who apparently had been tipped off about the covert refueling scheme.

PLANNING FOR the invasion of Cuba continued throughout February and into early March. Now there was great haste. The CIA warned of the impending arrival of first-rate Soviet MIG fighter planes flown by Czech-trained Cuban pilots. Moreover, the president of Guatemala, embarrassed and fearful from the avalanche of publicity, pressured the White House to get the Cuban exiles out of his country no later than April 30.

On March 11, seven weeks into his term, President Kennedy convened a meeting of his key cabinet members and other figures high on the governmental totem pole in a closely guarded room in the new wing of the State Department Building. The purpose was to discuss Operation Pluto. Faces were solemn. The stakes were enormous. A thin veil of tension hovered over the room.

Among those seated around a long, highly polished table were Secretary of Defense Robert S. McNamara; Secretary of State Dean Rusk; Secretary of the Treasury Douglas Dillon; Rusk's assistant for Latin American Affairs, Thomas Mann; Assistant Secretary of Defense Paul H. Nitze; CIA Clandestine Services chief Dick Bissell; and General Lyman Lemnitzer, chairman of the Joint Chiefs of Staff.

Bissell was the first to speak. He reviewed the military operation, praised the 2506 Brigade as a fighting force, detailed its array of weapons, told how Castro's air force would be wiped out by a B-26 attack just before the landing, and mentioned that Cuba's history was replete with rebellions and insurrections in which small forces triumphed over larger ones when the civilians joined with the liberators.

It was a curious position for the CIA to take. Weeks earlier, E. Howard Hunt, after a clandestine reconnaissance inside Havana, warned the Agency's top officials that most Cubans were solidly behind Castro and could not be expected to rise up once the exile brigade was ashore.

Bissell's plan called for a landing at Trinidad, a town on the south central coast. This site was favored by the Joint Chiefs of Staff, Bissell pointed out. If the invasion failed to trigger a major anti-Castro revolt, the exiles could slip into nearby mountains and fight indefinitely as guerrillas.

President Kennedy reputedly agreed to the overall invasion concept but wanted a different landing site. Three days later, CIA planners settled on a new target: the Bahía de Cochinos (Bay of Pigs), 100 miles west of Trinidad. The new locale was sparsely populated and swampy, thereby requiring less air cover to invade, the CIA concluded.

The Joint Chiefs of Staff looked on the new site with a jaundiced eye and preferred Trinidad. The military leaders' views were made known to Secretary of Defense Robert McNamara, who was a year older than Jack Kennedy, a graduate of the University of California and the Harvard Business School, and most recently, president of the Ford Motor Company. Perhaps through a bureaucratic snafu, McNamara never told the president about the Joint Chiefs' qualms. Eager to get rid of Castro, the military men apparently took the path of least resistance and put their stamp of approval on the Bay of Pigs plan.

On March 16, Kennedy and his advisers met again to mull over the latest invasion plan. Dulles and Bissell chose not to tell the conferees that if the invasion were to go awry, the exile soldiers would not be able to melt into the nearby mountains, where they could be resupplied indefinitely by air drops and be a rallying point for future actions against Fidel Castro. Some 85 miles of roadless swamps lay between the Bay of Pigs and the nearest mountains, the Escambrays.

An especially haunting question nagged at the conferees: Would Soviet armed forces be rushed to the island as Nikita Khrushchev had pledged, thereby conceivably touching off World War III? Dulles and Bissell admitted that they could not read the mind of the unpredictable Khrushchev.

With all the arguments concluded, President Kennedy pointed to each man and asked for his view. No one voiced an objection to the plan. A final meeting on the Bay of Pigs operation was scheduled for April 4.

In the interval, Jack Kennedy flew to his father's mansion in Palm Beach for the Easter holidays. When he returned to the White House, Arthur Schlesinger noted, the president seemed "more militant than when he left."[8] There was some whispering in the corridors that Jack's gung-ho attitude may have resulted from discussions with the conservative Kennedy Senior, who may have advised him not to pay attention to the views of what he called the eggheads and liberal wimps in his administration.

At the decisive conference, Dulles and Bissell reviewed the combat preparations. In response to a question, they projected heavily favored odds for the success of the invasion and the ultimate elimination of Fidel Castro. Again Kennedy asked each official to give his views. Only liberal Senator J. William Fulbright, chairman of the Senate Foreign Relations Committee who had been invited to sit in on the climactic session, vigorously opposed the entire scheme because it was "immoral."

Three days later, President Kennedy gave Operation Pluto the green light. He had grown impatient with doubters and labeled them as cowards. "I know everybody is grabbing their nuts on this one!" he growled to a confidant, Theodore Sorensen, who held the title of special counsel.[9]

ON APRIL 11, Kennedy was being interviewed on a television network when he made an incredible slip that sent shivers up the spines of those in the know about Pluto. When asked about a recent junket through Latin America by presidential assistant Arthur Schlesinger, the president responded, "I think Latin America is in a most crucial period in its relation with us. Therefore, if we don't move now, Mr. Castro may become a greater danger than he is today."[10]

It was I-Day minus 4 for Operation Pluto.

19

"The President Said 'No Deal'"

A T DAWN, three twin-engine B-26 bombers were winging toward the San Antonio de Los Baños airfield outside Havana, main base for Fidel Castro's air force. Piloting the lead plane was twenty-six-year-old, diminutive Salvador Miralles, a cocky Cuban exile known as the Evil Midget. The flight had taken off three hours and twenty-seven minutes earlier from a secret airfield (code-named Happy Valley) near Puerto Cabezas on the western coast of Nicaragua. It was Saturday, April 15, 1961—I-Day minus 2 for Operation Pluto.

As the three bombers neared the targeted airfield, Miralles's eyes widened in excitement as they took in the aircraft lined up on the runway. "Looks like another Pearl Harbor!" he called out gleefully to his copilot. The old crates made a pass over the airfield, dropped their bombs, banked, then returned to take several low-level sweeps with machine guns blazing.[1]

Meanwhile, other B-26s had fanned out over Cuba and bombed and strafed the airports at Santiago de Cuba, Ciudad Libertad, and San Julián, where Castro warplanes were based.

Landing back at Happy Valley, the Evil Midget was keyed up by the strike at Castro's air force. But he knew that not all of the warplanes had been destroyed, and he eagerly anticipated a second flight at dawn to finish the job. Soon his unbridled enthusiasm was dashed. A radio flash was received from Quarters Eye telling the airmen to "sit tight" for at least thirty-six hours to "assess public reaction."[2]

The Evil Midget and his fellow pilots howled in protest to the airfield's CIA air operations officer, who went under the alias Bill Carpenter. What did "public reaction" have to do with the task at hand, liberating Cuba from Castro's Communist yoke? Carpenter, too, was angry. Hoping that the Cuban exiles would take off for Cuba on their own without orders, the operations officer made himself scarce.

Bill Carpenter, the Evil Midget, and others in Nicaragua had no way of knowing that the halt order had resulted from decisions reached in Washington at the highest levels of government. After the Saturday bombing raids, the CIA had dispatched its supersecret U-2 spy plane to take bomb damage photographs. Quarters Eye was appalled. Photos revealed that only five planes had been hit on the ground, meaning at least eight of Castro's planes were undamaged, including three T-33 jet fighters, the most dangerous of them all, at the Santiago airfield.[3]

In drawing up operational plans, strategic masterminds had stressed that absolute control of the air over the Bay of Pigs was crucial to the success of the invasion. So the air operations officer at Quarters Eye began planning for a "cleanup strike" at dawn on Sunday, I-Day minus 1. He had just alerted Happy Valley to stand by when General Charles Cabell, deputy director of the CIA, fresh from a golf outing at the Chevy Chase Country Club, dropped in. "It seems to me that we were authorized only one strike at the airfields," Cabell said.

"Oh, no, sir!" the air operations officer replied. "The authorization was to knock out the Cuban air force. There was no restriction on the number of strikes."

Cabell was in charge in Washington. Allen Dulles was fulfilling a speaking engagement in Puerto Rico to conceal the fact that Something Big was in the wind. "Hold up until I check with higher authority," the general ordered.

Cabell quickly contacted Secretary of State Dean Rusk, who telephoned President Kennedy at his rural hideaway, Glen Ora, in Virginia. Already Fidel Castro was screaming over the airwaves about the "Yankee aggressors" bombing Cuban "civilian airports," and Kennedy had grown concerned that the U.S. involvement was in danger of being unmasked. Perhaps the president felt that another bombing raid could not be camouflaged under an all-Cuban charade.

"The President said 'no deal,'" General Cabell told the Quarters Eye air operations officer.[4]

If the Cuban exile pilots in Nicaragua were bewildered, Fidel Castro was not. Hardly had the bombs ceased exploding on the San Antonio de Los Baños airfield than he took to Radio Havana. "All commands have been put on alert," he declared in his strident voice. "If this air attack should be the prelude to an invasion, [Cuba] will resist and destroy with a mailed fist any force which disembarks on our soil. . . ."[5]

In a speech at memorial services for his troops killed in the air raids, Castro thundered: "If President Kennedy has one atom of decency, he will present the planes and pilots before the United Nations. If not, then the world has a right to call him a liar [for denying U.S. involvement]."[6]

Dick Bissell and other CIA officials began to panic, fearing that the invasion was doomed. They pleaded vigorously for Kennedy to reverse his decision to cancel the follow-up air strike. Their efforts were in vain. Pentagon leaders were appalled. General Lyman Lemnitzer, chairman of the Joint Chiefs of Staff, later referred to the president's action as "absolutely reprehensible, almost criminal."[7]

Meanwhile, Castro was convinced that the invaders had committed a monumental blunder. By bombing the airfields and not knocking out his air force, they had given him forty-eight hours' warning and time to mobilize his combat units. His spy network in the United States and Central America now paid off handsomely: He knew where the invasion would hit. Strapping on a .45 Colt, Castro rushed out of Havana and set up his battle headquarters in an old sugar mill, 15 miles inland from the Bay of Pigs in Las Villas Province.

From all parts of Cuba, long convoys carrying heavily armed soldiers began converging on Las Villas. Men and weapons, including artillery, mortars, and heavy tanks, quickly took up positions ringing the Bay of Pigs, a body of water some 11 miles wide at its mouth and tapering gradually inland for 17 miles from the Caribbean Sea. For 2.5 miles behind the shore, the terrain is level and firm. Then begins the Cienaga de Zapata, a massive swamp dotted with timber and extending 63 miles east and west and some 19 miles from south to north.

Operation Pluto called for landings at three points along 40 miles of coastline. Paratroopers would be dropped at the heads of the three causeways leading inland through the great Zapata swamp; the amphibious forces would rapidly push inland to link up with the parachute troops, thus giving the invaders an initial beachhead 40 miles long and 20 miles deep.

Meanwhile, Howard Hunt, CIA political-action officer for the invasion, launched a psychological warfare scheme he had concocted, one based on the BBC (British Broadcasting Company) aircasts beamed to the French underground to confuse the German high command prior to D-Day in Normandy. Over the CIA radio on Swan Island, Hunt's meaningless ditties in Spanish flowed toward Cuba:

Alert! Alert! Look well at the rainbow. . . . The first will rise very soon. . . . Chico is in the house. . . . Place notice in the tree. . . . The letters arrived well. . . . The letters are white. . . . The fish will not take time to rise.[8]

Castro's intelligence agency monitored the ditties, which were intended to convince the Maximum Leader that an underground army was about to emerge from the shadows. Castro was not deceived.

IN NEW YORK, Cuban Foreign Minister Raúl Roa charged in the United Nations that President Kennedy and the U.S. government were responsible for the bombing raids and were now on the brink of conducting a full-scale invasion of the island. Adlai Stevenson, whom Jack and Bobby Kennedy had called weak and indecisive during the 1956 Presidential election, took to the UN floor to strongly reject Roa's charges. His oration was passionate and sincere, as well it might have been.

Earlier, Kennedy aide Arthur Schlesinger and a CIA agent had briefed Stevenson on Operation Pluto in general terms, but the ambassador had "inadvertently" been led to gain the impression that any military action would not be launched until after the General Assembly adjourned.

When the bombers in Nicaragua had been preparing to take off for Cuba on I-Day minus 2, one plane was riddled with bullets while on the ground, and the markings of Castro's air force were painted on its tail. Then the pilot flew directly from Nicaragua to Miami. Carefully rehearsed, the Cuban exile told a swarm of jostling reporters and television film crews that he had joined with other defectors from Castro's air force in the bombing raids. It was a clever ploy to conceal U.S. participation.

Adlai Stevenson, unaware that the scenario was phony, read aloud in the UN the comments made by the exile pilot in Miami and held up photos of the bullet-pierced bomber and its Cuban Air Force markings.

ON APRIL 16—I-Day minus 1—some fourteen hundred partially trained recruits of the 2506 Brigade were packed like sardines on five small, black-painted vessels sailing toward the Bay of Pigs. Escorting the tiny flotilla were two U.S. Navy destroyers. The exiles slept where they could: on deck, in lifeboats, in hammocks. Many craved cigarettes; smoking was banned. Morale was high. The men sang and cheered each announcement. Be kind to prisoners, they are fellow Cubans, the men were told. More cheers.

Standing at the railing of one transport was twenty-eight-year-old Erneido Olivo, second in command of the Brigade. Olivo had been a loyal and dedicated army officer when Castro took over, so defecting had been an agonizing decision for him. His scorning of the revolution had been a particularly bitter pill for Castro to swallow; Olivo was a black man, and the Maximum Leader had projected himself as the champion of black people. In less than a year, Olivo, a tall, charismatic officer, had become convinced that Castro was using race as a cynical tactic to divide the Cuban people. As a devout Catholic, Olivo could not embrace Communism.

At sundown, the invasion fleet was 50 miles off the coast of Cuba. On the flagship *Blagar* Brigade leader Pepe San Román called his men to attention. They were a mixed bag, ages sixteen through sixty-nine. A few had been professional soldiers under Batista and Castro, a handful were mercenaries. But most had been ordinary civilians who had never held a gun until they joined the 2506 Brigade.

Standing at attention, the men on the *Blagar* saluted as the Cuban flag was raised. Most had tears in their eyes, including Dr. Manuel Artime, the physician and son of an avowed Communist but himself a devout Catholic, who was the Revolutionary Council's "delegate to the invading army."

IN THE MEANTIME, more than 1,000 miles to the north, CIA agents slipped José Miró Cardona, slated to be the new president of Cuba, and other members of the Revolutionary Council out of the Lexington Hotel in New York City and whisked them to a small airport in a remote area outside Philadelphia. Climbing into an unmarked plane with drawn curtains, the Cuban leaders were flown to Opa-Locka, a former Navy air base in southern Florida. There they were put under house arrest, guarded by sharp-eyed CIA men with orders to shoot if any of the detainees tried to get away. None of the Cubans had been told that the invasion was imminent. They were held in readiness to be rushed into the first slice of "free Cuba" to proclaim a new government.

One of those pacing nervously around the secret hideout was onetime Cuban Army Colonel Ramón Barquín, the Council's military expert. In 1956, he had received a six-year prison term for plotting against dictator Fulgencio Batista but was released in the confusion following Castro's takeover of the government. Barquín was puzzled and worried about the site chosen for the main landings, having had nightmares of the Army of Liberation becoming bogged down in the Zapata swamp.

AT 6:00 A.M. on I-Day, young Juan Luis Cosculluela and his frogmen finished their task, charting a path through the coral reefs. Twenty-five minutes later, leading elements of the 2506 Brigade were nearing the beaches in LCVPs (landing craft, vehicle-personnel) when the vessels crunched to a halt, stuck on coral 150 yards from shore. From this point, Murphy's Law took over: Everything that could go wrong would go wrong in Operation Pluto.

Men scrambled out of their landing craft into chest-high water, holding their weapons—including heavy mortars and shells—over their heads. Now a blue-coated B-26 with Cuban Air Force markings raced in and began bombing and strafing the ships and the men wading ashore. Minutes later, several of Castro's T-33 fighter planes and old British-made Sea Furies joined the attack. The struggling men trying to reach shore cursed loud and long. Wasn't Castro's air force supposed to have been wiped out before the landings?

When Castro's pilots had expended bombs and ammunition, they flew off to reload. During the ensuing lull, the invaders' lumbering old C-46 transport planes, carrying Alejandro del Valle's paratroopers, flew in low over the invading force. They were greeted by a torrent of "friendly fire" from invasion ships offshore. Bullets ripped through the C-46s' wings. The grim paratroopers cursed loudly. "What in the hell is going on—are those bastards crazy?" a man in del Valle's plane shouted.

Offshore on the *Houston*, the Fifth Battalion, an outfit so green that it had had only a few days of training, balked at heading for the beach. The bombing and strafing had unnerved the men. William "Rip" Robertson, the CIA leader of a team of frogmen, was furious. He began shouting at the cringing men to get into their landing craft. "It's your war, you bastards!" Robertson screamed. "Get the hell off!" Only ten men scrambled down nets and into landing craft.[9]

Now the *Houston*, with most of her troops still on board, came under attack by a Castro warplane. A rocket ripped through the ship, set small fires, and nearly panicked the green Brigade men. Water began pouring through a hole in her bottom, and the *Houston* captain headed the stricken vessel toward shore. Frenzied men, feeling that the ship was a sitting duck, jumped overboard. Some drowned, others were attacked by sharks. Only a few dispirited men crawled onto the beach. The *Houston* crunched onto a coral reef 300 yards from shore.

Minutes after the loss of the *Houston*, a Castro jet dived out of the sun and scored a rocket hit on the transport *Rio Escondido*, which was loaded with crucial supplies: ammunition, food, fuel, and medicine. There was an enormous blast, and the *Rio Escondido* became a roaring inferno. Literally going up in smoke was perhaps the most crucial item of all—the sole communications vehicle, carrying the means for the Brigade commander to keep in touch with the battalions on shore, the headquarters ship offshore, and the airfield in Nicaragua.

Despite the early disasters, Pepe San Román had reached shore and set up the Brigade command post. Almost at once, he received shocking news. Over a radio carried in by hand, he was told by the sea commander that the ships had been ordered to withdraw due to the heavy attacks. San Román cursed loudly. These freighters carried ammunition, food, medicine, and other supplies that had not yet been unloaded. The ships hurried off to the south, but their commander said that they would return that night to unload their cargo.

Inland, the C-46s with del Valle's paratroopers zoomed over their targets at the head of the three causeways and, according to plan, dropped the heavy equipment first. Swallowed up by the swamp, it was never seen again. Then the aircraft made another pass and the paratroopers jumped. Some landed in the swamps and drowned. Others dropped behind Castro's lines and were shot, one while still in his parachute harness and dangling from a tree. Scattered bands of parachutists landing on target began fighting Castro's soldiers.

Meanwhile, heavy firefights had broken out all around the Bay of Pigs. Castro already was massing some ten thousand troops to repel the invaders, and heavy reinforcements, including tanks, were streaming toward the battleground.

At 10:00 A.M., Pepe San Román recognized that less than four hours after the first invader had waded ashore, the operation had become totally disorganized and the situation desperate. His supply lines had been cut by the loss of the *Houston* and the *Rio Escondido*, his ships loaded with crucial supplies had fled, he had virtually no communications, and the Brigade's back was to the sea. And where were the hundreds, perhaps thousands, of eager Cubans on the island who were supposed to rush spontaneously to his colors?

Fidel Castro (center) and two of his guerrilla leaders, Juan Almeida (left) and
Ramiro Valdés (right) in the Sierra Maestra. Valdés reputedly oversaw the bull-
dozing of the fence at the U.S. Naval Base at Guantanamo in late 1963, a provocation that threatened to trigger nuclear war. (National Archives)

Raúl Castro (left) and Dr. Ernesto "Ché" Guevara were the two men closest to Fidel Castro. (National Archives)

Camilo Cienfuegos, whose popularity with Cubans rivaled that of Fidel Castro, mysteriously vanished after Castro seized power. (National Archives)

Radio Rebelde, Castro's hidden broadcast outlet, played a key propaganda role in the revolution. (Yale University Library)

U.S. Ambassador to Cuba Earl E. T. Smith repeatedly warned that Castro was a Communist, but the State Department ignored his views and fired him. (National Archives)

FBI Director J. Edgar Hoover (center) provided President Kennedy (left) and Bobby Kennedy (right) with the highest grade intelligence of Fidel Castro and Nikita Khrushchev by means of Operation Solo, the FBI's most spectacular espionage coup. (National Archives)

Joseph P. Kennedy Sr. was a driving influence and financial source behind the political careers of sons Jack and Bobby. (John F. Kennedy Library)

Richard M. Bissell Jr., CIA architect
of the Bay of Pigs operation.
(National Archives)

General Charles Cabell, deputy
CIA director at the time of the
invasion. (U.S. Air Forces)

Fidel Castro ordered leaders of the Bay of Pigs invasion force to be interro-
gated on Havana television after their capture. Seated left to right, wearing
camouflage uniforms: Erneido Olivio, Manuel Artime, and José San Román.
(National Archives)

Jack and Jacqueline Kennedy greet recently released Bay of Pigs prisoners in the Orange Bowl in December 1962. (John F. Kennedy Library)

CIA Director Allen Dulles, flanked by President Kennedy on the left and successor John McCone on the right, was singled out as the mandatory scapegoat for the Bay of Pigs fiasco and fired. (John F. Kennedy Library)

Eleanor Roosevelt raised funds for the ransom of the Bay of Pigs prisoners. Fidel Castro called her a "silly old woman." (Franklin D. Roosevelt Library)

The Soviet ship *Divinogorsk* departs from Cuba with a canvas-covered missile lashed to its deck. (National Archives)

Admiral John D. Bulkeley (squatting on left) watches as a section of water pipe is removed at Guantanamo. The dry pipe exposed Fidel Castro as a liar in front of the world. (Alice Bulkeley)

Some 250,000 *campesinos* (farm workers) who had been hauled to Santiago stood in the broiling sun for hours to hear Fidel Castro speak on July 26, 1964. Castro lambasted the United States and branded Admiral John Bulkeley, the Guantanamo commander, "a gorilla of the worst species." (National Archives)

20

"A Catastrophe
Is at Hand"

A S A BRILLIANT SUN burst over the Caribbean on April 17—I-Day—
the telephone jangled impatiently in the New York City apartment of Lem Jones, whose public-relations firm had been retained to
front for the Cuban Revolutionary Council as part of an elaborate
cover story to shield American participation. Drowsily, Jones picked
up the instrument. David Phillips, the propaganda expert at Quarters
Eye, was on the line. "Okay, take this down," Phillips said excitedly.
He then dictated Revolutionary Council War Communique Number
One: Invasion of Cuba reported begun by a rebel force. José Miró Cardona says groups of hundreds have landed in Oriente Province.

"Put on there, for immediate release," Phillips directed.

Phillips's war communique was a scheme designed to hoodwink
Castro, to convince him that a diversionary landing by a force of 168
men at Baracoa, in Oriente Province, not far from Guantanamo, was
the main effort, thereby luring Cuban defenders away from the Bay of
Pigs. The scheme collapsed. In one of the rash of communications
breakdowns that plagued Operation Pluto, Quarters Eye had been unaware that the Baracoa decoy had never taken place. It had been called
off at the final moment by its commander, Ninó Diáz.

Diáz, who had fought alongside Raúl Castro in the Sierra Maestra,
had trained his decoy force in a wild area north of Lake Pontchartrain,
in Louisiana. His unit had sailed for Baracoa from a berth on the Mis-
sissippi River below New Orleans in a creaking banana boat, the *Santa
Ana*, flying a Costa Rica flag. The old boat had been leased by the CIA,
using a dummy corporation for the transaction.

Three nights before the invasion, the *Santa Ana* arrived off Baracoa. The Brigade men were stiff and tired, having huddled in the cargo
hold during the long journey from New Orleans. Ninó Diáz sent a
reconnaissance patrol ashore, and it returned with curious tales of

burning cigarettes in the darkness and heavy vehicle traffic. Had the landing been betrayed?

Díaz, not noted for his daring, thought it had. "It would be suicidal to land," he declared. But his American CIA adviser on board, Curley Sanches, a former Marine, violently disagreed, and a hot argument erupted between the two men. But Díaz was in charge. He ordered the *Santa Ana* to head for the Bay of Pigs, where he would await new orders offshore.

As the veil of night fell over Cuba on I-Day, the beleaguered men of the 2506 Brigade were hanging on by their eyelids on a beachhead 35 miles long and a few miles deep. Castro's Soviet-trained troops, supported by artillery and fifty Soviet-built tanks, were attacking from three directions. Even Pepe San Román, the Brigade leader and a warrior of stout heart, had to face the grim facts. "Unless something drastic happens," he told his aides, "a catastrophe is at hand."

WHILE A ONE-SIDED BATTLE was raging in the Bay of Pigs region on I-Day, Secretary of State Dean Rusk stood before a battery of microphones in the State Department auditorium in Washington. In his southern drawl, he told a large group of journalists: "The American people are entitled to know whether we are intervening in Cuba or intend to do so in the future. The answer to that question is No. What happens in Cuba is for the Cuban people themselves to decide."[1]

Rusk's remarks provided another facet to the invasion cover story.

Before a tense session of the UN General Assembly, Raúl Roa, the Cuban foreign minister, charged angrily that the invasion had been conceived and orchestrated by the CIA with the full blessing of President Kennedy. Repeatedly, Roa referred to the CIA as "the American Gestapo."[2]

Ambassador Stevenson, meantime, had been clued in on what had been planned for months. He was angry about being set up as a front man in a deception scheme, but he loyally responded to Roa with a slashing verbal assault on Fidel Castro. "The United States has committed no aggression against Cuba and no offensive has been launched from Florida or from any other part of the United States," Stevenson added.[3]

In far-off Moscow, a spokesman for the Kremlin branded the invaders "American hirelings" and blamed President Kennedy for organizing and supporting the "devious operation."[4]

IN WASHINGTON on I-Day, CIA propaganda chief David Phillips was optimistic. From Quarters Eye, he telephoned Lem Jones and dictated another war communique from the Cuban Revolutionary Council. (Under house arrest in Florida, Council members knew nothing of the communiques until they heard them over a Miami radio station.) Marked for 7:15 P.M. release, the communique quoted a "Council spokesman" as saying: "I predict that before dawn the island of Cuba will rise up en masse in a coordinated wave of sabotage and rebellion which will sweep Communism from our country. . . . Much of the [Castro] militia in the countryside has already defected."[5]

It was the kind of stuff from which pipe dreams are made.

TUESDAY, I-Day plus 1, was the blackest day of Jack Kennedy's life to date. Like a tiger in a cage, he paced about the Oval Office, frustrated and worried. Each report from the beachhead brought with it new evidence of looming disaster. Not a single facet of Operation Pluto had gone as planned.

Kennedy's burdens became heavier when he received a threatening message from Nikita Khrushchev, hinting that Russian armed might was about to leap into the fray.

"It is not a secret to anyone," Khrushchev declared, "that the armed bands that invaded [Cuba] have been trained, equipped and armed in the United States. The planes, which bomb Cuban cities, belong to the United States, the bombs they drop have been made available by the American government. . . . As to the Soviet Union, there should be no misunderstanding of our position: We shall render the Cuban people and their government all necessary assistance in beating back the armed attack on Cuba."

Shortly before the clock struck midnight, the president met in the Oval Office with his top military and government advisers. Dick Bissell glumly briefed the group on the Bay of Pigs situation: Unless U.S. airpower was committed, an American-sponsored Dunkirk was certain.

A lively discussion erupted. Chief of Naval Operations Arleigh Burke, who had two aircraft carriers (*Essex* and *Boxer*), a flotilla of destroyers, and a combat-ready battalion of Marines standing by off Cuba, presented several proposals: Have a destroyer shell Castro's positions, send in a company of Marines, or post a picket line of jets at the 3-mile limit offshore. No deal, the president replied. Then how about sending in U.S. carrier-borne jets with their markings painted over to bomb and strafe? Negative, said Kennedy.

Dean Rusk, one of the more dovish advisers during the entire Cuban venture, strongly opposed any further aid to the invaders. Bobby Kennedy suggested sending U.S. reconnaissance jets to determine if hope remained for the hard-pressed 2506 Brigade.[6]

Jack Kennedy solemnly pondered the alternatives, one of which was to allow the entire Brigade to go down the tube. Finally, he reached a compromise: Sabrejets from the *Essex* could provide one hour of "dead cover" at dawn for a strike by B-26s from Nicaragua against Castro's military airfields. ("Dead cover" meant the U.S. jets would cruise between the Nicaraguan-based bombers and Castro's warplanes, but the carrier planes could not fire unless fired on first.)[7]

Quarters Eye promptly flashed orders for the dawn strike to Bill Carpenter, the CIA air operations officer at the Puerto Caezas airport in Nicaragua, and he began laying on the mission. His force had been seriously depleted: Nine of his sixteen B-26s had been shot down, and the others were barely serviceable. Ten pilots had been killed. Long before daybreak, Carpenter called his pilots to the briefing room, but some Cubans, leery of giving their lives for an apparently hopeless cause, refused to fly the mission.

Hearing of the defections, seven American instructors from the Alabama Air National Guard volunteered to fill the vacancies. Six of the old crates, two at a time at half-hour intervals, lumbered down the dark, dusty runway and lifted off for Cuba. Unbeknownst to the airmen, their mission represented the final desperate throw of the dice to achieve victory for the invasion.

In one of the two final B-26s to depart, Riley W. Shamburger Jr. of Birmingham was cheerful and confident. Just before he had taken off, General Doster, wing commander in the Alabama Air National Guard and a close friend, had leaped onto Shamburger's wing and jubilantly told him that a message had just arrived: Sabrejets from the *Essex* would provide an air umbrella at dawn.[8]

Now another incredible communications breakdown—this one between the CIA and the U.S. Navy—reared its ugly head. When the first B-26s reached the Bay of Pigs at about 5:30 A.M., just as the black sky was fading into gray, the air-umbrella jets were still perched on the flight deck of the *Essex*. The CIA had interpreted "dawn" as meaning the first glimmer of light, while the Navy defined it as 6:30 A.M.

First to arrive over the Bay of Pigs was a B-26 piloted by Cuban Gonzala Herrera. He was alone. When taxiing to take off in Nicaragua, his copilot had leaped from the plane and fled into the woods, and his companion bomber had developed engine trouble and turned back. Undaunted, Herrera flew inland to bomb and strafe a troop concentration and a gun battery.

A short time later, other B-26s manned by men of the Alabama Air National Guard neared the beachhead. Riley Shamburger was alarmed. He radioed Don Gordon in another B-26: "Where are our little friends [sabrejets from the *Essex*]?" Gordon was puzzled. "What little friends?" he replied. The message that the Navy would provide an air umbrella had reached Happy Valley after Gordon had departed.[9]

Meanwhile, Gonzala Herrera's bomber had been riddled by bullets; one engine had been knocked out and was smoking, and now he was limping back toward Nicaragua. Suddenly his radio picked up desperate distress calls: "Mad dog four! May Day! May Day!" Two speedy T-33s had pounced on a pair of American-manned bombers. One Castro fighter poured a stream of tracer bullets into Riley Shamburger's plane; one engine caught fire, and the plane began spinning crazily and plunged into the sea. Another B-26 was shot down and crashed on the site of an old sugar mill. Four Alabamans died in the two fiery crashes: Shamburger, Pete Ray, Leo Baker, and Wade Gray.

A B-26 piloted by Salvador Miralles (the Evil Midget) flew a final bombing run over the Bay of Pigs and, nearly out of gas, headed for Florida. He was choked with bitterness and frustration. Spotting the U.S. carrier *Essex* with its planes on deck, the Evil Midget cried out: "Damn you, Yankees, come on! They're *slaughtering* our boys on the beaches!" Miralles broke into tears.[10]

EARLY THAT AFTERNOON in New York, Lem Jones released to the media another upbeat Cuban Revolutionary Council war communique: "Peasants, workers and militia are joining the freedom front and aiding the rapidly expanding area already liberated by the Revolutionary Command."

IN FLORIDA in mid-afternoon—less than seventy-two hours after the 2506 Brigade had waded ashore with high hope—CIA monitors picked up a weak radio signal from the beachhead: "We are under heavy attack by artillery, tanks, and fighter planes. Do not see friendly air cover you promised. Need jet support immediately. Repeat, immediately."

Then there was silence. The Army of Liberation had been wiped out. The invaders lost 114 men. Castro captured about 1,200, along with a large cache of U.S. ammunition and equipment.

21

The Search for a Scapegoat

A S A ROSY SUN peeked over the glistening dome of the magnificent Capitol in Washington on April 20, 1961, Uncle Sam's ample whiskers could not hide the egg on his face. The Bay of Pigs venture that had ended in abysmal failure had been conceived and orchestrated by the CIA and given the blessing of President Kennedy—and the entire world now knew it.

America's leaders at the highest levels had been ensnared in a tangled web of fabrications designed to mask the true masterminds behind the invasion. Stung hardest by the catastrophe was President Kennedy, who was being hammered from all sides in the United States and abroad.

Kennedy was grief-stricken by the unexpected turn of events. Later, Arthur Schlesinger recalled: "The vision of [Cuban exiles] killed on the beach or hauled off to Castro's dungeons haunted him that week and for many weeks and months to come."[1]

It was also a crushing personal defeat for Jack Kennedy that tarnished his image of being all-wise, decisive, and a pillar of virtue. His three-month-old New Frontier, Schlesinger would later describe, "looked like a collection not only of imperialists but of ineffectual imperialists—and, what was worst of all, of stupid, ineffectual imperialists."[2]

As had been the case throughout much of his life, Jack Kennedy, when in trouble, sought advice—or morale boosting—from his father. When it became clear that Pluto had resulted in a debacle, Jack conversed several times on the telephone with Kennedy Senior in Palm Beach.

In between talks, Kennedy Senior told his wife, Rose, that he was unable to dispel Jack's gloomy outlook. In one telephone conversation, an exasperated father barked, "Hell, Jack, if that's the way you feel, give the job to Lyndon [Johnson]!"[3]

Kennedy, in the meantime, replied to Nikita Khrushchev's saber-rattling note with tough talk of his own. The United States had no plan to be directly involved in Cuba, but if the Soviet Union were to do so, the United States would "honor its obligations to protect the Western Hemisphere from external aggression," the president vowed.[4]

Clearly, Jack Kennedy and Nikita Khrushchev were on a collision course.

AT THE SAME TIME, Kennedy continued to embrace the Pluto cover story charade, even after much of the world knew that the fabrication had unraveled. On April 20, in a speech before the American Society of Newspaper Editors, the president continued to lie about U.S. involvement "in any way." Obliquely, he took a swipe at Fidel Castro, warning that U.S. "restraint was not inexhaustible" and declaring that he had no intention of abandoning Cuba to Communism.[5]

TWO DAYS EARLIER, on April 18, even before the invasion's outcome had been decided in the bloody Zapata swamps, Kennedy had been thinking about sacking Allen Dulles, the veteran masterspy who headed the CIA. At a private luncheon with Arthur Schlesinger and James "Scotty" Reston, a staunch supporter who was a correspondent for *The New York Times*, the president stirred his coffee and confided, "The Agency is in for some changes." He said that "Dulles is a legendary figure, but I must have someone from whom I know I will be getting the exact pitch."[6]

Jack had in mind just the right person to give him "the exact pitch" as CIA director—brother Bobby, the attorney general. "I made a mistake in putting Bobby in the Justice Department," he told Reston and Schlesinger. "He's wasted there."[7]

Bobby, for once, refused to accede to his big brother's wishes, turning down the job of CIA director on the logical basis that he was not qualified to handle it.

ELSEWHERE IN WASHINGTON on April 20, a thick pall of gloom and anger hovered over CIA headquarters. Allen Dulles knew that in Washington a scapegoat is mandatory after any disastrous venture, and he was aware that the finger of blame would point directly at him. But he had no intention of sprouting scapegoat's horns.

Low in spirit, Dulles held a postmortem with a dispirited Dick Bissell and other key figures in Operation Pluto. Their coroner's-jury verdict was unanimous: In sports jargon, President Kennedy had "choked up" at a crucial point in the game and canceled the second air strike. "As long as decisions by professionals can be set aside by people who know not whereof they speak, you won't succeed," J. D. Esterline, the CIA's director of planning for Pluto, later exclaimed.[8]

IN BALMY MIAMI that morning, a joyous crowd of some fifteen thousand wives, parents, sweethearts, relatives, and friends of the men of the 2506 Brigade had gathered in Bayfront Park for a "Thank You President Kennedy" rally. After a three-day, spoon-fed diet of glowing war communiques (those put out by Lem Jones in New York), the frenzied participants knew that victory was nearly at hand. Even before the ceremonies began, the shocking news arrived: The Army of Liberation had been wiped out. Stunned, most of those at the rally broke out in tears and screams of anguish.

RADIO HAVANA was jubilant. It trumpeted to Cuba and to the world: "The myth of Yankee invincibility has been destroyed by Fidel Castro." No doubt the Maximum Leader agreed with that analysis by his broadcasters. Stronger than ever, he exulted in his resounding triumph. Over television that afternoon, Castro blasted President Kennedy and "all the sages of the Pentagon and the government of the United States." Then he lashed out bitterly at the Cubans of the 2506 Brigade: "Mercenaries, thieves, smugglers, immoral and shameless people."[9]

WHILE CASTRO was scorching the airwaves with his diatribe, a long line of filthy, unshaven men, tied together and prodded by the bayonets of their guards, shuffled into the town of Girón, on the Bay of Pigs, where fighting had occurred. Clad only in ragged T-shirts and trousers, silent and grim, these were the survivors of the Army of Liberation. Weary, hungry, thirsty, they staggered through the town. Civilian men and women, faces contorted with anger, rushed out to spit upon and hurl curses at Pepe San Román's dispirited soldiers.

FOLLOWING the Bay of Pigs calamity, the telephone jangled in the Washington home of Richard Nixon. President Kennedy was on the line: "Dick, can you drop by to see me?" Replied Nixon: "Jack, I'll be right over."

As Nixon replaced the instrument, teenage daughter Tricia, who had taken the call, exulted, "I knew it! It wouldn't be long before he got into trouble and had to call on you for help!" Nixon only smiled. No doubt that was his precise sentiment.

In the Oval Office of the White House, Kennedy and Nixon labored to show no sign of the friction between them. Each had made slashing, often personal, attacks against the other during the fall campaign. Seated in the rocking chair that was to become his trademark, Kennedy told of his meeting the previous night with José Miró Cardona and members of his Revolutionary Council. "They were mad as hell at us," the president said, puffing on a cigar. "But today they have calmed down and, believe it or not, they are ready to go out and fight again if we will give them the word and support."[10]

As Kennedy talked, he became increasingly angry. He rose from his rocker and began pacing back and forth, all the while turning the room a deep shade of blue with the colorful vocabulary that he had polished to perfection during World War II service as a PT-boat skipper in the Pacific. He ranted against the CIA, the Joint Chiefs of Staff, and his own White House advisers and confidants. "I was assured by every son of a bitch I checked with that the plan would succeed," he declared.[11]

His full head of steam expended, President Kennedy asked calmly, "Dick, what would you do now in Cuba?"

Inwardly, Nixon may have gloried over this incongruous situation. Here was the man who had blasted Nixon for weeks on end during the recent campaign for "allowing" a Communist beachhead to be established on the front porch of the United States. Now Kennedy was asking the culprit for his advice on what action to take.

Nixon, who had been Eisenhower's contact man with what had been (and still was) known as the Cuban Project (the elimination of the Communist regime), replied immediately: "I would find a proper legal cover and go in. There are several justifications that could be used, like protection of American citizens living in Cuba and defending our base at Guantanamo."[12]

ACROSS THE UNITED STATES, meanwhile, liberals in academia were furious about the invasion. Arthur Schlesinger, whom Jack Kennedy had taken aboard in the White House to be a sounding board for liberals, received a jeering telegram from Harvard, where he had been on the faculty. Signed merely "graduate students," the message read: "Nixon or Kennedy. Does it make any difference?"

A Harvard professor, H. Stuart Hughes, spearheaded the drafting of an "open letter to the President." Signed by 70 other liberal academicians, the document demanded a restoration of diplomatic and economic relations with Fidel Castro and that Kennedy "reverse the present drift toward American military intervention in Cuba."

On more than fifteen college campuses, strident protest rallies praised Castro and damned the United States. In New York City, three thousand people were drawn to a rally sponsored by a group calling itself the Fair Play for Cuba Committee. At another Fair Play for Cuba protest demonstration in San Francisco, C. Wright Mills, a leading light in the intellectual community and long an apologist for Castro, sent a telegram that was read aloud to a wildly cheering crowd:

"Kennedy and Company have returned us to barbarism. [Arthur] Schlesinger and Company have disgraced us intellectually and morally. Were I physically able to do so, I would at this moment be fighting alongside Fidel Castro."[13]

Most Americans, following tradition, rallied behind Kennedy in this hour of national crisis and uncertainty when there were haunting clues that the United States and the Soviet Union could become involved in a major war over Cuba. Polls disclosed that 74 percent of the people stood behind the president.

Partisan assaults on Kennedy by the Republicans were muted or nonexistent. Just to make sure his political flanks were covered, however, he conferred with such GOP bigwigs as Barry Goldwater and Nelson Rockefeller. Each time Kennedy's spin doctors made certain that media photographers and television crews were on hand to capture the Republican/Democrat harmony over the Cuban situation.

Dwight Eisenhower accepted a personal invitation to visit Camp David, the presidential retreat in the Maryland mountains, and he listened intently as Kennedy briefed him on the Pluto military actions, including the president's controversial canceling of the second air strike in order to conceal U.S. involvement. The Old General was amazed, asking Kennedy how he had expected to fool the world into thinking the U.S. government was not involved.

"I believe there is only one thing to do when you go into this kind of thing," the Allied supreme commander in World War II added. "It must be a success!"

As a component of the Kennedy administration's damage-control operations, whispers were spread to media reporters that much of the responsibility for the Bay of Pigs debacle rested with Eisenhower. Plans for the operations had been developed and approved in early January 1961, before Kennedy took office, it was charged.

Eisenhower was furious, telling aides that the Bay of Pigs "could not have happened in my administration." His associates joined in a counterwhispering campaign, insisting that if Eisenhower had been president the Bay of Pigs would not have been conducted so sloppily, or if it had, Eisenhower would have called in U.S. air cover.

When a Pentagon general briefed him fully on the details of Pluto, Eisenhower stated privately that the operation "could be called a Profile in Timidity and Indecision."[14] The former president was making a sarcastic play on the book Jack Kennedy was said to have authored a few years earlier, *Profiles in Courage.*

IN THE MEANTIME, Nikita Khrushchev in Moscow and Fidel Castro in Havana were taking threatening potshots at the beleaguered Kennedy, who, Dwight Eisenhower would state, "looked on the presidency as not only a very personal thing, but as an institution that one man could handle with an assistant here and another there."

Khrushchev, who had never been overburdened with moderation, thundered that the United States had committed "a crime that has revolted the entire world." By arming the "criminal invaders," the Soviet leader declared, Kennedy had taken "a slippery and dangerous road which could lead the world to a new global war."[15]

Fidel Castro boasted over Radio Havana that the only thing that kept Kennedy from launching an invasion of Cuba by the U.S. armed forces was the military power of the Soviet Union.[16]

PERHAPS EVEN to a greater degree than his brother the president, Bobby Kennedy was humiliated and furious over the criticism being heaped on the White House, especially from domestic media. "If he hadn't gone ahead with [the invasion]," Bobby stated later, "everybody would have said that Jack had no courage."[17]

One thing seemed certain to White House aides. Jack Kennedy and Bobby emerged from the Bay of Pigs calamity unrepentant. They would become a two-man team to revamp the administration, ruthlessly chopping off heads at the top and using expanded clandestine, even illegal, activities to eliminate their hated adversary, Fidel Castro.

ALMOST BEFORE the smoke had cleared from the Bay of Pigs clash, Jack Kennedy was conferring in a conspiratorial tone with his vice president, rough-hewn Lyndon Johnson. The two men, so different in background and style, had no great love for one another, but each realized they were paddling the same canoe—if one end were to sink, so would the other end. The topic was the CIA. "I cannot understand how men like Dulles and Bissell, so intelligent and experienced, could have been so wrong!" Kennedy exclaimed.[18]

Lyndon Johnson, who hoped himself to occupy the president's chair one day, nodded vigorously and agreed that "something" would have to be done about the CIA. Dulles, a Republican, would have to go but would be kept at his post for the present time. It was a political decision designed to keep Republican leaders from attacking Kennedy over the Pluto fiasco.

Bobby Kennedy also scorched the CIA. Perhaps his views were shaped by a subconscious desire to protect his brother Jack and to absolve him from being a major cause of the disaster. "I think [the failure] was due to incompetency, lack of communications, and nervousness [by CIA officials]," Bobby stated later. "Dick Bissell always twists his hands and he was twisting them even more by the following week. Allen Dulles for the next six or seven days looked like living death."[19]

Conceivably the Kennedy brothers' distrust of and low regard for the CIA had been gained from their father. Five years earlier, Kennedy Senior had been appointed by Dwight Eisenhower as a member of a newly created President's Board of Consultants on Foreign Intelligence Activities. Those on the panel were prominent private citizens who, presumably, had some background and knowledge in the field. Now, after the Bay of Pigs, Kennedy Senior exclaimed, "I know that outfit [the CIA], and I wouldn't pay them a hundred bucks a week!"[20]

ELEVEN DAYS after the Bay of Pigs debacle, twenty-three-year-old Ramón Quintana and a comrade in the 2506 Brigade were captured and tied to an orange tree by thistles, not far from Girón. They had been roaming the Zapata swamps since the Brigade disintegrated, and, with no drinking water available, their tongues were swollen from drinking their own urine and from lack of food. Now their snarling captors spit on them and hurled vile insults. Quintana and the other man were receiving special treatment—both of them were black. Castro was particularly furious at the participation of blacks in the invasion force.

Scorched by the red-hot rays of the tropical sun, the captives remained tied for three hours while Castro's soldiers taunted them with shouts of "Niggers! Niggers! We're going to shoot you niggers and make soap out of you!"[21]

IN THE MEANTIME, the prisons, jails, and improvised internment centers of Cuba were crammed with civilians whom Fidel Castro's secret police had rounded up in a sweeping dragnet and charged with being counterrevolutionaries, traitors, and *gusanos* (worms). Hapless, bewildered men and women were hurled into LaCabána and El Principé prisons, the gloomy dungeons of historic Morro Castle, and sports centers, schools, and theaters. More than one hundred thousand were incarcerated, twenty thousand in Havana alone.

Those arrested existed in squalor, squeezed together like sardines in a can, often left standing for days without food or sanitary facilities. In Matanzas, eight thousand men and women were held in a poultry cooperative, one hundred persons in each chicken house.

Catholic churches and convents were raided, and scores of priests and nuns were flung into filthy jails crawling with insects and laden with human feces. Monsignor Boza Masvidal, Auxiliary Bishop of Havana who had become Castro's domestic Public Enemy Number One, and 135 priests were herded onto a weather-beaten old freighter and shipped to Spain. The Catholic Church in Cuba had been virtually wiped out.

OUTWARDLY CHEERFUL and self-assured in the weeks after the Bay of Pigs, Jack Kennedy privately was suffering from agonizing frustration. Away from the public eye, the fiasco even adversely affected his customary buoyancy and relish for the presidency. One day, he invited Paul "Red" Fay, his undersecretary of the Navy and crony going back to their PT-boat service in the southwest Pacific, to join him for a weekend at the Kennedy retreat near Middleburg, Virginia. As the presidential limousine drove through the White House gate, a number of sightseers were standing at the entrance.

Kennedy smiled and waved at the cheering crowd, but then he turned to Fay and in a solemn tone said, "By God, if they think they are going to get me to run for a second term, they're out of their minds. They can have this goddamned job when I finish my four years!"[22]

22

An "Assistant President"
Emerges

WHILE CHARGES and countercharges about who was to blame for the Bay of Pigs disaster flew back and forth in Washington, the CIA and the Pentagon were convinced that a mole (Castro sympathizer) in the Kennedy administration had provided Fidel Castro with inside knowledge about where and when the invasion would hit. Behind closed doors, CIA counterintelligence officers felt they knew his identity: one of Jack Kennedy's closest confidants in the White House. However, the Agency officials' suspicions were gained through circumstantial evidence and speculation.[1]

State Department security officials also had grown suspicious that the mole may have been within their building. It had long been the practice at State for incoming top-secret messages to be received and decoded in the building's communications center. Then copies were duplicated and hand-carried to the secretary of state, undersecretary, assistant secretaries, and others authorized to receive "for your eyes only" intelligence.

Consequently, the most secret information was sprinkled around the State Department like so much confetti. Couriers and others (presumably including the janitorial staff) could read these messages while they were being distributed.

In the Pentagon, the generals were convinced that Castro had been tipped off. His logistical feat of rushing troops, tanks, and artillery from throughout Cuba to the Bay of Pigs region, almost within hours, could not have been accomplished without prior knowledge of the invasion site, even if Castro had been a trained military commander, which he was not, Pentagon generals knew.

Behind the scenes in the White House, meanwhile, Jack and Bobby Kennedy planned action to even the score with Fidel Castro. In his anger and anguish in the wake of the Bay of Pigs, Jack had ranted to close staff members that he would like to "splinter the CIA into a thousand pieces and scatter [them] to the winds."

After venting his fury, however, he planned to place more, not less, clandestine responsibility in the hands of the CIA. To make sure that he received "the right pitch" from the Agency, Jack put Bobby in personal charge of what would become an ongoing secret war against Fidel Castro. In the time-honored tradition of the Fighting Irish, the Kennedy brothers were determined to win out over the man Bobby sneeringly called "that bastard with the beard."

Although ultimate responsibility for the secret war rested with the president, it would bear the stamp of Bobby, who plunged into the murky field of machinations with a passion an associate described as a "piano-wire hawk." A CIA official said that Bobby felt the "insult" Jack had received from Castro needed to be "redressed rather quickly."

There was no title for Bobby's ad hoc job as the president's ranch foreman to ride herd on the CIA the second time around. Soon, however, Washington insiders were calling him the "assistant president." Many involved in the Cuban Project were convinced Bobby felt he was conducting a holy crusade against the devil.

"Bobby was always for that kind of thing," Undersecretary of State George Ball later recalled. "He was fascinated by all that covert stuff, counter-insurgency and all the garbage that went with it."[2]

Ray Cline, who had been deputy director of intelligence at the CIA at the time, would recall: "Both Jack and Bobby were deeply ashamed after the Bay of Pigs, and they became quite obsessed with the problem of Cuba. They felt they had muffed it, and they vented their wrath on Castro. And, being good Fighting Irishmen, they vented their wrath in all ways that they could."[3]

No doubt there were other cogent reasons for Bobby's animosity toward Fidel Castro. One was that he had grown up hating Communism, a viewpoint gained from his father, Joe. Although the Soviets had been a U.S. ally during World War II, Kennedy Senior mistrusted and despised them. So he had offered his wartime services to a man he greatly admired, J. Edgar Hoover, and was assigned to use his extensive Hollywood connections to ferret out any infusion of Communism into the movie industry and report it directly to the FBI chief.

Bobby also was intimately exposed to an anti-Communism perspective when he was in law school at the University of Virginia at Charlottesville in 1951. Capitalizing on the power of the Kennedy name, Bobby was elected president of the Student Legal Forum (SLF) whose function was to bring prominent public figures to speak at the university.

As anticipated by those in the SLF, Bobby used his family connections to attract marquee names, one of whom was Senator Joseph McCarthy, then at the zenith of his clout. McCarthy had become a good friend of Joseph Kennedy Sr., who regarded the Wisconsin legislator as his kind of politician—a staunch conservative, an Irishman, a Catholic, and a zealous anti-Communist.[4]

After graduating from law school ranking 56th in a class of 124, and with a grade-point average of 2.54, Bobby had a difficult time finding a job. He eventually turned to his father. Kennedy Senior put in a telephone call to Senator Joe McCarthy, who was still being headlined in the media almost every day for what many called his Communist witch-hunt in the U.S. government. A month earlier, in November 1952, at the same time Jack Kennedy had been elected a U.S. senator, McCarthy had been reelected. Kennedy Senior had contributed a hefty sum to the Wisconsin senator's campaign.

Riding on the coattails of the immensely popular Dwight Eisenhower in 1952, the Republicans had not only captured the White House but the Senate as well. McCarthy was appointed chairman of the influential Permanent Subcommittee of the Senate Government Operations Committee. In his telephone call to McCarthy, Kennedy Senior pointed out that both Bobby and his wife Ethel were his fervent supporters, and that McCarthy's image would be enhanced with a bright, eager young man named Kennedy on his staff.

Typically, Kennedy Senior wanted his son, twenty-seven-year-old Bobby with a law degree on which the ink had barely dried, to start his career at the top—as McCarthy's chief legal counsel. McCarthy felt that Bobby was too inexperienced, but he offered to hire Bobby as an assistant to committee general counsel Francis D. Flanagan. Tactfully, the senator added that young Kennedy could move up as he gained more experience.

Kennedy Senior was disappointed. Yet he realized there would be heavy media exposure while the McCarthy probes for suspected Communists in the government were unfolding. Bobby reluctantly took the job but quit after only seven months, saying he was going into private law practice.

Years later, after Fidel Castro seized power in Cuba, Bobby's wife, Ethel, whom he had married in 1950, was outspoken in her anger against the Maximum Leader. She often expressed her negative views on Castro to Bobby, especially after he had ascended to a seat of immense power in the Justice Department and his brother was ensconced in the White House.

Most certainly Ethel had inherited her strident anti-Castro sentiment from her father, George Skakel Sr., a rich, conservative, highly successful businessman. When he was in his early twenties, Skakel had established the Great Lakes Carbon Corporation, a three-man firm, and built it into one of the largest privately held companies in the nation. On Wall Street in New York and in political and society circles in Washington, a common topic for conjecture was who was the wealthier, George Skakel or Joseph Kennedy Sr.

For many years during the Fulgencio Batista era, Great Lakes Carbon Corporation had an office in Havana and prospered by the sale of its products to the sugar industry. Great Lakes continued to do business in Cuba after October 1955 when George Skakel and his wife Ann were killed. Their private plane, a World War II bomber converted for passenger use, exploded in midair over Oklahoma en route to Los Angeles.

After Fidel Castro took over, two of the Skakel couple's sons, George Jr. and James C. III, visited Cuba periodically despite the dangers from the anti-U.S. stance of the Castro regime. George Jr. on occasion had as his companion on safaris into the Cuban bush to hunt for wild boar a good friend, Louis Werner II, who had come to the island as an executive with the U.S. Post Office Department to coordinate mail deliveries between the two countries.

In actuality, Werner's job was a cover: He was a bureau chief with the CIA. Utilizing his widespread business and social contacts in Cuba, George was able to provide Werner with a wealth of intelligence about Castro's plans and activities.[5]

Meanwhile, strong-willed Ethel Kennedy grieved for the many friends she had made in Cuba when visiting the island with her father or brothers during the Batista years. She prayed that Castro would soon be eliminated, and she never let Bobby forget how she felt about the Maximum Leader.

BOBBY'S FIRST TASK in energizing the secret war against Castro, beginning in May 1961, was to sit in with a four-man panel headed by retired four-star General Maxwell D. Taylor, who had led the crack 101st "Screaming Eagles" Airborne Division during World War II. Known as the Cuban Study Group, the panel had been hastily appointed by President Kennedy for a specific purpose: to assure that things would be done right the next time.

The Cuban Study Group convened mornings and afternoons (all through May) in a closely guarded room deep within the Pentagon. A parade of those involved with the Bay of Pigs debacle testified—generals, admirals, CIA officials, American paramilitaries, spooks, surviving 2506 Brigade leaders, and the Cuban Revolutionary Council. Shirtsleeves rolled up, tie knot loosened and askew, a shock of brown hair dangling over his forehead, Bobby Kennedy scribbled notes furiously, and late each day he would leap into his limousine, dash across the Potomac to the White House, and brief his big brother on the progress of the hearings.

"I remember that period so vividly," Ray Cline would recall later. "We were so wrapped up in what the President wanted. Bobby was as emotional as he could be, and he always talked like he was the President, and he really was in a way. He was always bugging the Agency about the Cubans."[6]

In mid-June, General Taylor submitted the Cuba Study Group's report, which he had written himself. It was precisely what the Kennedy brothers wanted to hear. "It is recommended," the document concluded, "that the Cuban situation be reappraised in the light of all presently known factors and new guidance be provided for political, military, economic, and propaganda action against Castro."[7]

In Congress, Senator Mike Mansfield, an outspoken dove on Cuba, was appalled by the thrust of the Taylor report. In a letter to President Kennedy, he stated, "If we must yield to the temptation to give vent to our own failure [in Operation Pluto], we will, ironically, strengthen Castro's position."

Mansfield recommended "gradual disengagement of the U.S. government from anti-Castro revolutionary groups . . . and a cessation of violent verbal attacks on Castro by officials of the U.S. government."[8]

Jack and Bobby Kennedy ignored fellow Democrat Mansfield's suggestion that the United States cut and run in the Caribbean. Rather, it was full steam ahead in the CIA.

23

Eleanor Roosevelt: "A Silly Old Lady"

IN EARLY JUNE 1961, Bobby Kennedy and Kenny O'Donnell, a former Harvard football player and a close friend of Jack Kennedy since college days, held a memorable conversation with the president in the Oval Office. As the president's appointments secretary, the tall, blunt O'Donnell held enormous clout. He used his position as keeper of the presidential keys to reward the loyal and punish the disloyal. No one could see the president of the United States unless O'Donnell gave his permission.

O'Donnell apparently considered himself to be the number-two man in the U.S. government, boasting privately, "The chain of command is from Jack to me to Bobby."

While sipping coffee, the president confided to O'Donnell and Bobby that he had trouble sleeping the night before. "I was thinking about those poor guys in prison down in Cuba," he explained. "I'm willing to make any kind of a deal with Castro to get them out."[1]

Bobby quickly agreed. "We want to do whatever is necessary, whatever we can, to get them out," he exclaimed.[2]

Through undercover sources, word reached Fidel Castro that President Kennedy wanted to cut a deal to get the Bay of Pigs prisoners released. The Maximum Leader was quite willing to comply—for a "ransom" of five hundred new bulldozers or $28 million. Kennedy accepted the offer.

Kenny O'Donnell, who one Washington reporter wrote would "die for Jack Kennedy if need be," later described this acceptance as "one of the most ill-advised moves in [the president's] career."[3]

Almost on cue, conservative Republican leaders denounced the Kennedy-cut deal. Barry Goldwater raged that Kennedy was "surrendering to blackmail." Richard Nixon charged that "human lives are not something to be bartered."

Fidel Castro was riding high in Havana and boasting over television that he had brought "that ignorant, beardless kid" (Jack Kennedy) to heel. He gloated repeatedly about the "indemnity" (a penalty for loss or damage) of five hundred bulldozers he was extracting from the imperialists in Washington.

The Kennedy brothers were angered by the use of the word indemnity. They preferred to talk about an "exchange."

Proud Uncle Sam was being humiliated by a dictator of a tiny Caribbean island. But Castro was holding the aces in this subtle card game. So Jack Kennedy organized a fund-raising committee. Among those accepting positions on the panel were Eleanor Roosevelt, the widow of the former president, and Dwight Eisenhower's brother, Milton, the head of Johns Hopkins University in Baltimore.

Soon a hassle erupted over the precise type of machinery to be sent to Cuba. Castro had stated specifically that he wanted D-8 Caterpillar bulldozers. However, to Pentagon intelligence, that type of dozer was admirably suited for the building of airfields and missile sites, not for farm use, as the Maximum Leader had inferred. So the fund-raising committee offered five hundred farm tractors instead.

To settle the wrangle, Castro announced that, out of the goodness of his heart, he would accept $28 million, his estimated cash value of the bulldozers. Again an impasse had been reached.

At the end of June, the designated term of the fund-raising committee expired. It went out in a blaze of verbal castigation of Fidel Castro, who apparently was delighted that he had stirred up so much fury among the *Yanqui* leaders.

Castro called in a group of the exile prisoners, offered them alcoholic drinks, and chortled, "Well, boys, the Kennedys are not going to give you those tractors!" Then he launched a long tirade during which he described Eleanor Roosevelt, the most visible and oft-quoted member of the fund-raising committee, as a *vieja chocha* (silly old lady).[4]

WHILE THE TRACTORS-FOR-PRISONERS project had fallen by the wayside, both the United States and Castro's Cuba focused on winning the hearts and minds of tens of millions of people in Latin America. Toward that end—Communism or democracy—a showdown took place in August 1961 at an Inter-American Economic and Social Council Conference held at Punta del Este, Uruguay.

"We live in a hemisphere whose own revolution has given birth to the most powerful forces of the modern age—the search for freedom," President Kennedy stated in his message to the conference. "We meet to carry on that revolution to shape the future," meaning "full recognition of the right of all the people to share fully in our progress."[5]

Douglas Dillon, head of the U.S. delegation, spoke in the same vein. "This is a revolutionary task," he declared. "The fruits of the American revolution have not yet been extended to all the people [in Latin America]."[6]

Ché Guevara, Fidel Castro's strong left arm since before the days of the Sierra Maestra, had a verbal confrontation with Dillon, in which he told the Latin American leaders, "You have Fidel Castro to thank for this sudden offer of massive United States aid." The Alliance for Progress was an "instrument of imperialism" and would fail, Guevara added.

The Alliance for Progress was a pet project of the Kennedy administration to unite the nations in Latin America against Communist expansion. When a vote was taken on creating the organization, Guevara abstained. But twenty republics pledged themselves to the new alliance and its goal of improving and strengthening democratic institutions through applications of the principle of self-determination by the people.[7]

Ché Guevara was regarded by the CIA as a firebrand and hot-eyed Communist. His rise to a high post in the Castro movement had not been by chance. Back in 1956, Guevara, the erstwhile Argentine physician, had gone to Mexico City, a hotbed of Communism in Latin America, and organized an espionage network called Asistencia Tecnica (Technical Assistance). Most of the "assistance" was earmarked for Soviet intelligence in Moscow.

The spy apparatus became known as A.T. and was funded by Moscow through Colonel Jaime Rosenberg, who had been chief of the security police in Guatemala before fleeing to Mexico City just prior to being arrested for malfeasance in office. When he linked up with Guevara in the mid-1950s, Rosenberg's goal was to "liberate" Guatemala from "the yoke of the lackey of the United States," President Carlos Castilo Armas (who was later assassinated).

In the months ahead while rebel leader Fidel Castro and his forces were holed up in the Sierra Maestra, Guevara extended his A.T. network to Cuba and soon had an array of agents, cutouts, and couriers collecting intelligence that enabled Castro to know of Batista's military plans in advance and take countermeasures.

ON NOVEMBER 4, 1961, less than four months after the establishment of the Alliance of Progress, top officials from the executive branch, the

CIA, and the Pentagon met with President Kennedy in the Oval Office. The urgent topic: Fidel Castro. Almost daily, the Maximum Leader was launching tirades against Kennedy and other "Yankee imperialists."

While Castro's verbal blasts against the president stung Jack and Bobby, they were much more concerned that the Maximum Leader was making headway in his plan to export his Communist revolution throughout Latin America. Over Radio Havana, whose equipment had been purchased from Swiss and Czech sources for $35 million and which was the most powerful transmitter in Latin America, Castro bombarded tens of millions of listeners with more than one hundred hours a week of Communist propaganda in Spanish, Portuguese, French, and English.

Among those present at the Oval Office discussions were Defense Secretary Robert McNamara; the CIA's Dick Bissell, the Bay of Pigs architect whose head would soon be placed on the chopping block; Attorney General Bobby Kennedy; and Brigadier General Edward G. Lansdale, a legendary CIA spook now back serving in the U.S. Air Force.

Although Bobby Kennedy had no background in covert operations and international intrigue, he was the most vocal at the conference. His goal was to "stir things up" inside Cuba with "espionage, sabotage, and general disorder," all carried out by groups on the island other than Batista followers and Communists.[8]

Bobby asked McNamara to "loan" Lansdale to him for the purpose of making a study of the Cuban situation and recommending actions. McNamara, of course, granted the request.

Lansdale, a swashbuckling type long involved in the dangers of intrigue, had been a CIA operative in the Philippines after World War II. There he worked closely with President Ramón Magsaysay, who had been a guerrilla leader during the conflict against Japan, and orchestrated a campaign to defeat the Hukbalahap, the Communist armed force trying to overthrow the Philippine government.

In South Vietnam in the early 1950s, Lansdale had been active in helping a little-known nationalist politician, Ngo Dinh Diem, ward off the violent efforts by the Communist underground (later known as the Viet Cong) to take over the government.

WHILE GENERAL LANSDALE was developing plans for ousting Fidel Castro and his regime, Tad Szulc, the Latin America correspondent for *The New York Times*, was in the Oval Office for a discussion with President Kennedy. Szulc, who had covered Castro's seizure of power and ensuing actions in Cuba, had been recommended for a post in the administration. Kennedy talked about the Cuban situation and asked what might be done about it. He asked Szulc, "What would you think if I ordered Castro to be assassinated?"

Szulc replied that killing the Maximum Leader would not necessarily change things. Kennedy hurriedly assured the reporter that he was only testing him, and that he felt the same way as did Szulc. The president added that he had been under "enormous pressure" to "okay a Castro murder."[9]

A few days later, Richard Goodwin, the president's confidant, asked Kennedy about his conversation with Tad Szulc, and the Castro murder question came up. Goodwin said it sounded like a "crazy idea" to him. "If we get into that kind of thing," the president was said to have replied, "we'll all be targets!"[10]

24

Top Secret: Agents CG-5824S and NY-694S

A FTER THE BAY OF PIGS DEBACLE and the decision made on high to step up the secret war, thirty-four-year-old Ted Shackley arrived in Miami from his post in Berlin to take charge of JM WAVE, the CIA station where covert operations were developed and launched against Cuba. Shackley would be, in essence, a field marshal in the unprecedented covert conflict against the Castro regime devised by the Kennedy brothers and implemented through the CIA.

Shackley, who was regarded in Washington as one of the CIA's brightest young stars, had been with the CIA for nearly thirteen years. After graduating from the University of Maryland in 1950 and preparing to enter law school, he was called to active duty as an army lieutenant after the Korean War broke out. Soon, he was assigned to the CIA and had been with it since that time.[1]

Miami was one of the few cities in the United States in which JM WAVE's covert empire could function and largely escape widespread public attention. The city already resembled Istanbul, Lisbon, Madrid, and Stockholm of the World War II era; it was a hotbed of intrigue. Miami swarmed with spies, Mafia mob bosses, soldiers of fortune, gun runners, exiled dictators, smugglers, refugees, and criminal fugitives. The CIA operatives did not stand out at all in the Florida city's curious mix.

Among the CIA veterans greeting Shackley on his arrival was William "Rip" Robertson, the paramilitary who had become something of a living legend in the hazy domain of clandestine activities. Despite President Kennedy's strict orders that no Americans were to land in the Bay of Pigs operation, Robertson had been one of the first men ashore. Later, he explained with a straight face that somehow he had missed hearing about the no-Americans order.

Despite his forty-eight years, Robertson had been a dynamo during the landings. When Castro's overwhelming force began to drive many of the invaders off the beaches, Robertson on his own volition had gone back ashore under fire to rescue wounded survivors.

While a stunned official Washington was trying to figure out what had gone wrong at the Bay of Pigs, Robertson was called to explain his actions. There he had a lengthy private discussion with Bobby Kennedy, who did not mention that the gung-ho paramilitary had violated strict orders by taking part in the assault.

Returning to Miami, Robertson told his CIA Cuban agents that Kennedy was "okay." They rightly took this to be a compliment because Robertson had often stated that he hated all politicians.

Perhaps Robertson's high regard for the young Kennedy came from the fact that Bobby had hinted to the CIA operative that, while Castro had won the first round, the fight against the Cuban dictator was only beginning.[2]

Meanwhile, 1,200 miles north of Miami, Morris Childs, the number-two official in the Communist Party USA, arrived at Idlewild Airport in New York City after a trip to Moscow and Havana. Moments after he stepped off the plane, a pair of FBI agents who had been awaiting his arrival escorted him to a nearby building. There the wiry, gray-haired Childs gave a detailed report of his conversations with Fidel Castro in Cuba and Nikita Khrushchev in the Soviet Union.

Morris Childs and his younger brother Jack were double agents. Ostensibly, they were hard-core Communists laboring constantly toward the party's goal, the violent overthrow of the U.S. government. Actually, they were spies for the FBI and provided President Kennedy with a direct pipeline to Castro and Khrushchev, permitting Kennedy to read the minds of these Communist leaders, to anticipate their actions, and to exploit their problems.

Code-named Solo, the Childs brothers' espionage operation was orchestrated by the FBI under the overall supervision of Director J. Edgar Hoover. Tactical oversight was by Assistant Director William Sullivan, who was in charge of COINTELPRO, the FBI program to combat subversion and terrorism within the United States. Day-to-day planning and coordination was in the hands of FBI agents assigned permanently to Solo.

Born Morris Chilofsky of Jewish parents in 1902 near the Polish-Soviet border, Morris, along with his younger brother Jack, was a child when the family came to the United States. By the late 1920s, Morris Childs (the last name had been Americanized) was driving a milk wagon in Chicago, where his outspoken political views earned him the moniker Red Milkman.

Among his superiors in the Communist Party USA, Morris was regarded as a promising leader, and in 1930, he was one of the persons around the world whose expenses were paid to travel to Moscow and attend the Lenin School, where he was trained in Communist doctrine and goals.

After returning home, Morris plunged into a vigorous effort to expand the Communist Party, first as an organizer in Milwaukee, then as state secretary for the party in Illinois and as organizer for the Chicago region. At the age of thirty-five, in May 1938, he was elected to the national committee of the party. A year later, he was appointed editor of the *Daily Worker*, the newspaper of the Communist Party USA, based in New York City.[3]

Morris Childs had become a public figure. Stories about him appeared in the U.S. media, he was often featured and his photograph displayed in the *Daily Worker*, and his name and activities filled the pages of testimony recorded at Congressional investigations into domestic Communism.

All the while, Jack Childs also had been a Communist Party stalwart. He enrolled new members, raised funds, and organized rallies. Unlike his brother, however, Jack preferred to keep a low profile. So his name was never mentioned in public print, although he was widely known within the party.[4]

Morris had been editor of the *Daily Worker* for only a year when he found himself the unwitting centerpiece of a bitter dispute that had erupted between two factions of the party. Childs was aligned with the majority group, headed by Eugene Dennis, a good friend whom Morris had known since both attended the Lenin School in Moscow. William Z. Foster was leader of the minority clique.

Dennis decided he would demonstrate his strong desire to restore unity and harmony in the party by sacrificing one of his own, Morris Childs, on the altar of expediency. So Childs was summoned to a meeting of the national committee, of which he was a member, in New York City on June 27, 1947.

Soon after the session began, Dennis stood and recommended that Childs be given "a leave of absence" as editor of the *Daily Worker*. Childs's jaw dropped and his face turned ashen. Dennis even had a replacement in mind: John Gates, who had fought on the Communist side in the Spanish Civil War and was an enthusiastic worker in the party.

Dennis's rival for power, William Foster, then leaped to his feet and seconded the motion. The committee approved unanimously. Childs abstained from voting.

John Gates would later state that it had been "an inhuman way to treat a person, but it was also a common practice in the [Communist] party."[5]

Both Morris and Jack Childs were shocked by the unexpected turn of events. After twenty-five years of dedicated service to the Communist Party, Morris had been booted out of his post. During the next few years, the brothers apparently underwent a dramatic shift in political sentiment and steadily drifted away from the party.

In the early 1950s, agents of the FBI, which was contacting former and inactive members of the party, interviewed Morris and Jack individually. Finding the brothers disillusioned, the agents suggested that Morris and Jack reactivate themselves within the party and pass along to the FBI as much information as they could acquire. After much soul-searching, the brothers agreed to become double agents.

The FBI gave Morris the code designation CG-5824S and Jack was designated NY-694S. In conversations in the field or at FBI headquarters on Pennsylvania Avenue in Washington, Bureau officials and agents referred to Morris as "58" and Jack as "69." Their true names were never mentioned.

Within an amazingly brief period of time, the Childs brothers had worked their way back into the hierarchy of the Communist Party USA. Eugene Dennis, who had figuratively stabbed his good friend Morris in the back a few years earlier, now appointed Morris his number-two man with the assignment of dealing with Cuban, Soviet, Chinese, and other Communist leaders around the world. Jack Childs was designated to be his brother's assistant.

In 1960, Dennis was diagnosed with an incurable disease, and he was replaced as head of the domestic party by Gus Hall, who, like Morris, had been a pupil at the Lenin School in Moscow. Hall had a violent career as a party organizer in the Midwest and had been convicted in the 1930s for being involved in a bombing during a union strike.

After taking office, Hall kept Morris as his deputy and Jack as his brother's assistant. Morris continued to make numerous trips to Havana, Moscow, Peking, East Berlin, and Prague. In keeping with his status in the party in the United States, he received the red carpet treatment in each capital.

Always there was the danger of being unmasked, which would have resulted in Morris's torture and execution in some foreign land.

When he was unable to take a planned trip to a Communist capital because of the chronic heart ailment that had plagued him for many years, Jack Childs went in his place. On one visit to Moscow, Jack had a seat of honor next to Fidel Castro at a banquet and returned home with a bonanza of high-grade intelligence for the FBI.

Castro in Havana, Nikita Khrushchev and his successor, Leonid Brezhnev, in Moscow, and Mao Tse-tung and Chou En-lai in Peking trusted Morris without reservation. After all, he was the second highest ranking leader in the Communist Party USA. So they spilled their innermost thoughts, ambitions, strategies, apprehensions, and opinions on world events.

All of the Communist dictators denounced the United States, but they did so mainly along ideological lines—Communism versus capitalism. Castro aimed his heaviest salvos on a more personal basis—against President Kennedy.

During his trips to Moscow, Morris Childs was often given heavy amounts of cash, ranging from $50,000 to $350,000, for the Communist Party USA. These funds, packed in suitcases, could be smuggled into the United States only because FBI agents were at the airport to get customs agents to look the other way as Morris trudged past with his heavy burden of money.

Meanwhile, the Soviets had been bringing large amounts of money into the United States, probably in sacrosanct diplomatic pouches; these were funds destined for the Communist Party USA. On at least six occasions, KGB spies, most of them masquerading as employees of the Soviet delegation to the United Nations, held rendezvous with Morris at various secluded places around greater New York City and gave him a total of $500,000. The KGB men said there would be larger amounts to come.

Before the money was put into Gus Hall's treasury, FBI agents orchestrating Solo recorded the serial number of each bill. As anticipated by the FBI, many of these bills showed up later in the bank accounts of Fidel Castro's agents in the United States.

In 1961, the FBI was approached by Victor M. Lessiovski, a Soviet citizen who was working in the United Nations building as a special assistant to Secretary-General U Thant of Burma. Lessiovski said he was angry because his superiors in Moscow told him he could not keep both his salary as a KGB agent and as an assistant to U Thant. So Lessiovski volunteered to become a double agent for the FBI.

Although the FBI accepted his offer, it was wary of his true loyalty. Would he be an FBI-controlled double agent, or was he acting under

KGB orders to serve as a conduit for the KGB to plant false stories with the U.S. government through the FBI?[6]

One day, Lessiovski, code-named Fedora by the FBI, informed Solo handlers that Jack Childs was going to rendezvous with a KGB agent at a certain place and time in New York City. Gus Hall had assigned Jack the added duty of keeping track of party funds. Fedora said the secret meeting would be held to discuss money.

Solo's handlers were suspicious. Did Fedora or his KGB superiors in Moscow suspect or know that Jack Childs was spying for the FBI? Did Fedora tip off the Solo handlers to see what the FBI reaction would be? If Jack failed to show up for the meeting it would be clear to the KGB that Jack and Morris were involved with the FBI. That knowledge would have caused the FBI to cancel Solo and thereby end the wealth of intelligence it had been generating.

A decision was finally reached. Jack would go to the rendezvous. If his true role with the FBI had been made known to the KGB, Jack perhaps would be dispatched at the scene. However, the discussion was routine. All the KGB men wanted was to settle on plans for sneaking more funds to the Communist Party USA.

After Morris and Jack Childs returned from trips to see Castro, Khrushchev, or other global Communist leaders, President Kennedy was briefed by FBI officials on the intelligence collected. On occasion, J. Edgar Hoover sent hand-carried summaries of Solo intelligence to a designated presidential aide in the White House. Kennedy (and future presidents) apparently were told only that the information came from an unimpeachable source. The names of Morris and Jack Childs or their code designations, Agent 58 and Agent 69, were never mentioned to the president.

25

The Dominican Republic Connection

I N THE FALL OF 1961, the secret war between the Kennedys and Fidel Castro spilled over into the Dominican Republic, the country that makes up the eastern two-thirds of the island of Hispaniola, in the West Indies, about 575 miles southeast of Miami. Although the 2.2 million Dominicans lost much of their personal freedom when General Rafael Trujillo seized power in 1939, a social welfare program had given the Republic many new hospitals, free maternity care, low-cost housing projects, and a pension plan.

Therefore, most citizens were satisfied with the Trujillo regime. However, rumors were now being whispered in Washington that the Dominican's right-wing strongman was on some group's hit list. But who were the conspirators? Trujillo's own generals, who wanted a larger slice of the financial pie? The CIA? Or could Castro be instigating the murder of his rival for power in the Caribbean? It was widely known that the Maximum Leader detested Trujillo because he had given sanctuary to Fulgencio Batista and for his friendly relationship with the United States.[1]

These assassination rumors soon reached the ear of Bobby Kennedy, who quickly passed them along to brother Jack. Consequently, it was decided to have presidential aide Richard Goodwin probe into the allegations about a murder plot against Trujillo.

Goodwin called on Allen Dulles at CIA headquarters and obtained details of the Agency's covert operations in the Dominican Republic. Documents disclosed that the Special Group, on January 12, 1961, eight days before Kennedy took office, had approved supplying a small number of pistols and rifles to conspirators inside the Republic plotting to overthrow Trujillo.

It had been a curious action. The plotters were generals and therefore should have had available a large number of army weapons. Pre-

164

sumably, the clandestine arms shipment was designed to imply symbolic support to the conspirators by Washington.

When Richard Goodwin showed President Kennedy the CIA reports on covert activities in the Dominican Republic, Jack merely remarked, "Well, if Trujillo goes, he goes!"[2]

IN CIUDAD TRUJILLO (formerly Santo Domingo, the city's ancient name), the Dominican leader was well aware that Cuba was the main concern of Washington, but that the United States, while drawing a bead on Castro, was catching Trujillo in the line of fire.

"Look," Trujillo told confidants, referring to the Kennedy administration, "those bastards want to use me as the instrument to pull down Castro, and I'll do it because Castro is no friend of mine. But I know also that the [Americans] want to pull him down in order to pull me down afterward."[3]

JACK KENNEDY'S INTEREST in the political situation of the Dominican Republic may have been aroused by his father, who had been involved in a secret mission to contact General Trujillo a few months earlier. At that time, Kennedy Senior had been approached by Igor Cassini, who was more widely known as Cholly Knickerbocker, the name under which he wrote a gossip column for the Hearst newspapers aimed at the high-society crowd.

Cassini informed the Kennedy clan patriarch that a revolution was brewing in the Dominican Republic to overthrow Trujillo, who, the journalist stated with some merit, was quite friendly to the United States. If the revolt were successful, Cassini pointed out, the next regime might swing over to Fidel Castro.

A high Dominican official (no doubt Trujillo himself) had suggested to Cassini that it would be most beneficial in stabilizing his government and heading off the revolution if a prominent American were to meet with the dictator on the sea between Florida and the Dominican. Such a conference would convey to his people that the United States supported the Trujillo regime, Cassini said. Would Kennedy Senior take the role as the prominent American?

Kennedy, a wise old owl, was cautious. What was Cassini's interest in becoming involved in this machination? Only a desire not to see a friendly Caribbean country's government overthrown and replaced with a Communist regime, the journalist replied piously.

What Cassini did not tell Kennedy was that he was an agent in the United States for the Dominican Republic and had cashed in handsomely in that role. (Two years later, Cassini would be indicted by the

U.S. Justice Department for representing the Trujillo regime without registering as a foreign agent as required by law.)

Kennedy Senior accepted the clandestine assignment and presumably relished the task. At the appointed time, a U.S. Navy ship (no doubt arranged for by Kennedy Senior's contacts in the Pentagon) was to carry him to the designated point off the Dominican coast. There he would rendezvous with Trujillo, who would arrive on his personal yacht.

Word of the Kennedy/Trujillo meeting reached Porfirio Rubirosa, Trujillo's ambassador to Cuba, while he was vacationing in Palm Beach, Florida. A husky, handsome man, Ruby, as the diplomat was known to friends, was socially involved with Hollywood glamour queens Zsa Zsa Gabor and Kim Novak, and therefore, he spent more time in the United States than at his official post in Cuba. A wheeler-dealer, he had once received a $50,000 fee (equivalent to $500,000 in 1997) from a major Hollywood operative for a mystery-shrouded "public relations" task.[4]

Presumably, Rubirosa was leery about the Kennedy/Trujillo engagement because he rushed to the West Palm Beach home of Arthur Gardner, the former U.S. ambassador to Cuba whom the State Department had booted out for his constant warnings that Fidel Castro was a Communist. Gardner had gathered a number of unidentified but influential Americans to discuss the meeting with Trujillo suggested by Igor Cassini.

After lengthy conversation, the group decided that sending Kennedy Senior on the clandestine mission was too risky, that unmasking of the partisan role played by the father of the president might backfire against the United States. So Robert D. Murphy, a veteran spook who had first gained wide recognition in the U.S. intelligence community for his undercover work against the Nazis in World War II, would go in Kennedy's place.

For whatever reason, the sea rendezvous was abandoned and Murphy instead traveled to Ciudad Trujillo. With him was Igor Cassini, who, of course, did not disclose his true connection to the Dominican leader. Murphy's mission was to try to get Trujillo to liberalize his total authority, thereby gaining wider approval for his regime in Washington. The task was futile. Dictators, especially one in absolute power for three decades, do not give up their iron-fisted rule.

Not long after Murphy and Cassini left for the United States, two Dominican groups that had been scheming to murder Trujillo for several months began to move into the operational stage. The plot was being developed by two entities, neither of whom trusted the other.

Plans called for the Action Group to kill Trujillo and take his corpse to the Political Group as proof of the deed. Then the Political Group would seize the government and the armed forces. Several generals and high civilian officials were part of each band.

On the night of May 30, 1961, the plot was triggered when Lieutenant García Guerrero, a trusted member of the military guard at the National Palace, sent word to the other conspirators that Trujillo had departed by automobile for Estancia Fundación, his huge estate on the outskirts of Ciudad Trujillo.

Shortly after 10:00 P.M., Trujillo was seated in the back of his chauffeur-driven limousine as it sped along the highway. Both he and his driver carried a pistol, and there were three submachine guns in the car. Suddenly, from an automobile that had raced alongside, came a staccato of automatic-weapons fire. Bullets riddled the limousine.

Trujillo called out weakly, "Please stop. I'm wounded." After the vehicle pulled to the side of the road, the dictator said, "Take the machine guns—we have to fight!"[5]

Seventy-year-old Trujillo, blood spurting from his back, crawled out of the door with his .38 caliber pistol in hand and began firing. Meanwhile, the automobile carrying the conspirators whipped around, came back, and halted. Four men scrambled out and began shooting. Struck several more times, the dictator pitched forward onto his face, quite dead.

AT THE SAME TIME General Trujillo was drawing his final breath, President Kennedy and his sizeable entourage were in Paris on a state visit. Pierre Salinger, his thirty-six-year-old press secretary, informed reporters that the Dominican leader had been assassinated.

Later in Washington, that seemingly routine announcement touched off widespread speculation among the media personnel covering the White House. How had Salinger known that the murder had taken place when the news had not yet reached Paris? To some of the curious, it indicated that there were those in the Kennedy inner circle who had prior knowledge that the assassination had been scheduled to take place that night.

Whatever may have been the case, President Kennedy on his return to Washington discovered that Joaquin Balageur, who had been the figurehead president under Trujillo, had proclaimed himself the head of government, and the slain dictator's playboy son, Rafael Leonidas "Ramfis" Trujillo, had seized control of the armed forces.

Now the question confronting the White House and the CIA was: How would these new leaders deal with Fidel Castro and Cuba?

Balageur, a man of morality and deep religious convictions, had impressive credentials. Educated in the Dominican Republic and Paris, he had earned a law degree from the University of Santo Domingo. Short, wiry, and soft-spoken, he was regarded by the CIA as holding moderate political views, meaning he might well seek to accommodate both the democratic United States and Communist Cuba.

Privately, the Kennedy brothers were also concerned about Ramfis Trujillo's political views and whether he might lean toward supporting Fidel Castro's revolutionary regime. As chief of the armed forces, he held the clout to overthrow Balageur and substitute a Communist or left-wing president in his place.

Ramfis Trujillo had a checkered military background. In 1957, at the invitation of the U.S. government, he enrolled at the Command and General Staff College at Fort Leavenworth, Kansas, where the U.S. Army sends its best and brightest young officers. Ramfis's doting father had no trouble in finding behind-the-scenes sponsors for his son in Washington. It had long been the dictator's habit to donate $100,000 to $200,000 to both the Republican and Democratic parties at presidential election time, thereby making him certain to back the winner.

The elder Trujillo also ladled out substantial funds to individual members of the U.S. Senate and House and to key officials in the executive branch. Code names were used by Trujillo and Manuel de Moya, an aide, when they were engaged in telephone conversations about which politicians in Washington would get what amount of money.

In Washington, moreover, twenty civilians, mostly Americans, were on Trujillo's payroll and registered as agents of the Dominican Republic. One of them, a retired U.S. Army major general, received $270,000 from Trujillo in a single year for "tourist promotion."

While enrolled at the Command and General Staff College, Ramfis Trujillo's lifestyle amazed U.S. Army officers and Kansans alike. In the nearby city of Leavenworth, he rented a mansion for $450 (equivalent to $4,500 in 1997) per month for his weekday pleasure. The ornate structure was guarded by six detectives, several Dominican army men, and special patrols with shortwave radio facilities connected to his weekend headquarters in Kansas City, Missouri—the entire top floor of the plush Ambassador Hotel. That hideaway was secured by heavily armed guards and sophisticated electronic devices.

Fort Leavenworth routines proved to be dreary for Ramfis, as was life in the cornbelt. So he prevailed on another playboy with connections in Hollywood, Porfirio Rubirosa, the Dominican Republic ambassador to Cuba, to write the film star Zsa Zsa Gabor, tell her Ramfis was going to visit Hollywood, and suggest that she introduce him around. Zsa Zsa was delighted. Hobnobbing with international jet-setters was a special passion of hers.[6]

Zsa Zsa and Ramfis hit it off well. He had a bright red Mercedes flown in from Kansas City for her. A few weeks later, he had a luxury automobile delivered to Kim Novak, another reigning Hollywood sex goddess.[7]

When young Trujillo gave Zsa Zsa a $17,000 ($170,000 in 1997) chinchilla coat, the media sniffed out the transaction. Angry voices were raised in Congress, demanding that the U.S. Foreign Aid Program, which was pouring tens of millions of dollars annually into the Dominican Republic, be investigated. Nothing came from the demands.[8]

Ramfis's diversions in Hollywood and the Ambassador Hotel penthouse in Kansas City were not conducive to the strict academic requirements at Fort Leavenworth, so when his class graduated in June 1957, he was given only a certificate of attendance instead of a diploma.

Ramfis's father was furious, not at his carousing son, but at the U.S. government. After funneling an estimated $10 million into the pockets of numerous Washington big shots during the previous five years, he could not understand why Ramfis had been washed out of the Command and General Staff School. To salvage his son's bruised ego, the dictator elevated thirty-five-year-old Ramfis to the rank of four-star general and head of the newly created Combined Chiefs of Staff.

NOW, FIVE YEARS LATER toward the end of 1961, Ramfis Trujillo, under heavy pressure from Washington, agreed to abdicate his post and make his home in another country, leaving Joaquin Balaguer in complete charge. A day after Ramfis agreed to depart, the CIA informed President Kennedy that two of his uncles, who had fled the island after the assassination, had unexpectedly returned. Ramfis immediately canceled his departure from the Republic.

These developments upset the applecart in Washington: U.S. leaders had envisioned that Balaguer would have a moderate government and be a Caribbean bulwark against Fidel Castro's plan to spread Communism throughout the region. It appeared that the ingredients were present for a military coup by Ramfis Trujillo and his uncles to overthrow Balaguer. Consequently, Kennedy decided to employ gunboat diplomacy.

Eight U.S. Navy warships, with 1,800 combat-ready Marines on board, were dispatched to the waters off the Dominican Republic, where the small fleet sailed back and forth just outside the 3-mile limit, clearly visible from Santo Domingo. (Cuidad City had reverted to its ancient name after the Trujillo assassination.)

No doubt the message was clear to the three Trujillos: The Marines would storm ashore at once if called in by President Balaguer. Perhaps the presence of Uncle Sam's striking power offshore, combined with undercover manipulations by CIA operatives in the Dominican Republic, energized General Pedro Rodriguez Echavarria, leader of the Dominican Air Force, to launch a move against Ramfis Trujillo. Seeing the handwriting on the wall, Ramfis fled the island, taking his two uncles with him.

IN HAVANA, Fidel Castro took to television to make his views known. No doubt seeing a golden opportunity for a propaganda coup throughout Latin America, he denounced President Kennedy and his "clique of gangsters" for their "brutal, naked aggression against the peaceful people of the Dominican Republic."[9]

IN MID-NOVEMBER, seven months after the Bay of Pigs fiasco, CIA Director Allen Dulles's head fell into the basket. Fired by the Kennedys after eight years on the job, Dulles had been aware for many weeks that the guillotine was being sharpened. His requests for routine discussions in the Oval Office had been politely turned down.

The Kennedys handled Dulles's departure with as much grace as the situation allowed. He was permitted to retain his chauffeured, bulletproof limousine, and on his final day, the president awarded him the National Security Medal and showered him with public praise.

A few days later, on November 28, President Kennedy dedicated the new home of the CIA, a monstrous building across the Potomac in Langley, Virginia. Agency wags labeled it the Pickle Factory. That same day, Dulles's successor, Republican John A. McCone, took over the CIA reins. McCone, a wealthy shipbuilder and for the past three years chairman of the Atomic Energy Commission, was considered by many to be a curious choice for the post of America's chief spymaster: He was devoid of experience in clandestine activities.[10]

An energetic taskmaster who was astute enough to recognize Washington's minefields and avoid most of them, McCone had not been President Kennedy's first choice; brother Bobby had turned down the job to continue as "assistant president." General Maxwell Taylor had been considered, among others. But Jack Kennedy decided that McCone would fit the bill: He would give Kennedy "the exact pitch."

Dulles was not the only Bay of Pigs fixture to be swept out the door. General Charles Cabell was replaced by Major General Marshall "Pat" Carter, and General Lyman Lemnitzer, chairman of the Joint Chiefs who had approved the military plan, was shifted to Paris as commander of NATO (North Atlantic Treaty Organization). Lemnitzer was succeeded by Maxwell Taylor. Dick Bissell, mastermind of the Bay of Pigs, was banished to a niche at the Institute of Defense Analysis, a so-called think tank.

Bissell was replaced as chief of CIA Clandestine Services by his number-two man, forty-eight-year-old Richard Helms. A survivor, Helms had emerged unscathed from the Bay of Pigs wreckage. A 1935 graduate of Williams College, where he was voted by classmates most likely to succeed, Helms spent two years in Europe as a correspondent for United Press. On returning home, he took a job with the *Indianapolis Times* and rose to national advertising manager.

With the outbreak of World War II, Helms volunteered for the Navy, received a commission, and a short time later was recruited into the OSS by its founder, the legendary William J. "Wild Bill" Donovan. Helms quickly earned a reputation as one who would "get things done" by developing innovative intelligence techniques used against Germany.

Now, sixteen years later, Helms would play a key role in the secret war against Fidel Castro.

26

A Green Light for
Operation Mongoose

ENERAL EDWARD LANSDALE, the sophisticated, worldly-wise CIA
spook who had been "borrowed" from the Pentagon by Bobby
Kennedy to energize the secret war against Fidel Castro, rapidly drew
up a scenario and a timetable for overthrowing the Maximum Leader.
His plan called for infiltrating Cuban exiles from Florida into the island to contact Cubans who had opposed both Fulgencio Batista and
Castro and organize them into underground cells.

The goal was to bring down the Communist dictatorship from
within, culminating in a massive march on Havana by the Cuban people on October 31, 1962. Special care would be taken to give the impression that Castro was being ousted by his own people rather than
by actions engineered by the United States.

In late November 1961, President Kennedy gave the green light to
Lansdale's plan, which was code-named Operation Mongoose. To
smooth the way for its implementation, Kennedy sent a top-secret
memo to key figures in his administration to "use our available assets
to help Cuba overthrow [Fidel Castro]."[1]

Those in the CIA involved in Cuban matters, the Pentagon chiefs,
and top officials in the Kennedy administration rightly interpreted
Mongoose to mean that actions were to be kept small. Known in the
spook craft as a low noise level, the idea was to keep Uncle Sam's head
below the parapet.

Bobby Kennedy, no doubt still smarting over what he perceived to
be the slap in the face Castro had given brother Jack in the Bay of Pigs
fiasco, apparently did not subscribe to the low-key approach. When
briefed on Mongoose at the Justice Department, he said that "no time,
money, effort or manpower [should] be spared." The plan was to be
given "top priority," he added.[2]

For his part, Ed Lansdale never doubted his number-one task. Later, he would be quoted as telling a journalist that "acting on orders from President Kennedy, delivered through an intermediary, [my] job was to develop plans for removing Fidel Castro by any means, including assassination."[3]

Lansdale's fertile brain hatched a multitude of schemes designed to generate internal unrest and then revolution in Cuba. One of his ideas was to play upon the devout Catholicism and rampant superstitions of the peasants. Cuba would be flooded with rumors that the Second Coming was at hand, that Christ had chosen the island of Cuba for His return. Castro, the rumors would have it, was the anti-Christ and would have to be eliminated. On the night foretold for the Second Coming, a U.S. submarine would surface off the Cuban shoreline and begin pumping starshells into the sky, heralding The Arrival.

Other Lansdale machinations included encouraging "criminal elements" to launch repeated attacks on Cuban police officials; using nonlethal chemicals to temporarily incapacitate sugar workers, thereby striking a heavy blow at the already fragile Cuban economy; and coercing defections from "the top echelon of the Communist gang" in Havana.

Lansdale concocted the overthrow plan and would prescribe policy, but the CIA would carry out operations under a newly formed Task Force W. Howard Hunt, who had been the Agency's political-action officer for the Bay of Pigs venture, was the first choice to head the task force. But he was still furious at President Kennedy for canceling the second air strike and declined the offer.

William Harvey, the next candidate, accepted the job, although he was not entirely in tune with Lansdale's idea for fomenting a Cuban revolution solely from within. Harvey had begun his cloak-and-dagger career as an FBI counterespionage agent during World War II. In 1947, according to Washington gossip, he fell into disfavor with J. Edgar Hoover, left the Bureau, hooked on with the new CIA, and became one of its most effective operatives.

Harvey's greatest covert exploit was known in the CIA as the "Berlin Tunnel," which permitted the CIA in 1955 and 1956 to eavesdrop on communications between Moscow and Soviet-occupied East Berlin.

A huge man with a deep, gravelly voice, Bill Harvey was one of the few CIA operatives—perhaps the only one—in Washington who packed a gun at all times. "If you ever know as many secrets as I do," he would say in a mysterious tone, "then you'll know why I carry a gun."[4]

Harvey had a reputation in the Agency as a bulldog—once he sank his teeth into a covert job, he refused to turn loose. So it came as no surprise in the CIA that Harvey, while conducting other covert anti-Castro operations, began building an underground network code-named Amblood. Its purpose was to keep the CIA—and the Kennedy brothers—abreast of what Castro was doing inside Cuba.

Based in the vicinity of Santiago in Oriente Province, Amblood was headed by Luis Toroella, who had been spirited out of Cuba months earlier, given clandestine training at a secret base in Florida, and slipped back into his homeland. Amblood was supplied by the CIA with good-sized sums of money, weapons, and even a yacht.

Contact with Quarters Eye was maintained through Quito, Ecuador. An Ecuadorian army officer working hand-in-glove with the CIA station in Quito rented several post office boxes there in the names of Amblood members in Santiago, and messages, written in secret ink, were mailed back and forth between Quito and Santiago. At Quito, the Amblood letters were collected and put in the sacrosanct U.S. diplomatic pouch and flown to the CIA station in Miami, forward command post for directing Mongoose.[5]

Bill Harvey had high hopes that Amblood would serve as the nucleus for an islandwide underground network whose work would culminate in the envisioned massive march by the people on Havana, much in the manner that angry citizens of Paris had stormed the Bastille, the hated symbol of the oppression of the people of France, on July 14, 1789. However, Harvey grew alarmed when the CIA ceased getting letters from the Quito post office boxes.

Frantic efforts to reach Luis Toroella by radio were futile. Harvey feared the worst—and it was not long in coming. Radio Havana trumpeted that Castro's secret police had smashed the Amblood underground, the "tool of Yankee imperialists."

Twelve members of Amblood were charged with plotting to kill Fidel Castro by firing bazooka rockets from a building across the street from the Havana Sports Palace when the Maximum Leader arrived to speak at a rally. Most of those put on trial, including the Amblood chief, Luis Toroella, were executed.[6]

Undaunted by the Amblood disaster, Bill Harvey began preparing for an especially daring clandestine operation—blowing up the Matahambre copper mines, the largest ones in Cuba, in Pinar del Rio Province. If the raid were to succeed, production would be halted for at least a year, causing a severe jolt to Castro's already shaky economy. Leading the mission would be Roberto San Román, the brother of the Bay of Pigs brigade leader Pepe, who was still in a Castro dungeon.

Rigorous training for the sabotage operation got under way in the Florida Everglades. Under CIA direction, preparations were as meticulous as had been those of British Commandos when they raided German-occupied territory across the British Channel in the early years of World War II. There were precise models of the mine shafts, and training was done with a wide array of demolition charges. The Cuban raiders practiced paddling rubber rafts and scrambling off of and back onto mother ships. Morale was high among the raiders: They were going to land a knockout punch on Castro's bearded jaw.

On the evening of the Matahambre raid, Roberto San Román and six others climbed onto a battered old vessel and headed for Pinar del Rio. San Román was furious. After all the strenuous training, why were they put on such a dilapidated boat? His fears soon proved to be valid. A short distance out to sea, the battery went dead, one engine gave out, the radio failed, and the ship began leaking badly.

Now the five Cubans and their two American CIA supervisors (one was Grayston Lynch, who had taken part in the Bay of Pigs and was known to his charges as Gray) drifted aimlessly for three days. They were out of food and water. Grayston and the other American (known as Bob) climbed into the little catamaran brought along for the landing and paddled off in an effort to reach Key West. Gray and Bob were finally picked up by a freighter—and taken to Texas. But they managed to contact the U.S. Coast Guard, which rescued the five stranded exile commandos between Key West and Cuba.

Reaching Florida, Roberto San Román was, in his words, "mad as hell." He took a jet to Washington, stormed into the CIA headquarters, and was directed to a high-ranking officer involved in Mongoose. Don't despair, the officer soothed his angry visitor. Things will get better.[7]

SAN ROMÁN was not the only one furious over the failed mission. So was Bobby Kennedy, who had taken a direct interest in the sabotage operation. At a session of the Special Group in the Pentagon, he disclosed that he had grown impatient with Mongoose's seeming lack of concrete results. Bobby wanted more boom-and-bang in Cuba.

With jaws clenched and the steely-eyed glare for which he had become known when riled, Bobby told the Special Group, "A solution of the Cuban problem carries top priority in the United States government. . . . Yesterday the President indicated to me that the final chapter has not yet been written."[8]

MEANWHILE, a personal tragedy struck the Kennedy family. On December 18, 1961, Joseph Kennedy Sr. was relaxing and soaking up the warm winter sun in Palm Beach when he suffered a massive stroke. Although he would stay alive for nearly eight years, he would never again be able to speak. Now Jack Kennedy was not only president of the United States but, as the oldest son, patriarch of the clan.

IN HAVANA, Fidel Castro decided it was time to abandon the masquerade that he was only a "nationalist" and an "agrarian reformer," descriptions that he had projected and many in the U.S. media, academia, the Kennedy administration, and the Congress had accepted. During a five-hour speech on television, the Maximum Leader exclaimed, "I am a Marxist-Leninist, and I will be a Marxist-Leninist to the last day of my life!"

Castro continued: "Now, then, do I believe in Marxism? I absolutely believe in Marxism! Did I believe in Marxism on the first of January [1959]? I did believe on the first of January! Did I believe on the 26th of July [1953]? I did believe on the 26th of July! Do I have some doubts about Marxism? I have not the least doubt!"[9]

Castro's "confession" had curious repercussions. Despite the fact that his marathon oration had been televised, the portions dealing with his Communist past were omitted from the next day's story in his own print mouthpiece, *Revolución*. The Communist hierarchy in Moscow apparently strongly disapproved of his remarks as imprudent, so *Pravda* ignored Castro's televised speech.

Three weeks later, on January 7, 1962, in an address before a graduating class of the revolutionary instruction school for militiamen, Castro unveiled his reasons for deceiving the Cuban people about his true colors. By concealing the nature and objectives of the revolution, he said, "we acted in the Marxist-Leninist manner. If we had told the people [the truth] it is possible that we never would have been able to descend [from the Sierra Maestra] to the plains."[10]

IN WASHINGTON and in Las Vegas in the spring of 1962, the witches' brew stirred by the CIA plot to use the Mob to murder Castro started to boil again. For many weeks, Lawrence Houston, the CIA's general counsel, had been urging the Justice Department to drop charges against Sam "Moo Moo" Giancana, the crime boss, for Giancana's role in the bungled bugging of television star Dan Rowan's room in Las Vegas. Houston called on Attorney General Bobby Kennedy and explained why absolving Giancana of legal consequences was so crucial to national security.

Houston assured Bobby that the Mob plot aimed at the Maximum Leader had been "terminated completely." What Houston presumably did not know was that the Mob operation was still in force: Big Bill Harvey had resurrected the scheme and passed on a new batch of poison pills to John Roselli, Giancana's representative in Las Vegas and Los Angeles.[11]

The ongoing scheme for the Mob to murder Fidel Castro took on an amazing new twist. FBI Director J. Edgar Hoover learned from his agents' wiretapping activities that President Kennedy was unwittingly skirting a messy scandal that would link him to the Mob and, indirectly, to the Castro assassination plot. The centerpiece in the unfolding scenario was twenty-five-year-old Judith Campbell, a beautiful divorcée. She and Jack Kennedy, Hoover would discover, had been introduced at the Sands Hotel in Las Vegas in 1960 by showbiz celebrity Frank Sinatra. At the time, Kennedy had been campaigning for the presidency.

Hoover was given evidence that Judith Campbell at the same time was also "involved romantically" with two mobsters in the Castro assassination plot, Sam Giancana and John Roselli. Moreover, during a two-year period, Campbell had made several visits to the White House, and telephone logs recorded more than seventy calls, presumably to Jack Kennedy, the FBI learned.

On March 22, 1962, J. Edgar Hoover called on President Kennedy in the Oval Office where he reportedly laid out the entire CIA-Giancana-Roselli-Campbell-Sinatra-Castro connection. Whatever the two men discussed will never be known for certain. But from that hour onward, Kennedy reportedly received no more telephone calls from the black-haired beauty Judith Campbell. Clearly, word had been passed to her that the proverbial cat was out of the bag with regard to her affair with the president of the United States.

Jack Kennedy set about disentangling himself from the sordid mess. The day after his secret session with Hoover, the president flew to California where he had intended to spend a weekend at the ornate Palm Springs home of his old pal, Frank Sinatra. The singer/actor had long looked forward to the occasion and had had a heliport built on his estate, wired his mansion to be able to handle sophisticated communications equipment, and added two large guest rooms to his manor.[12]

Before departing Washington, however, Kennedy had telephoned another crony of both his and Sinatra's, Hollywood star Peter Lawford, who was married to the president's sister. "I can't stay there," the president told Lawford. "You know as much as I like Frank, I can't go there, not while Bobby is handling this [Giancana] investigation."[13]

Sinatra was livid. He later complained to Hollywood movie queen Angie Dickinson (who was said to have been an occasional but quite discreet intimate of the president), "If he would only have picked up the telephone and called me and said it was politically difficult to have me around, I would understand."[14]

What Sinatra didn't understand was that his telephone might have been bugged by FBI agents probing into organized crime—a fact that President Kennedy, far more attuned to political minefields, no doubt had been aware of when he called Peter Lawford instead of Sinatra.

If Sinatra was livid, Sam Giancana was nearly stricken with apoplexy over the close scrutiny he was receiving from FBI agents. So closely had the G-Men stuck to their target that when Giancana played a round of golf, four of the Feds were playing right behind him. Exasperated, Giancana sent his lawyer into a federal court to seek a restraining order against the FBI and won a partial victory. The judge ordered the FBI agents to play the golf course no closer than two foursomes behind Giancana.

MEANWHILE IN CUBA on March 29, 1962, twelve hundred men of the 2506 Brigade were led from filthy cells in the old Príncipe Castle and taken to the courtyard in the center of the prison for trial. The accused men had to sit on rows of narrow benches, facing the boiling sun, without food or water. Outside the walls, some five hundred Cuban women knelt and prayed for their loved ones among the prisoners.

Castro had expected this to be a showcase trial; television cameras were on all sides, including atop the walls. Brigade members were expected to stridently denounce the United States and President Kennedy. Only two of them did so.

In their summations, the prosecutor and the "defense" attorney vied with one another in damning the Brigade members and Kennedy. The accused men were "traitors to their country" and the "direct instigators" of the Bay of Pigs invasion, the prosecutor charged.

"As far as the other instigator, United States imperialism and its president, Kennedy, who admitted this great crime, they will not be tried here," the prosecutor declared. "But Kennedy will have to answer for his crime before the court of the peoples of the world which will punish him fully as his crime merits."

Antonio Cejas, the defense counsel, spoke for nearly ninety minutes, calling his "clients" traitors and cowards. He quoted long passages from Fidel Castro's speeches and said, "The crimes for which the defendants are charged have been proven amply."

After four days, the mockery was concluded, and the tribunal judges left to reach a preordained verdict.

Four days later, Fidel Castro appeared at the cell holding Pepe San Román, the Brigade commander. He had come to announce the tribunal's finding. "To prove that we are truly generous, we are not going to kill you," the Maximum Leader said, stroking his beard. "Instead you will be given thirty years in prison."

Castro then announced that he was going to ask for a $62 million ransom for release of the Brigade members.

WHEN WORD of the trial's verdict reached Roberto San Román in Miami, he flew to Washington to call on Bobby Kennedy. The attorney general was sympathetic but pointed out that the U.S. government could not legally pay ransom to a foreign entity to gain release of prisoners. He suggested that San Román form a committee of Cuban exiles in Florida to raise the $62 million ransom.

"It won't be easy to raise all that money," Bobby said in a masterpiece of understatement.

27

Tension Grips Washington

ARLY ON SATURDAY MORNING, April 14, 1962, throngs of Cuban exiles began arriving at Miami International Airport. It was precisely one year since the 2506 Brigade had sailed from Nicaragua to the Bay of Pigs. By mid-afternoon, twenty thousand persons stood in the sweltering heat, eyes periodically sweeping the sun-splashed sky.

Earlier, in another move on the strategic chessboard, Fidel Castro had agreed to release fifty seriously wounded men from the invasion force to prove that he would turn loose all the Brigade prisoners if the $62 million ransom were paid. When the funds had been raised, they were to be placed in a designated bank in Canada, Castro specified.

Suddenly, there was a roar from the crowd gathered at the Miami Airport as a large commercial airplane winged in, circled, then glided to a landing. One by one, the prisoners left the plane. Most wore bandages. Arms, legs, and eyes were missing. Some were on crutches. Screams of joy from the well-wishers echoed for great distances across the landscape.

AS BOBBY KENNEDY had recommended, a Cuban Families Committee was organized from among the exiles in Florida and New York City. Ostensibly, it would be a grassroots fund-raising group, with donations solicited from the private sector. In reality, the entire enterprise would be a quasi-government activity spearheaded behind the scenes by the tenacious attorney general.

Also at Bobby's suggestion, the Cuban Families Committee retained the services of James G. Donovan, a partner in the law firm of Watters & Donovan, with offices in New York City and Washington, to initiate negotiations with Castro for the release of the Bay of Pigs prisoners.[1]

Jim Donovan seemed the ideal man for the job. Off and on, he had been involved in cloak-and-dagger affairs since his graduation from Harvard Law School. During World War II, he had been with the hush-

hush agency that had created the atom bomb, and later he had joined the OSS. In 1960, Donovan negotiated with the Soviets to secure the release of Gary Powers, pilot of the CIA's high-flying U-2 spy plane that had been shot down over Russia.

While the negotiations were in progress, the CIA tried to get into the act. An Agency spook suggested to Donovan that he give Fidel Castro a scuba diving suit contaminated by a tubercle bacillus and dusted inside with a fungus designed to produce a serious skin disease. Somehow there was a mix-up. Donovan had no knowledge of CIA efforts to get rid of the Maximum Leader, so he innocently gave Castro an ordinary diving suit on his own.

ALTHOUGH THE CIA had recently sent many Cuban exiles to death or imprisonment at the Bay of Pigs, there was no shortage of Cuban volunteers for sabotage and espionage missions. They were convinced that Fidel Castro could be overthrown only with the clandestine assistance of the United States. All were eager to strike another blow at the Communist regime in their homeland.

Consequently, as JM WAVE mushroomed into the largest CIA station in the world, the Agency spread its machinations against Castro around the globe. Agents were sent to Europe to discourage shipping lines from transporting goods to Cuba. At ports in Europe and the Far East, cargoes bound for Cuba were contaminated or otherwise sabotaged as they sat on docks. Untraceable chemicals were poured into lubricating fluids that were being shipped to Cuba, thereby causing machinery to break down.

"It was all planned economic retrogression for Castro," a former CIA official at JM WAVE would later explain. "Before we sabotaged a product, we would contact the manufacturer to see if we could convince him to do it. If he wouldn't, then we would just put the science fiction crap in ourselves when the shipment was en route."[2]

One of JM WAVE's most notable successes was in convincing a ball-bearing manufacturer in Frankfurt, West Germany, to make a large order of crucial ball bearings off center, so that these items would be useless when they arrived in Cuba. A similar success was scored with a manufacturer of balanced wheel gears in Lyon, France.

These achievements forced the CIA to cough up heavy money, because a manufacturer had to remake his entire mold. But money was no problem for JM WAVE, not with Jack and Bobby Kennedy solidly backing nearly any scheme to dethrone Castro.

JM WAVE agents also were able to sabotage buses manufactured in England and shipped to Cuba. When these shiny new vehicles arrived, they were impressive to behold. However, when put into service, the red-painted buses were constantly breaking down, giving Castro an image of ineptness in the eyes of many Cuban citizens.

SOON AFTER darkness fell over the Florida Keys on August 24, the 31-foot powerboat *Juanin* headed to sea to set a course for Havana. On board were six Cuban exiles led by Carlos "Batea" Hernandez, who had returned only a week earlier from a covert mission to Helsinki, Finland, where the CIA had sent him to try to disrupt the annual international Communist Youth Conference, sponsored by the Soviet Union.

Armed with recoilless rifles, two .50-caliber machine guns, and a small cannon—all purchased by the exiles from Mafia weapons dealers in Miami—the *Juanin* team was on a dangerous mission. Each Friday night, large numbers of Soviet military officers, along with their wives or Cuban girlfriends, gathered for wild parties in the magnificent ballroom of the bayfront Blanquita Hotel in the upscale Havana suburb of Miramar. Hernandez and his commandos were bent on shooting up the building.

Just before midnight, under a star-spangled sky, the *Juanin*, cruising slowly on a muffled engine, stole into Havana Harbor and headed for Miramar, whose lights could be seen twinkling in the distance. Off to one side, the raiders discerned the dim silhouette of the graystone Morro Castle, built by the Spaniards in the sixteenth century to protect the harbor entrance.

Hernandez and his men, perspiring profusely from nervous tension, watched intently for Castro's swift police boats, which had been patrolling the harbor since the Maximum Leader announced that the "war mongers in Washington" were preparing to launch an invasion by U.S. armed forces. Detection and capture would mean certain torture and agonizing deaths for the nocturnal intruders.

Suddenly, Hernandez and his men heard a frightening sound: the hoarse putter of a powerful speedboat. The *Juanin*'s engine was cut off and the craft drifted aimlessly. Then the exiles detected the outline of a Castro patrol boat, including the snouts of machine guns. They held their breath as the craft, its blue lights now plainly visible, headed directly toward the *Juanin*. For whatever its reason, the patrol boat sharply altered its course and soon was swallowed by the night.

Hernandez and his men issued sighs of relief. Their craft's engine was restarted, and a short time later, the *Juanin* halted 200 yards offshore. Peering through binoculars, Hernandez could see the Soviet officers in their dress uniforms, dripping with medals, dancing with their female companions in the Blanquita ballroom.

Moments later, the quiet was shattered by a cacophony of bullets whistling toward the hotel. Windows in the stately structure were smashed and chunks of concrete and brick were ripped loose. Through binoculars, Hernandez gleefully watched the Soviet officers and their guests scurry for cover. After a five-minute fusillade, the *Juanin* dashed back out of the harbor at full speed and headed for the Florida Keys.

Meanwhile, many of the 1.3 million residents of greater Havana had been jolted awake by the roar of the gunfire. Most thought the Yankee invasion had struck. Bedlam erupted. Men and women of the militia leaped out of beds, threw on uniforms, grabbed weapons, and rushed to their predesignated assembly points. Bars emptied as if by magic, and late drinkers staggered home. The eerie wail of sirens split the night. Searchlights sent long white fingers into the black sky in search of nonexistent U.S. warplanes. Throughout the island, Castro's regular army was put on full alert. So was the Cuban Air Force.

Although no one had been killed or wounded in the shoot-up of the Blanquita, Castro was embarrassed and furious. After daylight, his newspaper, *Revolución*, devoted the entire front page to his condemnation of the episode. Castro called the attack "a treacherous and cowardly act" and stated that the "United States of North America government and the hoodlum [President] Kennedy are responsible for the terrorism."[3]

So loudly did Castro denounce the raid that the relatively minor incident became front-page news around the world. In London, the Communist *Daily Worker* ran a blaring headline: U.S. WARSHIPS BOMBARD HAVANA. A subhead stated: "Civilian Casualties Are Heavy."

In Moscow, Nikita Khrushchev remained strangely quiet, because he had long denied that Soviet officers and troops were in Cuba.

In Washington, a White House spokesman expressed the proper amount of abhorrence over the Blanquita shoot-up and speculated that the raid had been the work of Cuban exiles acting on their own.[4]

IN FLORIDA, Big Bill Harvey was worried. All through July and much of August, the Task Force W spies he had infiltrated into Cuba were sending back alarming reports that the Soviets had fifteen missile bases completed or under construction, and that some five thousand Soviet military technicians had descended onto the island. The Washington intelligence community tended to dismiss these reports as having come from unqualified sources. The prevailing wisdom in early fall was that Harvey's spies had seen SAMs (surface-to-air missiles) deployed by Castro for defensive purposes.

Based on the fragmentary reports out of Harvey's spy network in Cuba, CIA Director John McCone was also concerned. On August 22, he called at the White House to brief President Kennedy on his view that "something new and different" was going on in Cuba. McCone admitted that he had no hard intelligence to back up his claim. But, he added undiplomatically, "Perhaps Senator Keating is right."

The remark about Keating irritated Kennedy, for the conservative Republican from New York, a frequent critic of the liberal Democratic president, had been noisily proclaiming that Soviet missiles were in Cuba. Kennedy had gone to great pains to deny the charge; frequent high-altitude sweeps over the island by U-2 spy planes had produced no sign of these lethal weapons, the president declared.

CIA and military surveillance of Cuba was intensified, however. On October 10, Major Rudolf Anderson Jr., cameras grinding furiously, swept over the island in a black-bodied U-2 at a height of 13 miles. On returning to his Texas base, his camera magazine was rushed to Washington by a waiting jet. Interpreters poring over the aerial film detected frightening clues: new roads slashing through tall stands of timber and Soviet-style tents mushrooming in remote areas.

For four seemingly endless days, tension gripped official Washington as Hurricane Ella ripped through the Caribbean and grounded all aircraft. Finally, on October 14, Navy fighter pilots, knifing over Cuba at deck level, provided the clinching evidence. Thousands of photographs revealed without a doubt that almost overnight a bristling missile complex had been built on the front porch of the United States.

Chillingly clear to the expert eye were some forty medium-range missiles, many of them already angled skyward and aimed at the United States. With a range of 1,200 miles, and if armed with one-megaton nuclear warheads, each missile was fifty times as powerful as the Hiroshima bomb and could rain destruction on New Orleans, Houston, St. Louis, and Washington.

The bases were located at ten sites along Cuba's northern coast and at the western tip of the island. Nearing completion were another six bases for 2,500-mile, five-megaton missiles, which could pulverize U.S. cities from the Atlantic to the Pacific. There was more. The aerial film disclosed that the Russians had sneaked into Cuba at least twenty-five twin-jet Ilyushin-28 bombers capable of carrying nuclear bombs.

At 4:00 A.M. on October 16, John McCone received a telephone call at Seattle, where he had gone because of the death of his stepson. The CIA chief was jolted wide awake by the shocking impact of the grave news. He ordered the photos to be rushed to President Kennedy immediately.

As the pictures were being prepared for the president, CIA officials by phone briefed McGeorge Bundy, Kennedy's national security adviser. The grim-faced Bundy hurried out of his office in a wing of the White House and upstairs to the president's living quarters. Kennedy had just finished breakfast as Bundy spun out the electrifying revelations.

It was 10:30 A.M. when Kennedy first saw the telltale aerial pictures. Outwardly calm and collected, he rapidly created an advisory group, later dubbed the Executive Committee of the National Security Council (ExCom for short). It consisted of brother Bobby and ten other confidants.

In the meantime, Jack sent Bobby to the Operation Mongoose orchestrators to emphasize that the president was not happy with the results, or lack of results, of the machinations. Bobby declared that he wanted the heat turned up on the Maximum Leader and that he planned to meet daily with the CIA overseers to assure more clandestine action.[5]

ExCom convened for the first time later that afternoon with the president presiding, and members were briefed on the developments in Cuba. Jack was convinced that Nikita Khrushchev was testing his toughness and that the United States would have to react forcefully. The president was "very clipped, very tense," an ExCom member would later recall.[6]

Time was fast running out—perhaps two weeks—before the Soviet missiles became operational. So Jack ordered more U-2 flights over Cuba. After the session, he told Bobby that he would not attend ExCom meetings for a time so that members would feel more inclined to speak freely. Then the president decided to continue his campaign schedule on behalf of congressional candidates in the November elections to present a public portrait that everything was under control.

During the remainder of the week, ExCom assembled daily to discuss developments and options. People came and went as their regular duties allowed. They listened, talked, and scribbled notes. While Jack was away on the political hustling, Bobby presided. He was hawkish, suggesting that an "incident" be invented to warrant direct involvement by the United States in Cuba. Perhaps there could be a cooked-up altercation at the Guantanamo naval base or an "attack" on U.S. vessels.

Thirty-seven-year-old Bobby was undaunted at being the driving force in the deliberations with far more experienced officials who were much older. He asked sharp—some felt rude—questions and forced one protagonist or another to defend his chosen position on what action to take. Adlai Stevenson, the UN ambassador who was still seething inwardly over the Kennedy brothers keeping him in the dark about the Bay of Pigs plans, later compared Bobby to "a bull in a china shop."[7]

Another participant would later recall: "We all knew that little brother was watching—and keeping a little list of where everyone stood."[8]

Rancor erupted in one ExCom session when an option was advanced that jet bombers be used to wipe out the Soviet missile sites. Undersecretary of State George Ball argued strongly against the air-strike scheme. If the United States were to launch a sneak bomber attack, it would be violating its own sterling traditions, Ball declared.

Bobby quickly agreed. Recalling Pearl Harbor, he said with a tinge of anger: "My brother is not going to be the Tojo of the 1960s!"

Dean Acheson, the tall, mustachioed, sharp-tongued former secretary of state and architect of President Harry Truman's Cold War policies, took violent exception to Bobby's remark. For more than a century, the sixty-nine-year-old Acheson declared in his clipped accent, the Monroe Doctrine had made it clear to the world that the United States would not tolerate the intrusion of any European power into the Americas.[9]

There was a sharp exchange between the two strong-willed men, Bobby and Acheson, but the duel was not resolved that day. In any case, it would be the president's decision—and he would most likely listen to Bobby.

On Saturday, October 20, President Kennedy was back from his campaign swing and presiding over an ExCom session. It was a long and acrimonious deliberation. The choices put before Jack were a naval blockade of Cuba or an air strike, followed almost certainly by an invasion of U.S. forces. Tempers flared. Adlai Stevenson disapproved of the proposals, suggesting diplomatic moves instead. The president, he declared forcefully, should consider offering to abandon the U.S. Naval Base at Guantanamo, as Fidel Castro had long been demanding, as an ingredient in a plan to demilitarize, neutralize, and guarantee the territorial integrity of Cuba. Guantanamo, the ambassador added, was of little value to the United States, a view stridently disputed by the Joint Chiefs of Staff.

Jack Kennedy rejected Stevenson's proposal, which a Kennedy booster, syndicated columnist Stewart Alsop, would later write was a "Munich settlement with Khrushchev."[10]

Bobby was furious at Stevenson for suggesting an accommodation with Khrushchev. "He's not strong enough or tough enough," he told Jack after the meeting, "to be representing us at the UN at a time like this." The young brother recommended: "Why not get him out of there and put someone like John McCloy in his place?"[11]

McCloy was a hard-nosed Republican, a Washington insider, and long experienced in international machinations. Jack Kennedy, as Bobby had suggested, promptly called McCloy back from an assignment in Europe and sent him to the United Nations to "help stiffen" Stevenson, as Jack put it.

ALL DURING THE WEEK, Cuba was kept under a photographic magnifying glass. Navy jets swept low over the coastline, and U-2s and Air Force RB-47s circled high over the island with cameras whirring. Each hour of each day was crucial as the Soviet missile installation mushroomed.

At the Pickle Factory in Langley and in the intelligence domains in the Pentagon, officials were stunned by the speed and scope of the missile buildup. It was agreed that the Soviets must have been planning the project for a year and poured at least a billion dollars into its all-out effort.

28

"Our Blood Ran Cold"

A S THE CLOCK TICKED ON in these tension-racked days in Washington, a puzzling question continued to haunt President Kennedy: Why had the Soviets spent this enormous amount of money and time to plant missiles in Cuba? He was fully aware that the Soviets already had intercontinental missiles in the homeland aimed at the United States. Former ambassador to Moscow Charles "Chip" Bohlen, in a hasty discussion, gave Kennedy a clue. A Lenin adage that Nikita Khrushchev was fond of quoting, Bohlen pointed out, stated that "if a man sticks out a bayonet and strikes mush, he keeps on pushing, but when he hits cold steel he pulls back."

Khrushchev's missile caper, it seemed to Kennedy, was just such a bayonet probe. The Soviet boss hoped to rapidly establish a missile arsenal in Cuba and confront the United States with a fait accompli to test the resolve of the Kennedy administration. If Kennedy responded weakly and fearfully, then Khrushchev would be emboldened to plant the Communist banner at other key points in Europe and elsewhere, the president concluded.

In Moscow, Khrushchev held a relaxed three-hour talk with U.S. Ambassador Foy D. Kohler on the same day that Kennedy had first seen the aerial photographs of the Cuban missiles. The weapons sent to Castro were merely defensive, the rotund Khrushchev explained. Two days later, Soviet Foreign Minister Andrei Gromyko showed up at the White House with the same soothing assurance.

The macabre melodrama being acted out by Khrushchev and Gromyko, both grizzled veterans of the Cold War, convinced the president that the Soviet leaders had embarked on a "bayonet probe." Kennedy was determined that the bayonet would strike not mush but steel.

Mulling over the options presented by ExCom, the president had to be cautious so as not to excite the volatile Khrushchev into plunging the world into a nuclear conflagration. For this reason, proposals to bomb the missile sites and invade Cuba were ruled out—for the time being. Rather, Kennedy approved, as a first step, a "quarantine" in which ships of the U.S. Navy would encircle Castro's island and intercept Soviet vessels carrying offensive weapons to Cuba. Such an action would provide the Soviet boss with food for thought and perhaps cause him to pull back his bayonet. If the quarantine failed, a full-blooded U.S. invasion of Cuba seemed inevitable.

THE BURDEN of making the quarantine work fell on the shoulders of fifty-five-year-old Admiral George W. Anderson Jr., the chief of naval operations. Anderson, who replaced Arleigh Burke as the Navy's top sailor, had seen heavy combat in the Pacific during World War II, had flown fighter planes from the carrier *Lexington,* and had been landing signal officer on the carrier *Yorktown.* On Anderson's desk in the Pentagon rested a plaque that read CHARGER—his radio code when he later commanded the Sixth Fleet in the Mediterranean. Those who had served under and with him swore Charger described Andy Anderson to a tee. And now he began charging directly into the path of what could prove to be a thermonuclear hurricane—if he failed in his mission.

Risks were enormous. Speed was crucial. Intelligence, much of it provided by the CIA, had revealed that some twenty-five Russian and Soviet-bloc vessels, loaded with missiles and UL-28 bombers, were plowing through the Atlantic for Cuba. Navy planes shadowed the oncoming ships, and monitoring stations listened to their wireless messages. Then Admiral Anderson sent his warships to intercept the Soviet vessels.

ALL OF THESE DRAMATIC—and potentially perilous—activities took place under an eerie veil of secrecy and outward normality. As a key component of the security cover, President Kennedy, flashing his boyish smile, flew out of Washington on a campaign tour. On October 20, he was scheduled to speak in St. Louis, but the flow of intelligence reports convinced him that he could remain away from the capital no longer.

The St. Louis date was suddenly canceled. Press Secretary Pierre Salinger lied to the media that the president "has a bad cold." Conscientiously, Kennedy bundled up in an overcoat and even pulled on a hat (he hated headwear), climbed into the presidential jet, and sped back to Washington. There was urgency to his flight: He had to prepare for breaking the shocking news to the American people.

EACH DAY during the crisis, CIA officials were meeting regularly with ExCom. Because of the gargantuan intelligence bonanza pulled off two years earlier, the CIA was able to provide the committee with precise answers on questions of enormous concern. How long would it take the Soviets to get a missile site operational a second time if it were knocked out by bombings? The CIA furnished the answer: only a few hours.[1]

The information on missiles had been obtained from Soviet Colonel Oleg Penkovskiy, whom the CIA had recruited as a Kremlin spy in 1960. Penkovskiy had smuggled to his American contact in Moscow nearly ten thousand pages of Soviet military documents, including high-technology manuals and blueprints on current missiles.

As a result, the CIA was able to provide President Kennedy and the Pentagon with the precise range of the missiles and techniques for bringing the weapons into operational readiness. Until this point, little of the Soviet top-secret documents had been of practical value, but now, with the assistance of the U-2 cameras, the CIA knew nearly as much about the Cuban missile buildup as did the Soviets.[2]

EVEN WHILE Jack Kennedy's jet was winging back to the capital, an order went out for Congressional leaders to be rounded up and flown back to Washington immediately: House Republican Leader Charles Halleck from pheasant hunting in South Dakota, Senate Republican Whip Thomas Kuchel from a campaign visit in San Diego, House Speaker John McCormack from Boston, and House Democratic Whip Hale Boggs from fishing in the Gulf of Mexico, among others.

As the Congressional leaders were flying toward Washington, Kennedy convened his cabinet. All wore solemn faces. They were briefed and quietly left the room. On their heels came the Congressional leaders, some still wearing outdoor clothing. They were shown the telltale photographs. Said one after leaving the room: "Our blood ran cold."

The president outlined his initial plan of action: a quarantine. A fellow Democrat, Richard Russell, chairman of the Senate Armed Forces Committee, declared that a quarantine would not get the job done. "Why fiddle around?" he asked. Russell was for a U.S. invasion—now. Kennedy stuck to his guns, or rather, quarantine.

It had been one of the most gut-wrenching conclaves in U.S. history, for national survival was at stake. But as the session broke up, Kennedy, grinning and fidgeting with his tie, turned to Senator Hubert H. Humphrey, who had sought the Democratic presidential nomination in 1960. "Hubert," quipped Kennedy, "if I had known this job was going to be so tough, I'd have let you beat me in West Virginia [where a crucial presidential primary to select delegates had been held]."

Humphrey, never at a loss for words, beamed and shot back, "Well, I *knew* how tough it was going to be—that's why I let you beat me!"

Laughter rocked the room.[3]

THAT AFTERNOON of Monday, October 22, a black Cadillac carrying Soviet Ambassador Anatoly Dobrynin rolled up to the State Department. Seemingly relaxed, the Russian alighted and went inside to answer a summons by Dean Rusk. Formalities between the two men were brief and strained. The secretary of state handed Dobrynin a copy of Kennedy's television speech to be made that night and a personal letter from the president to Nikita Khrushchev.

Returning to his limousine, the Soviet ambassador, face ashen and shoulders sagging, was swarmed by news reporters. "What happened?" they called out. "You'll know for yourselves soon enough!" Dobrynin snapped.[4]

MEANWHILE, a thousand miles to the south, a routine DEFEX (Defense Mobilization Exercise) was in full swing at Guantanamo. Fighting men at the naval base had grown accustomed to these field exercises, which had been held every six weeks for the past two years. On October 20, Rear Admiral Edward J. O'Donnell, base commander, received an urgent signal: Guantanamo was being put on a war alert. He was notified to prepare to receive reinforcements.

At Camp Pendleton, California, a beehive of activity erupted, as bronzed, tough men of the 1st Marine Division received orders to "mount out." They would be the first reinforcements to reach Guantanamo and would land with weapons and in combat gear, ready to fight. Nine hours after the alert, the Pendleton Marines were ready to go. The next day, company officers and noncoms were briefed and told their destination. "And put on body armor [bulletproof vests]," they were told.

Three hours later, the first huge transport jets, crammed with Marines, weapons, and supplies, lifted off from the Pendleton airfield for the six-hour flight to Gitmo. Unknown to the Marines on board, most of whom could be facing combat for the first time, an ominous order had gone out to all commands involved in the massive airlift: Planes were to carry sufficient fuel to return to the U.S. mainland if need be without refueling at Guantanamo. The implication was clear: By the time the aircraft reached Cuba, the naval base might be overrun by Cuban or Soviet forces.

Each plane carried 125 Marines—two platoons plus support elements. On some aircraft, the men knew where they were going; on others, they did not. As a result, in-flight rumors abounded: They were heading for Hawaii, the Philippines, the Panama Canal, even India.

Beginning at 5:27 A.M. on October 21, the transports began touching down at Gitmo at eight-minute intervals. The Marines were hustled into trucks and driven directly to the MLR (main line of resistance), a series of bunkers, trenches, and foxholes strung out along the 26-mile fenceline that separated the base from Cuba.

On the following day, leading elements of the 2nd Marine Division from Camp Lejeune, North Carolina, began pouring into Gitmo by sea, and they, too, were rushed to the MLR.

In a period of seventy-eight hours from dawn on October 21, the skies over Guantanamo Bay were pierced almost constantly with the roar of U.S. jets and propeller-driven aircraft. Perspiring, bone-weary sailors and airmen unloaded and serviced 187 military cargo and transport aircraft at the Leeward Point airfield on the west side of the bay entrance and at McCalla Field, with its 4,800-foot runway hugging the cliffs on the other side of the bay.

Within a few days, Guantanamo had some ten thousand fighting men—Marines, sailors, and airmen—to contest any effort by Fidel Castro to storm and overrun the naval base. The speed of the Gitmo mobilization amazed even Admiral Robert L. Dennison, commander of the Sixth Fleet with headquarters in Norfolk, Virginia, and his staff officers who worked on the operation. To these Old Salts of World War II and Korea, the lightninglike buildup was not only a source of pride but wonderment as well.

Despite the tremendous firepower of the Gitmo Marine force, backed by land-based and carrier-borne jets and the big guns of warships, Admiral Bob Anderson in the Pentagon and Admiral "Denny" Dennison in Norfolk were concerned. Not only had Nikita Khrushchev clandestinely created a mighty missile base in Cuba, but over the months, he had armed and equipped Fidel Castro's once ragtag army until it was a potent force. CIA and military intelligence in the Pentagon estimated that the Soviet Union, Czechoslovakia, and other Communist-bloc nations had sent Castro 150 to 250 medium and heavy tanks, from 50 to 100 assault guns, 20,000 small arms, some 1,000 artillery pieces, and about 750 antiaircraft guns, plus an unknown number of the new high-altitude SAMs that were thought to have brought down a U.S. U-2 spy plane in the Soviet Union.

There was more. In excess of one hundred of Russia's late-model MIG jet fighters, flown by skilled pilots, were in Castro's arsenal, as were a number of earlier model MIGs. And the Cuban armed forces were estimated to number two hundred thousand men, most well trained by Soviet advisers, brainwashed into hating America, and under tight Communist discipline. Reports of Soviet long-range submarines cruising underwater in the vicinity of Gitmo did nothing to relieve the worries of Navy leaders in the Pentagon and in Norfolk.

As men of the 1st and 2nd Marine Divisions, augmented by two battalions of Seabees (Navy combat engineers), braced for a potential onslaught along the fenceline perimeter, arrayed on the other side of the barrier were an unknown number of Cuban soldiers. A Marine veteran described them as "old pros, real bastards." These were disciplined regular troops who wore Soviet-style uniforms and helmets. A few months earlier, they had replaced a force described as militiamen (civilian soldiers), whose main goal in life had been to return to their farms and villages.

Reuben the Cuban, the Gitmo fighting men called their cross-fence foes.

"At night, Reuben gets a little playful," a teenaged Marine explained to a visiting reporter. "Old Reuben slips up to the fence in the darkness, shakes the fence violently, and shouts loud curses about Yankee bastards and the like." The fence-rattling always brought the Marines to full alert, weapons clutched tightly, trying intently to pierce the veil of darkness. For the rattling set off Marine-built "burglar alarms" made of empty beer cans.

At 10:00 A.M. on the day after the first Marine reinforcements had landed, Gitmo's commander, Admiral O'Donnell, announced that U.S. civilian employees and dependents would be evacuated. Housewives were caught off guard—many had the Monday wash on the line. "You can take only one suitcase each," O'Donnell said over the Gitmo radio station. "Tie pets in the yard, leave house keys on your dining room table, and stand in front of your house and wait for a bus to pick you up."

The outward flow of dependents and civilian workers began at once. Buses carried 2,777 of them to the piers, where they boarded four ships that were under way by 5:00 P.M. Meanwhile, many of the cargo planes that had been bringing in Marines flew off with evacuees, including expectant mothers and hospital patients. Ten Navy nurses and a Red Cross representative were the only women remaining at Gitmo.

EARLY ON MONDAY, October 22, the U.S. television and radio networks carried an ominous sounding announcement: President Kennedy would address the nation that night "on a matter of the highest national urgency." Afternoon newspapers published similar statements. An alarmed citizenry was abuzz with speculation and deep concern.

THAT SAME MONDAY in Washington, the Joint Chiefs of Staff issued "maximum alert" orders. Men assigned to intercontinental ballistic missile sites in the Western states, capable of launching a devastating counterstrike against the Soviet Union, went on a seventy-hour work-week.

At noon, from his underground headquarters at Offutt Air Force Base near Omaha, Nebraska, General Thomas S. Power of the Strategic Air Command (SAC) started dispersing his B-47 bombers to forty civilian airports around the nation. Power was taking no chances that a Soviet missile attack would wipe out his permanent bases. All bomb-bay doors were shut, meaning that each B-47 carried nuclear bombs.

THAT NIGHT all America seemed to be watching as President Kennedy went on television. It was perhaps the nation's most anxious moment since its citizens were stunned on December 7, 1941, on hearing that the U.S. fleet virtually had been destroyed at Pearl Harbor. A grim president delivered a grim speech. The United States had two goals, Kennedy said: "To prevent the use of these [Soviet] missiles against this or any other country, and to secure their withdrawal or elimination from the Western Hemisphere."

Outwardly calm and firm, America's youngest president warned that "any nuclear missile launched from Cuba against any nation in the Western Hemisphere" would be regarded by the United States as an attack by the Soviet Union and would bring full-scale retaliation against the Soviets.[5]

The world teetered on the brink of a nuclear holocaust. But most Americans applauded their leader's bold and decisive stand: After all, they had elected him to "do something about Communist Cuba."[6]

ON THE FOLLOWING NIGHT in Havana, streets were virtually empty. Citizens were home listening to radios or watching television sets. Fidel Castro, it had been announced earlier in the day, would address the nation. From a small studio, backed by military and civilian leaders, the Maximum Leader spoke for more than ninety minutes. The carefully selected studio audience laughed or snickered as Castro lambasted President Kennedy and U.S. senators.

In his television talk, Castro said, Kennedy had presumed to speak to the Cuban people—"as a friend," to a "captive people," a "betrayed people." What gall, what effrontery, he declared loudly. "Kennedy must think your leaders are no longer Cubans," he said. "Maybe they are Martians!"

Castro guffawed. So did the audience.

"At the end, this gentleman [Kennedy], because he is so good, so saintly, after writing all those perfidies, commits a deed that is a violation of law and morals," Castro declared.

Now Castro's voice began to rise. "Kennedy even asks God to bless all the crimes he intends to commit and has committed. . . . These were the words not of a statesman, but of a pirate! No state could, with impunity, stop the ships of another country on the high seas."[7]

29

"If We Want to Meet in Hell"

WITH THE ARRIVAL OF DAWN on Tuesday, October 23, an almost audible collective sigh of relief wafted through official Washington. The world was still at peace. A nuclear holocaust had not been triggered. "We had taken the first step," Bobby Kennedy would state later, "and we were still alive."[1]

Still, neither Bobby, Jack, the military, nor ExCom deluded themselves into believing that the supercrisis had ended. In fact, the most dangerous period lay ahead.

ExCom continued to meet each day to discuss details of new developments in Moscow, Cuba, and elsewhere around the globe. New haunting specters arose. Nikita Khrushchev issued a blunt statement calling the U.S. quarantine "an act of piracy."

ON WEDNESDAY, the Soviet dictator invited William Knox, president of Westinghouse Electric, in Moscow on business, to call on him in the Kremlin. Khrushchev told the American in frank terms that Kennedy had embarked on an extremely hazardous action and warned that if the U.S. Navy halted and searched Soviet commercial vessels bound for Cuba on the high seas, he would order his submarines to sink the American ships.[2]

At the root of the present crisis, Khrushchev told Knox, was the president's immaturity. "My oldest son," the Soviet leader remarked, "is older than Kennedy."[3]

Khrushchev scoffed at Kennedy's charge that the missiles in Cuba were put there to threaten the United States with nuclear destruction. "Soviet weapons in Cuba are defensive," he insisted, pounding his desk for emphasis. However, Khrushchev emphasized, if Kennedy wanted to learn more about the weapons, he had only to invade Cuba.

"I'm not interested in destroying the world," he told Knox, "but if we all want to meet in Hell, it is up to Kennedy."[4]

MEANWHILE in his spacious, blue-carpeted office in the Pentagon, Admiral George Anderson, calm and collected, but red-eyed and haggard from lack of sleep, methodically went about the task of directing the quarantine. (The word "blockade," long recognized internationally as an act of war, was shunned in Washington as scrupulously as the Devil shuns holy water.) As paintings of historic sea battles looked down on him from his office walls, the chief of naval operations waded through a conveyor belt of incoming reports and, in turn, fired off a blizzard of top-secret cables. Tension hung heavily in the air: Seldom had a military man been saddled with such an awesome mission.

As the pressure mounted, an aide handed Anderson a plain white envelope. Marked on it in red letters were the words "Urgent—to the Chief of Naval Operations—Private." Curious, Anderson ripped open the envelope to find a greeting that only an Old Salt could cherish. A card read, "In Times of Stress, Keep a Cool Head!" Inside was a drawing of a Navy "head"—a toilet—perched on a huge block of ice. The card was signed, "Your Sometime Wife" (Mary Lee, whom the admiral had seen only fleetingly since the crisis erupted).

All the while, Soviet vessels continued toward Cuba on a collision course with U.S. warships sent out to intercept them. In the Oval Office of the White House, in Admiral Anderson's domain in the E-Ring of the Pentagon, in Admiral Dennison's Atlantic Fleet headquarters in Norfolk, at the Pickle Factory on the banks of the Potomac, at the Gitmo command post, nerves were taut and stomach butterflies were flapping their wings furiously. What would the unpredictable Nikita Khrushchev do? Would he get rattled and punch the nuclear-missile button? What would Castro do? Would he assault Guantanamo?

As Admiral Dennison paced the floor, his nimble mind retraced the Navy's problem—his problem. The approaches to Cuba were somewhat funneled toward the island, so Dennison knew the Soviet ships' routes. "We really won't have too much difficulty in finding them [the Soviet ships]," he told a reporter who had joined in the vigil. "We have plenty of force. A lot of our ships are down there [in the Caribbean]."[5]

Those "plenty of ships" were commanded by fifty-three-year-old Vice Admiral Alfred G. Ward, a gunnery expert. His specialty might soon be put into play. Under Ward were some eighty vessels, including the nuclear-powered carrier *Enterprise*, its flight deck jammed with jet fighters. Navy patrol planes, taking off from bases in Florida and all along the eastern seaboard, as well as from carriers now encircling Cuba, scanned the vast ocean.

Admiral Ward knew exactly what was expected of him. All Soviet and Communist-bloc vessels heading for Cuba would be approached by U.S. ships and ordered to heave to (halt). If a ship ignored the command, a shot would be fired across its bow. If it still sailed onward, it would be sunk, by naval gunfire or by jet bombs and rockets. Ships that heeded the order to heave to would be boarded by Ward's men and searched for offensive weapons. If these were found, the ship would be ordered to turn away from Cuba and go to a non-Cuban port selected by its captain. If it had no offensive materials, the vessel would be allowed to continue to Cuba.

Soviet cargo aircraft bound for Cuba would be intercepted and forced to divert to a landing at a U.S. airport. There they would be searched for offensive war materials. Soviet submarines would be detected by sonar and radar, then notified by "harmless" depth charges, while U.S. ships radioed the international signal for "rise to the top"—the code letters IDKCA.

DURING THE CRISIS, Secretary of Defense Robert McNamara had been catching catnaps on a cot in his ornate third-floor office on the Pentagon's E-Ring, the outermost in a series of concentric corridors, where the decision-making power is concentrated. Now forty-four years of age, McNamara was regarded by uniformed officers in the Pentagon as "our resident egghead." That label was based on his background as a statistician with a knowledge of psychology and sociology since his days as a Phi Beta Kappa and an economics major at the University of California at Berkeley in the mid-1930s.[6]

Now, at 10:00 P.M. on Wednesday, October 24, fifty-one hours after President Kennedy's televised speech, McNamara, with his deputy, Roswell Gilpatric, went to the fourth floor to find out if Admiral George Anderson was carrying out Kennedy's instructions. The civilian leaders found Anderson in the Navy flag plot, the command post for the quarantine operation under constant guard by armed Marines.

Anderson, who had had hardly any sleep for three days, was far from happy over the unexpected visit from the "visiting firemen," McNamara and Gilpatric. McNamara, never overburdened with tact, spotted a marker on one of the huge wall maps showing a U.S. ship off by itself on the vast ocean. "What's it doing there?" he demanded to know.

Visibly annoyed, Anderson did not reply. There were many others in the flag plot who were listening. Eventually, the admiral took Mc-

Namara aside. "That ship is sitting on top of a Soviet submarine," Anderson explained.[7]

The discussion grew more antagonistic. McNamara wanted to know what the Navy would do with the first interception of a Soviet-bloc vessel. Anderson replied that there was no need to discuss that matter, that the Navy had known about operating a blockade since the days of the legendary John Paul Jones in the late 1700s.

McNamara was not to be put off, continuing to quiz the four-star admiral on details of the quarantine. These were the kinds of details generals and flags (admirals) insisted that civilian overseers need not concern themselves with. It was doubtful if any secretary of defense ever had spoken so sternly to a chief of naval operations.

"Is there a Russian-speaking officer on each ship [in the blockade]?" McNamara asked.

Anderson admitted that he did not know the answer. "Then find out!" McNamara snapped. (Navy planners already had assigned U.S. Naval Academy language instructors to blockade vessels.)

Some thirty Navy officers were in the flag plot at the time, and they tried to go about their duties as though the loud dispute were not raging. Admiral Anderson was red-faced and struggling to keep his temper under reasonable control. Squinting through his glasses, McNamara was equally furious and trying to hold his temper in check.

Suddenly, the encounter ended when Anderson said to McNamara: "Now, Mr. Secretary, if you and Mr. Gilpatric will go back to your offices, the Navy will run the blockade."

McNamara made no reply but spun on his heels and, with Gilpatric trotting along behind, stalked out of the flag plot.[8]

THERE WAS RELIEF in Washington official circles sixty hours after President Kennedy's television address when a few Soviet cargo ships altered course, away from Cuba. But the others plowed onward. The *Bucharest*, an oil tanker, was intercepted on Thursday, Quarantine Day plus 3, but Jack Kennedy, not wanting to push the volatile Khrushchev too far, permitted it to continue uninspected to Cuba.

Sixteen hours later, the destroyers *John R. Pierce* and *Joseph P. Kennedy, Jr.* (by happenstance it carried the name of the president's older brother who had been killed in World War II) got on the tail of a Soviet-chartered Lebanese cargo ship named the *Marucla*. At dawn on Friday, in a scene reminiscent of a Hollywood movie version of seafaring men of centuries before, the *Kennedy* lowered a whaleboat and sent a heavily armed search party aboard the *Marucla*. Clad in crisp dress whites, Lieutenant Commander Kenneth C. Reynolds, executive officer of the *Kennedy*, and Lieutenant Commander Dwight G. Osborne, executive officer of the *Pierce*, led the boarding party.

Marucla's captain was Greek, friendly and cooperative. He had even lowered a ladder for the boarding party, then served coffee to the Americans. A diligent search found only rolls of paper, trucks, truck parts, and drums of sulfur. With handshakes all around, Lieutenant Commanders Osborne and Reynolds and their men departed the *Marucla* and it sailed on to Cuba.

IN WASHINGTON on Saturday, October 27, FBI Director J. Edgar Hoover informed his boss, Bobby Kennedy, of an alarming discovery by G-Men. Soviet officials, diplomatic and KGB, in New York City were getting ready to burn secret documents in the event they had to depart for the Soviet Union in case an armed conflict were about to erupt.

Bobby rushed to the White House to break the news to Jack. It seemed clear to both men that Khrushchev, whose mood swings were legendary in the Soviet Union, was thinking of something other than a peaceful resolution of the missile crisis.

THAT SAME DAY, the already tension-packed situation grew worse. Word arrived in Washington that a U-2 spy plane had been shot down over Cuba by a Soviet SAM missile, killing the pilot, Major Rudolf Anderson Jr. Elsewhere over the island that same day, four other U.S. surveillance planes had been shot at but missed.

Now war—nuclear war—seemed probable. ExCom had agreed earlier, and President Kennedy had not ruled out the idea, that if a U-2 were shot down, the SAM site responsible would be wiped out by an air attack. If a second U-2 were downed, ExCom had envisioned that all the SAM sites in Cuba would be destroyed from the air.

"There was a feeling that the noose was tightening," Bobby Kennedy would state later, "on all of us, on Americans, on mankind, and the bridges to escape were crumbling."[9]

Then the intense anxiety was stepped up yet another notch. While on a routine flight over the North Pole, a U-2 pilot inadvertently strayed into Soviet territory. Russian fighter planes scrambled. American aircraft lifted off from Alaska to meet the looming challenge. Soon the erring American pilot righted his misdirection and returned to his base without incident.

Jack and Bobby Kennedy, ExCom members, and Pentagon officials resumed breathing—and waiting for the next unexpected snafu.

THAT EVENING in a private conversation, the president and Bobby decided, in order to meet Khrushchev halfway and permit him to save face, the United States would quietly withdraw its nuclear-capable Jupiter missiles from Turkey and Italy, as the Soviet dictator had been demanding. The next morning, Bobby summoned Ambassador Dobrynin to his office and informed him that the Jupiters would be dismantled in a relatively short time after the crisis concluded.

Jack and Bobby may have had a trick up their sleeves. As soon as the Jupiters were removed, they would be replaced by submarine-launched Polaris missiles.

Moreover, the president allegedly made a secret pledge to the Soviets. If Khrushchev removed the missiles, the United States would not invade Cuba.

AFTER MANY DAYS of sailing directly toward the U.S. warships while a fearful world held its collective breath, the Soviet cargo ships carrying missiles to Cuba suddenly reversed courses and headed back to home ports.

Jack Kennedy and Nikita Khrushchev for a tension-filled week had been eyeball to eyeball. The Soviet leader blinked first.

But the war of nerves and the global peril were not over. Kennedy still had to get the missiles out of Cuba. There was urgency to the task, for Khrushchev had not yet withdrawn entirely from the confrontation. Low-level Navy reconnaissance planes revealed that construction of the missile sites had been accelerated.

As part of the U.S. strategy, U Thant of Burma, the acting secretary-general of the United Nations, was asked to contact Khrushchev and stress that the missiles had to go—immediately. Khrushchev hemmed and hawed. Kennedy stepped up the war of nerves. Swarms of supersonic jet fighters descended on Florida's MacDill and Patrick Air Force Bases. Twenty-four troop-carrier squadrons—fourteen thousand men—of the Air Force Reserve were called to active duty. By air, train, and long vehicle convoys, infantry, tank, and artillery units poured into southern Florida. The threat was clear: If Khrushchev would not remove his missiles, the United States would invade.

To leave no doubt in the Russian bear's mind that he meant business, President Kennedy fired off a letter to the Kremlin: The missiles had to go—at once. The next day, two weeks after Kennedy had first seen the incriminating aerial photographs, Khrushchev gave in. He sent the president a mild message: "I understand very well your anxiety and the anxiety of the people of the U.S. in connection with the fact that the weapons which you describe as offensive are in fact grim weapons. Both you and I understand what kind of weapons they are."

An elated—and relieved—President Kennedy replied within three hours: "I welcome Chairman Khrushchev's statesmanlike decision to stop building bases in Cuba, dismantling offensive weapons and returning them to the Soviet Union under United Nations verification. . . ."[10]

It appeared that in the potentially explosive duel between the two heavyweights Kennedy had won a clear-cut decision. But the president was under no such illusion. Only days after U-2 cameras confirmed that the missiles were being dismantled and put on Soviet ships, Kennedy told a press conference: "I am sure we face possibly bigger decisions [over Cuba]."[11]

IN HAVANA, Fidel Castro heard of his friend Khrushchev's agreement to pull out the missiles from a secondary source: a telephone call from Carlos Franqui, editor of *Revolución*, who received the information on a teletype. Castro reportedly pitched a temper tantrum, kicking the walls and breaking a window. His ego had been battered. How dare the superpowers make decisions regarding the fate of Cuba and leave him out of the consultations?

Less than four hours after word of Khrushchev's decision reached him, Castro, not willing to be cast aside, defiantly listed his own conditions for peace in the Caribbean: five "demands" made of the United States. President Kennedy would have to halt (1) the economic sanctions against Cuba and such subversive actions as sabotage; (2) the financing and organizing of "mercenary invaders"; (3) the violations of Cuban sea and air space; (4) the "pirate attacks"; and (5) the "illegal occupation of Cuban territory" at the Guantanamo naval base.

Until his five demands were accepted by Kennedy, Castro asserted, the president's "guarantees" with regard to Cuba would be meaningless.[12]

30

Shake-up in the Secret War High Command

A HEAVY SNOW BLANKETED MOSCOW, and icy gales ripped through the wall-enclosed Kremlin as Nikita Khrushchev waddled to the podium to address the Supreme Soviet (legislature). It was December 12, 1962, less than one month since President Kennedy had learned of the missile threat. Khrushchev had a tough job on his hands: trying to explain to the Soviet people why he had backed down in Cuba. In a long, rambling speech, during which most of the delegates sat on their hands, he stressed that sneaking missiles into Cuba had been an act of peace, and withdrawing them was in reality a Soviet victory over the United States.

The Soviets "never had any intention of attacking the United States with the missiles and bombers," Khrushchev exclaimed, pounding the podium for emphasis. "We stationed rockets in Cuba precisely for the protection of the Cuban revolution."[1]

MEANWHILE, in Havana, Fidel and Raúl Castro and Ché Guevara were furious at Khrushchev. It was a real blow to their pride when the Soviet chief suddenly, and without consultation with them, packed up his missiles in Cuba and shipped them back to the Soviet Union.

Fidel Castro complained bitterly that Khrushchev lacked *cojones* (balls). Guevara was even more apoplectic than the Castro boys. At a session with a reporter from the Communist London *Daily Worker* in mid-December, the Argentine physician-turned-professional-revolutionist fumed, "If the rockets had remained, we would have used them all and directed them against the very heart of the United States, including New York City."

Guevara worked up a full head of steam. Cuba's purpose, he declared, "was to fight to the death, to inflict the maximum damage on the enemy [the United States]."[2]

Guevara's rocket-rattling outburst horrified the editors of the London *Daily Worker*. They had on their hands a story that would have pointed to the clash between Moscow and Havana over the missile caper. Big Bear Khrushchev, only three days earlier, had set down the Communist line in his speech before the Supreme Soviet: The nuclear missiles, which could have reached nearly to Seattle, Washington, had been sneaked into Cuba for solely defensive means. Now the hot-eyed Guevara was trying to tell the world that Khrushchev was all wet, that the Cuban honchos had hoped to pulverize U.S. cities.

The London *Daily Worker* editors resolved the party-line clash in the only way possible: They blue-penciled and toned down Guevara's remarks to bring them in line with those of the Big Bear in the Kremlin.[3]

MEANWHILE, James Donovan, the New York lawyer, had been pursuing his often frustrating task of negotiating with Fidel Castro over the release of some twelve hundred Bay of Pigs survivors being held for more than a year and a half in the Old Príncipa Castle and a prison on the Isle of Pines off southern Cuba. Finally, in mid-December 1962, his efforts paid off. Castro agreed to release the prisoners—for a king's ransom of $53 million in medical equipment, baby food, and medicinal drugs (the latter largely contributed by U.S. pharmaceutical giants).

Bobby Kennedy had been the moving force behind raising the goods, telephoning corporate tycoons, twisting arms, coercing, even threatening on occasion. Jack was being blamed for the prisoners' horrendous plight, Bobby knew, and he had been conducting almost a crusade to secure their freedom.

In Cuba, members of the 2506 Brigade were shaven and given haircuts, shoes, and fresh uniforms at the dungeons. Then they were herded to airfields and flown to Miami, which they reached on Christmas Eve. Euphoric exile leaders planned a gigantic welcome-home rally for the Bay of Pigs veterans to be held at the Orange Bowl four nights later.

President Kennedy was invited, but his close aide, Kenny O'Donnell, urged him not to accept. "You can't go there and pay tribute to those rebels," O'Donnell warned. "It will look like you're backing them for another invasion."

"You're absolutely right," Kennedy replied. "I shouldn't go. But I'm going."[4]

On Saturday night, December 29, the president and his wife, Jacqueline, entered the Orange Bowl in a white convertible. An earsplitting din went up from the forty thousand persons in the stadium, and a blizzard of small Cuban and American flags, most of them homemade, were furiously waved. Dismounting, Kennedy moved along the lines of Brigade members, all standing at rigid attention, and shook hands.

At the formal ceremonies, the Brigade commander, Pepe San Román, turned to Kennedy and said, "Mr. President, the men of the 2506 Brigade give you their banner—we temporarily deposit it with you for safekeeping." The folded gold and blue flag was handed to Kennedy who unfurled it. Visibly racked with emotion, he stepped to the microphone.

"Commander, Doctor, I want to assure you that this flag will be returned to the Brigade in a free Havana!" he declared.[5]

Rousing cheers and chants of *Guerra! Guerra!* (War! War!) rang through the huge stadium.

ON JANUARY 1, 1963, Fidel Castro celebrated the fourth anniversary of his seizing power. By almost any standard, the Maximum Leader put on quite a show. In Havana's Plaza de la Revolucion, he and some four hundred Communist notables from many nations (including Soviet spaceman Pavel R. Popovich) beamed down from the reviewing stand on a two-hour parade of Soviet-supplied sinews of war.

Overhead, flights of sleek MIG fighters zoomed past in tight formation, while medium and heavy tanks, artillery pieces, and heavy trucks towing long rockets rumbled over the pavement. Castro's display of military hardware was on an even larger scale than U.S. intelligence agencies had estimated it had been prior to the missile crisis.

After the parade, Fidel Castro took to the podium to blast President Kennedy for the heroes' welcome given the Bay of Pigs prisoners a few days earlier in Miami. The Maximum Leader was shaking with rage when he lit into Kennedy. "Never," he thundered, "has a President [of the United States] so degraded the dignity of his position. This hoodlum acted like a vulgar pirate chief and freebooter to meet with these cowards [the Bay of Pigs prisoners] and then say . . . that their flag would return to a free Havana."[6]

The Plaza de la Revolucion rocked with the resounding cheers of several hundred thousand Fidelistas. Castro threw in a crowd-pleaser. "What Kennedy must have meant," he shouted, "was a bar in Miami called the Free Havana. Perhaps he had had too much to drink!"[7]

IN THE MEANTIME, Bobby Kennedy had been taking a new look at the results from Operation Mongoose and didn't like what he saw. It seemed clear to him that the primary achievements of the secret war against Castro had been the blowing up of a few sugar refineries and bridges.

So once again heads fell into the basket at the CIA. First to feel the guillotine blade was the gun-toting chief of Task Force W, Big Bill Harvey. He was banished to the post of CIA station chief in Rome, 3,500 miles away from Bobby Kennedy, who detested him.

Harvey had been on Bobby Kennedy's black list since early 1962. While inspecting JM WAVE, the bustling CIA station in Miami at that time, the attorney general had noticed an item on the teletype that linked the station to the Pickle Factory in Langley, Virginia. Kennedy ripped it out of the teletype and headed for the door with the message paper in his hand. Harvey spotted him and called out gruffly, "Hey, where in the hell do you think you're going with that?"

Harvey knew that the internal CIA document contained secret operational codes. He strode over to Kennedy and snatched the sheet of paper from his hand. Kennedy's face flushed crimson with anger. Bill Harvey became a marked man.

Shortly after Harvey was given the heave-ho, General Ed Lansdale, the legendary spook who had been the Kennedy brothers' choice to spearhead Mongoose, quietly vanished from the scene. It was announced that he was retiring.

As part of the Kennedys' shake-up of clandestine groups, Task Force W was dissolved and replaced by a group called the Special Affairs Staff. Desmond FitzGerald, who was with the Agency's Far East Division, was named to replace Harvey.

Known in the Agency as Des Fitz, he was steeped in cloak-and-dagger machinations. After graduating from Harvard Law School, he was recruited into the OSS during World War II and served in China as an adviser to Chinese officers fighting the Japanese.

Unlike bluff, blunt Bill Harvey, Des Fitz melded nicely with the carefully cultivated Camelot image of the Kennedy administration. Before joining the CIA, he had been a member of a prestigious law firm, had married the socially prominent Marietta Tree, and was a leading light in Washington's high-society whirl.

Soon after replacing Harvey in early 1963, FitzGerald hatched a bizarre scheme to eliminate Fidel Castro. He ordered the CIA's Technical Services Division to create an exploding seashell. This would be placed on the sea floor at Varadero Beach, a spot where Castro, protected by sharp-eyed guards with automatic weapons, loved to skin-dive. The idea was for the explosive device to be detonated remotely as Castro plunged underwater and picked up the seashell.[8]

Des Fitz's associates looked on the gadget with a jaundiced eye. How could it be certain that Castro would pick up this particular seashell from the hundreds naturally on the beach? Eventually the scheme was dropped, partly because the implied policy of the Kennedy brothers, in the wake of the pledge to Nikita Khrushchev not to invade Cuba, was to cease clandestine operations against the Maximum Leader.

AT THE SAME TIME that the CIA lineup was being revamped, Jack and Bobby Kennedy greatly downsized ExCom and renamed it the Standing Group. Its members now included only Bobby Kennedy, Robert McNamara, John McCone, and the president's confidants, Ted Sorenson and McGeorge Bundy. From the first meeting of the Standing Group, there was a wide division on the approach to take toward Cuba, from holding out an olive branch to perpetrating mayhem.

Jack Kennedy always had trouble with Bundy's name. On occasion he referred to him as McBundy, at other times as George. A former dean at Harvard College, Bundy was bright, ambitious, and energetic. He now proposed that the United States should try to establish "some form of accommodation" with Fidel Castro.[9]

At the other end of the spectrum, the Pentagon recommended "increasing degrees of political, economic, psychological, and military pressures" to cause the "overthrow of the Castro/Communist regime." Privately, the generals and admirals were convinced that "we missed the big bus"—that is, not invading Cuba with U.S. forces during the missile crisis.

31

Shooting Up a Soviet Ship

A NTI-CASTRO EXILES IN FLORIDA, embittered by the peaceful resolution of the missile crisis that left their homeland in the hands of
the Maximum Leader, launched a keenly orchestrated campaign to coerce the Kennedy administration into invading Cuba with U.S. armed
forces. Components of this covert project were rumors, armed raids,
and other clandestine activities.

In Washington, the CIA began receiving a rash of reports about European embassies in Havana being "plagued" with anonymous telephone calls and letters claiming that Castro had hidden in caves a
large number of long-range missiles that Nikita Khrushchev had secretly left behind. Mysterious visitors were calling at the embassies
with sketches of the caves and crude drawings of the missiles.

As intended, these reports reached the Capitol in Washington. On
January 31, 1963, Senator Kenneth Keating declared that the Soviet
Union had cunningly filled Cuba's caves with nuclear-tipped missiles.
Two days later, he demanded that President Kennedy come up with a
plan to get the seventeen thousand Russian troops out of Cuba.[1]

Dick Nixon, sensing political mileage to be gained, rushed to get
in his licks. "We have goofed an invasion, paid financial tribute to
Castro for prisoners, then given the Soviets squatters rights in our
backyard," the former vice president exclaimed.[2]

Using such designations as Alpha 66, Commando L, and the Second Front of Escambray, Cuban exiles in swift powerboats were dashing from locales in the Florida Keys and the Bahamas to fire at Castro's
merchant ships. These "unauthorized raids" greatly complicated matters, Jack Kennedy told a syndicated columnist.[3]

On March 18, a powerboat manned by Cuban exiles roared into
the harbor at Port of Isabela de Sagua, about 150 miles east of Havana
on the north coast, and poured fusillades of machine-gun fire into the
Soviet freighter *Lgov*. Eight days later, the Soviet merchant ship *Baku*
was fired on during another exile raid into the nearby port of Caiba-

iarien. These attacks resulted in major damage to the two Soviet ships and, reportedly, some casualties.

In Miami, leaders of Alpha 66 and Commando L noisily took credit for the raids.

In Moscow, Nikita Khrushchev denounced the hostile actions and warned that the Soviet Union was holding Washington responsible.

In Havana, an irate Fidel Castro declared that he might be forced to acquire long-range bombers and naval units (from the Soviet Union) to protect his supply routes.

In Washington, Bobby Kennedy, wearing yet another hat as a member of the National Security Council, heard CIA chief John McCone speak at length about the possibility that Cuban military leaders might revolt against the Maximum Leader if covertly nudged in the right direction.

As was his custom, Bobby immediately fired off a terse summary of the NSC session to Jack in the White House:

> John McCone described the possibilities [of a military revolt] in rather optimistic terms. What can and should we do to increase the likelihood of this kind of action? . . . Do we have evidence of any break amongst top Cuban leaders and if so, is the CIA or USIA [U.S. Information Agency] attempting to cultivate that feeling. I would not like it said a year from now that we could have had this internal breakup in Cuba but we just did not set the stage for it.[4]

Jack Kennedy apparently was not as eager as Bobby to reignite the secret war against Fidel Castro. For once, he did not reply to his brother's memo suggesting increased covert actions. What concerned the president was that the attacks by Cuban exile mavericks might bring about Soviet armed intervention and retaliation by Castro against U.S. merchant ships. However, the raids continued.

A week later, the National Security Council convened again to discuss the current Cuban situation. Bobby then informed the president that a decision had been made to formulate a plan to shut down the hit-and-run attacks from Florida locales.

On the following day, the president announced that he would "take every step necessary" to clamp down on the exiles' excursions against Cuba. In rapid order, Bobby Kennedy's Justice Department, with much fanfare, indicted several Cuban exile leaders for "violating U.S. neutrality laws," and the CIA was ordered to cut off financial support to Miró Cardona and his anti-Castro Cuban Revolutionary Council.[5]

A YEAR EARLIER, in March 1962, J. Edgar Hoover had appointed W. Raymond Wannall, a twenty-year veteran of the FBI, as chief of a group in the Intelligence Division known as the Nationality Intelligence Section. Its function was to handle intelligence and investigative matters relating to all countries outside the Soviet/Communist bloc. One of Wannall's units, consisting of three men, concerned itself with events in Central and South America and the Caribbean region.

There were about twenty special-agent supervisors in the Nationality Intelligence Section, and their reports all came across Wannall's desk, keeping him closely advised on developments in Cuba, Latin America, and the Caribbean.

Now, on March 29, 1963, Wannall was returning to his office from lunch when a woman staffer rushed up and said breathlessly: "Mr. Belmont wants to see you—*immediately!*"[6]

Wannall hurried to the office of Alan Belmont, assistant to the director, and found him talking earnestly with Courtney Evans, who was the FBI liaison with Bobby Kennedy in the Justice Department and Jack Kennedy in the White House.

For two years, Evans had been saddled with an almost impossible mission: explaining J. Edgar Hoover to Bobby Kennedy and vice versa—and keeping them both happy. Nicholas Katzenbach, who was the assistant attorney general at the time, later said that the only way Evans could do his job was to "explain something to Bobby one way and to Hoover another way."

Belmont told Wannall that Bobby was holding a crucial meeting in his office at three o'clock that afternoon and that he and Court Evans were to represent the FBI. The topic would be the hit-and-run raids by Cuban exiles against Cuban and Soviet ships.

A spark of urgency was injected into the subject when it was learned that two "unidentified" MIG jets had fired their weapons near a privately owned U.S. ship in international waters off the northern coast of Cuba. From southern Florida, U.S. fighter planes scrambled, flew to the site of the armed attack, and escorted the vessel to Miami.

Bobby had mobilized representatives of nearly all the might of the U.S. government for the meeting. Along with the two FBI agents, there were officials of the CIA, Immigration and Naturalization Service, Navy, Coast Guard, Customs Service, the Internal Security Division of the Justice Department, and the State Department.

Coatless, sleeves rolled up to elbows, and tie askew, Bobby explained that the president wanted to put a halt to the exile raids against Cuba. Sixteen of the officials present were ordered to leave promptly for Florida and to convene there early in the morning to decide what measures could be taken.

Then Bobby turned to General Joseph Carroll, director of the Defense Intelligence Agency, and instructed him to have an Air Force plane ready at 7:00 P.M. to fly the group to Miami.

When the meeting adjourned, there was a scramble to get out of the room: Less than three hours remained before the Air Force jet was to lift off from Andrews, just outside Washington. Since no one knew how long they would be in Miami, they had no idea how much extra clothing to take along.

From his office, Ray Wannall telephoned his wife, Trudie, at her place of business and told her that he had just been "awarded an unscheduled vacation in Florida—all expenses paid." He asked her to pack a suitcase for him and bring it to his office no later than 6:00 P.M.—about ninety minutes away. "How long will you be gone?" Trudie asked. "I don't know," was the reply.[7]

Trudie rushed out of her office, leaped into her car, sped home, and rapidly threw wearing apparel into a large suitcase. She glanced at her watch. It was 5:30 P.M. Only thirty minutes were left—and she had to make an 11-mile drive through Washington's rush-hour traffic blitz.

At 5:45 P.M., Ray Wannall went down to the street in front of his building to meet his wife and collect the suitcase, taking one of his special agents with him. Trudie's auto, meanwhile, had bogged down in the crush of thousands of vehicles, so at five minutes after six, Wannall, minus any extra clothes, caught a cab for Andrews Air Force Base.

When Trudie finally drove up to the building, the FBI agent Wannall had left to wait for her grabbed the heavy suitcase and made a breakneck dash to Andrews, arriving just before the jet lifted off.

Most of Miami was asleep when Wannall and the other federal officials arrived at 12:10 A.M., March 30. The FBI man promptly went to the local field office and talked about the exile problem with the special agent in charge (SAC) until 1:30 A.M. After stealing a few hours sleep, Wannall returned at 7:15 A.M. for the conference, which lasted until noon.

Among the steps proposed to halt or discourage Cuban exiles from launching violent actions against Cuba or Soviet ships were serving restriction notices on certain exile leaders to prevent them from leaving the United States, refusing reentry to the United States to any exile who went beyond the 3-mile limit offshore, increased surveillance by the Coast Guard of the Florida coastline, and intensified FBI intelligence coverage of Cuban exile groups to ascertain and abort plans for future raids.

Eighty minutes after the session adjourned, Ray Wannall and the other conferees climbed aboard an Air Force plane that winged them back to Washington. Instead of being gone for a week or a month on the open-ended assignment, the FBI official had been away for nineteen hours and fifty minutes—all the while lugging a large, heavy suitcase that he had never opened.[8]

In the days and weeks following the Miami conference, the various federal agencies carried out their tasks. In numerous raids, agents of the FBI shut down exile camps and seized large amounts of weapons, ammunition, and explosives.

PRESIDENT KENNEDY had publicly blamed anti-Castro groups in Florida for the raids on Cuba and the attacks on Soviet and Cuban ships. But had these groups alone financed, orchestrated, and conducted these attacks? Or had individual operatives in the CIA, acting on their own volition, masterminded these covert missions despite White House policy to lie low?

Army Captain Bradley E. Ayers, who had been assigned to the CIA, would later recall that Lieutenant General Victor "Brute" Krulak, a highly decorated Marine hero in World War II and later the Pentagon's counterinsurgency chief, told him in March 1963 that the raids publicly attributed to Cuban exile groups were "planned and conducted by the CIA from bases in southern Florida."[9]

32

"We Must Do Something about Castro"

A T 4:22 P.M. ON JUNE 3, 1963, Fidel Castro's plane touched down at the Havana airport after the Maximum Leader had spent nearly six weeks in the Soviet Union. There he was wined and dined and had his ego massaged by Nikita Khrushchev and other bigwigs in the Kremlin. He had a terse comment for waiting reporters: "You can say we pinned the tail on the North American donkey!"[1]

Twenty-four hours later, Castro was on television, being interviewed by Cuban reporters who knew what questions to ask and which ones not to bring up. For nearly three hours, he rambled on, much of the time speaking in praise of Big Bear Khrushchev. As for the Soviet Union, he claimed everything there was "the best"—the leaders, the government, the people, the military, the schools, the subways.

Castro, in closing, suggested that he might consider restoring normal relations with the United States and opening discussions on paying for the U.S.-owned corporations' properties he had stolen in Cuba.

At the White House, Jack Kennedy was not impressed. He told journalists that the United States would not and could not accept peaceful coexistence with a Soviet satellite. "No satellite leader had ever spent forty days in Russia," the president declared.[2]

Back in Havana, Castro was furious about Kennedy's remarks and denied vehemently that Cuba was a Soviet satellite. "To be a satellite one must be exploited," he said. "The Soviet Union has exploited no one."[3]

IN WASHINGTON, the Standing Group was convened to discuss the significance of Castro's jaunt to the Soviet Union and his syrupy remarks about Khrushchev on his return. Why the sudden mood shift of the Cuban from anger at the Soviet boss over his missile-crisis handling to eulogizing him? Had Khrushchev promised Castro a whole range of new and sophisticated weapons?

CIA chief John McCone declared that it was now "a whole new ballgame" and that a sabotage campaign against Cuba using Cuban exiles directed by Agency operatives should be launched. Defense Secretary Bob McNamara favored overt economic pressures against Cuba. Bobby Kennedy was the most militant, exclaiming that the United States "must do something about Castro."

Two weeks after the Standing Group recommended a resumption of the secret war, President Kennedy gave the green light to a CIA plan to launch sabotage raids by Cuban exiles against Castro's communications and power facilities, oil refineries, and the railroad and road systems. For the first time, the president approved hitting targets that had been off-limits—U.S. corporation–owned facilities that had been stolen by Fidel Castro.[4]

Neither Jack nor Bobby Kennedy nor the CIA held any illusions that these hit-and-run strikes would result in Castro's government crashing down. Rather, the raids reflected a growing frustration in official Washington and a need to "do something" to chip away at the Communist bastion in the Caribbean.

Apparently, there had been no CIA-sponsored effort to kill Fidel Castro since the clandestine moratorium had been ordained after the missile crisis. Now, however, CIA operatives got in touch with Rolando Cubela Secades, an Agency secret agent in Havana who had been ignored since President Kennedy promised Khrushchev that Cuba would not be invaded.

Cubela was a soldier of fortune, a zealot, who had led a band of students that fought under Castro in the Escambray Mountains. He had been credited with murdering Fulgencio Batista's military intelligence chief, an act that catapulted Cubela into prominence in the 26th of July Movement. Ahead of Fidel's triumphant entry into Havana in the first week of January 1959, Cubela and his young guerrillas seized the Presidential Palace. Eventually, Cubela became disillusioned with Castro, and he had eagerly accepted an offer to be a mole in Havana for the CIA.

Now, after the missile crisis, Cubela was anxious to get back into a CIA harness, perhaps for the hefty salary he received, but also to strike another blow at his hated foe, Fidel.

FIDEL CASTRO now had but two symbols of "Yankee imperialism" remaining in Cuba on which he could vent his wrath: the U.S. Embassy building and the naval base at Guantanamo. The tenth anniversary of the 26th of July Movement (date of the attack on Moncada Barracks) was approaching, and the Maximum Leader, always conscious of his image with his people and those of Latin America, needed to embarrass the United States prior to the big holiday.

Castro sensed that opportunity on July 8, when the U.S. Treasury Department, citing recommendations made by the Organization of American States (OAS) aimed at curbing Communist-Castro subversion in Latin America, ordered all Cuban assets (about $33 million) in U.S. banks to be frozen.

On July 26, tens of thousands of perspiring Fidelistas and some 950 guests from foreign countries packed Havana's José Martí Plaza to hear Castro speak. A large group of U.S. students had defied a State Department ban on travel to Cuba. Three of the students had been recruited by the FBI to report back on activities.[5]

Castro said that he was "willing to discuss differences with the United States," but President Kennedy had refused all offers to negotiate. He also expressed "sorrow" for the American people who had to pay for Kennedy's "stupid, incorrect policy.

"This gentleman [Kennedy], like a horseman, is riding from blunder to blunder, stupidity to stupidity," the Maximum Leader declared.

Then the plaza rocked with cheers when the Maximum Leader thundered that he had taken over the empty U.S. Embassy building "in the name of the Cuban people."

Now Castro had but one domestic target at which to take aim: the mighty U.S. Naval Base at Guantanamo. That "bastion of Yankee arrogance" would have to go.

IN MID-1963, Special Agent James P. Hosty Jr. of the FBI's Dallas field office noticed that a local ne'er-do-well, Lee Harvey Oswald, had subscribed to the *Daily Worker*, a Communist newspaper. Earlier, Hosty had interviewed Marina Oswald, a Russian citizen whom Lee had married before returning from a year-long stay in the Soviet Union. It also had been learned that Lee Oswald was active in the Fair Play for Cuba Committee, a Communist front in the United States, and had been passing out pro-Castro propaganda on the streets of Dallas.

Oswald moved to New Orleans, which was a hotbed of anti-Castro activities. In a carefully conceived raid, FBI agents seized over a ton of dynamite and a cache of weapons that anti-Castroites had stockpiled outside New Orleans.

On August 7, Oswald tried to join an anti-Castro group, then was detected distributing pro-Castro materials by a member of the group. A fight broke out, and Oswald was arrested. Oswald, possibly acting under instructions from an unknown party, apparently had been trying to infiltrate the anti-Castro group.

Later in the month, Oswald was a panelist in a heated radio debate during which he spoke highly of the Maximum Leader, defended Castro's actions, and proclaimed himself a Communist.

Oswald left New Orleans for Mexico City in early September. There he was spotted meeting with a Soviet diplomat who, the FBI believed, was an officer in the KGB, the secret police organization. After learning that Oswald had returned to Dallas, Special Agent Hosty interviewed Oswald's wife, Marina. She came across as almost terrified, Hosty reported.

Two days later, Oswald stormed into the FBI's Dallas office and left a written message for Hosty that threatened to blow up the FBI if Hosty didn't cease harassing Marina.

MEANWHILE, early in September, Rolando Cubela, the onetime Fidel Castro confidant and now undercover agent in Havana for the CIA, was given secret instructions to fly to São Paulo, Brazil. There, one night, he met on a deserted street corner with another CIA spook and told him that he had an assignment to do an "inside job" on Castro's life.[6]

On the following day in Havana, Fidel Castro was attending a party in the Brazilian Embassy. In a conversation with Daniel Harker of the Associated Press, he took a few verbal potshots at President Kennedy. "He is the Batista of our time, and the most opportunistic President of all time," Castro declared. Kennedy was more demagogic than Dwight Eisenhower, he asserted, and, moreover, he was a member of an "oligarchic family" that controlled several top posts in the U.S. government.

Puffing on a cigar and casually blowing smoke rings, he said that Kennedy paid more attention to being reelected than to the needs of the American people. "He thinks only of Kennedy and nothing else," Castro observed.

Jabbing the air with his cigar for emphasis, the Maximum Leader blamed Kennedy for raids by Cuban exiles and "their CIA sponsors" on the coasts of the island.[7]

Was it a coincidence that Cubela, who was plotting to assassinate Castro, was in Brazil at the precise time that the Maximum Leader was in the Brazilian Embassy? As Castro continued talking with Harker, it seemed as though he had been tipped off about Cubela's mission. He told the reporter that Kennedy should be careful about launching "terrorist plots to eliminate Cuban leaders."

"We are fully prepared to answer in kind," Castro exclaimed. "United States leaders should think that if they assist in terrorist plans, they themselves will not be safe!"[8]

Three weeks later, after a marathon speech to a revolutionary group, Castro held court for a bevy of reporters. Cuba was the innocent victim of an "undeclared war," he declared, one for which President Kennedy was responsible. This war consisted of an economic blockade, piratical attacks by Cuban exile cutthroats, and sabotage, he explained.

"They [Kennedy and his government leaders] are our enemies, and we know how to be their enemies," Castro stated emphatically.[9]

ON THE DARK NIGHT of October 21, the former U.S. Navy subchaser *Rex* dropped anchor softly a half mile off the Cuban coast. A team of twelve CIA-trained Cuban exile commandos, heavily armed, faces painted black, and burdened with explosives, climbed over the railing, slipped into a pair of rubber rafts powered by muffled motors, and headed for the beach. The raiders felt reasonably secure. Cuba has over two thousand miles of coves, harbors, bays, and inlets, so it would be impossible for Castro forces to guard the entire coastline.

Suddenly the silence was shattered. A hundred yards from shore, the rafts were raked by streams of machine-gun tracers. The commandos had paddled into an ambush; Castro had been tipped off to their coming. Bullets ripped into one craft, spilling its dead and dying men into the black waters. Seeking desperately to escape the deadly fusillades, the raiders in the second raft made it to shore where they were collared by Castro soldiers.

Captain Alejandro Brooks, skipper of the *Rex*, had been watching from the bridge as the brightly colored tracers knifed into the rafts. Heavy at heart, Brooks knew that he would have to abandon the commandos to their fate; his CIA orders had been to avoid at all costs the capture of the *Rex* and its sophisticated electronic surveillance equipment.

Captain Brooks gave the order to flee—just in the nick of time. Soviet-built helicopters clattered over and headed directly for the precise spot where the *Rex* had been anchored. Castro's spies had been thorough. There the choppers dropped brilliant parachute flares that lit up the seascape for miles. But the *Rex*, running in total blackout, had sneaked down the murky coastline and made her escape, even though Soviet-built patrol boats, with searchlights playing over the water, were dashing about in pursuit.

Minutes later, the 32,000-ton freighter *J. Louis* by happenstance was cutting through the search area, on her way from Jamaica to Corpus Christi, Texas. The *J. Louis* was flying a Liberian flag but was owned by an American corporation. Despite the fact that the *J. Louis* was several times larger than the *Rex*, it was apparently mistaken for the CIA spy craft. Five MIG-21 jets zoomed in and began pouring machine-gun and rocket fire into the *J. Louis*, making perhaps ten to fifteen passes.

Even though bullet holes had made a sieve out of the *J. Louis* and rocket explosions had ignited several small fires, none of those on board had been hit. Out of ammunition, the Cuban (or Soviet) pilots flew off, and the *J. Louis*'s bewildered captain resumed the trek toward Texas.

Four CIA commandos had been captured in the ambush. Fidel Castro was gleeful: He knew that Uncle Sam once more had been caught in the act. Castro, the high priest of high drama, milked every drop of propaganda from the *Rex* episode. On the night of October 30, he held a "news conference" at the Havana television studio, where the four wretched captives were put on display, and each dutifully confessed his "misdeeds."

As with all Castro news conferences, the Maximum Leader did most of the talking. He ripped into the CIA, the "miserable worms" (exiles) who he said were constantly trying to sabotage the Cuban revolution, the *rufián* (hoodlum) President Kennedy, and the U.S. Red Cross, which Castro claimed had "swindled" him out of $10 million in the Bay of Pigs prisoner ransom.[10]

IN THE MEANTIME, Rolando Cubela, the CIA's assassin-designee, had returned to Havana from Brazil and demanded a meeting with Bobby Kennedy. The topic? Cubela wouldn't say. CIA leaders were leery about bringing the Cuban in direct contact with the attorney general. He could be a double agent (that is, feigning being a CIA spy and saboteur but in reality working for Castro).

Richard Helms, the CIA's director of Clandestine Services, solved the dilemma by taking it upon himself to send Desmond FitzGerald to speak in Bobby Kennedy's name.[11]

Des Fitz rendezvoused with Cubela at an undisclosed location on October 29 and said that he had been sent by Attorney General Kennedy. The Cuban, it developed, had been unable to hatch a scheme to kill Fidel Castro, who was cagey and always closely watched by heavily armed bodyguards. Even while Castro was riding in his limousine, there were clever arrangements to make certain an automobile carrying assassins could not drive alongside and open fire at pointblank range.

Now Cubela pleaded with Des Fitz for the CIA to come up with a means for killing Castro where Cubela wouldn't be killed himself.

Three weeks later, in Paris, the two men met again and the CIA official was said to have offered Cubela "everything you need—telescopic sight, silencer, money."

Then Des Fitz gave Cubela an assassination gimmick that was currently being made famous around the world in James Bond movies. It was a ballpoint pen containing a hypodermic needle so thin that the victim presumably would not even feel its insertion. Cubela was not impressed. Surely the vaunted CIA could come up with some gadget better than that, he complained.[12]

This latest plot to murder Fidel Castro collapsed when the secret police in Havana arrested Cubela, who was tried, convicted, and sentenced to death by a Havana court. Castro, for whatever his reason, commuted the penalty to thirty years in prison.

IN THE MEANTIME, President Kennedy apparently had become steadily more incensed at the verbal attacks made against him by Fidel Castro. On November 18, he spoke to a gathering of the Inter-American Press Association in Miami. Stressing that the Alliance for Progress, an idea he had nurtured into being, did not dictate to any Latin American nation "how to organize its economic life," he went on to say that a "small band of [Cuban] conspirators had attempted to subvert" democratic nations in the Western Hemisphere.

By "conspirators," Kennedy had been taking a potshot at Fidel Castro. This "conspiracy" was dividing Cuba and the United States, the president said, adding that once Cuba's sovereignty was regained, the United States would "extend the hand of friendship and assistance." Translation: If the Cuban people kicked out Castro, the United States would pour in massive funds to restore the island's anemic economy and thereby upgrade the lot of its people.

33

"The President's Been Shot!"

TWO THOUSAND MILES from Havana on November 22, 1963, the same day that Desmond FitzGerald and Rolando Cubela had held their secret session in Paris, President Kennedy was in Texas and spoke at a breakfast of the Fort Worth Chamber of Commerce. Along with the customary presidential entourage, he had flown to Texas to try to patch up a rancorous feud that had erupted between factions of the Democratic Party in the Lone Star State.

Later that morning at the Texas Hotel, Kennedy was engaged in conversation with his wife and Kenneth O'Donnell, his Harvard roommate and now a special assistant. The role of the Secret Service, the elite group traditionally assigned to protect a president from harm, was brought up. All the Secret Service agents could do, Kennedy said resignedly, was to protect a president from boisterous crowds. If someone really wanted to kill a president, it would be relatively simple: Put a sniper with a telescopic rifle on a high building, and there would be nothing the Secret Service could do to defend a president.[1]

An hour later, during the short flight to Dallas aboard *Air Force One*, the presidential jet, the subject of violence and assassination was discussed again. At 11:31 A.M., the plane touched down at Love Field. Congressman Henry Gonzalez of Texas joked to those aboard the plane, "Well, I'm taking my risks. I haven't got on my steel vest yet!"[2]

Within minutes, the president and Jacqueline, together with Texas Governor John Connally and his wife, began riding in an open limousine into the city for a scheduled presidential luncheon address at the Dallas Trade Mart.

Throngs lined the streets and cheered as the motorcade made its way through the city. Mrs. Connally turned and said, "Mr. President, you can't say Dallas doesn't love you." Flashing his famous grin, Kennedy replied, "That is very obvious."

At 12:32 P.M., the vehicle was passing the Texas School Book Depository. On one of the upper floors, a would-be assassin poked a 6.5 Mannlucher Carcano Italian carbine with scope out through an open window. He had purchased the weapon by mail for $19.95.

AT THE SAME TIME that the presidential convoy was heading toward the Dallas Trade Mart, Bobby Kennedy and two colleagues were getting out of a limousine at Hickory Hill, the estate in toney McLean, Virginia, that Bobby and Ethel Kennedy had occupied since 1956. With the attorney general were Robert Morgenthau, the U.S. attorney in New York, and Silvio Mollo, the chief of the criminal division in the Justice Department's Manhattan office. Bobby had brought the two men home for lunch to develop strategy for the attorney general's ongoing battle against union corruption and organized crime.

Hickory Hill had a two-and-a-half-story, white brick mansion and six acres of beautifully manicured lawn. The premises were concealed from the road by huge trees and neatly trimmed shrubbery. Joe Kennedy Sr. had bought the estate as a gift for Jack and Jacqueline Kennedy after Jack had been elected to the U.S. Senate. But in 1956, Jack and Jacqueline decided to move to the Georgetown enclave in Washington, so Kennedy Senior gave the property to Bobby and Ethel.

On this pleasant November early afternoon, Hickory Hill was relatively serene. While Bobby, Robert Morgenthau, and Silvio Mollo were eating lunch, the attorney general was summoned to the telephone.

"This is Edgar Hoover," the voice said. "I have news for you. The president's been shot!"

Stunned, Bobby mumbled something like, "What?"

"The president's been shot."

"Oh. Is it serious?"

"I think it's serious. I'll call you back."

A short time later, the FBI chief telephoned again. "The president was pronounced dead at Parkland Memorial Hospital in Dallas," he said.

Later, Bobby would recall that Hoover did not seem upset.[3]

Hoover's seeming lack of compassion would be eventually interpreted by Bobby and his friends as calculated coldness. It was far more likely that the FBI boss, faced with solving a presidential assassination and not knowing if a massive conspiracy was under way to murder other leading government officials, had countless other matters on his mind.

IN HAVANA, Jean Daniel, a reporter for the French newspaper *L'Express*, was interviewing Fidel Castro when a telephone call came about the president's fate. Daniel was surprised that the Maximum Leader displayed no emotion over the sudden demise of his bitter Yankee foe, not even asking the caller who had performed the deed. It was almost as though Castro was expecting it, Daniel later reflected.

"I'll tell you one thing," Castro told Daniel, "at least Kennedy was an enemy to whom we had become accustomed."[4]

Castro began pacing the floor as Daniel listened. "Who is this Lyndon Johnson?" the Maximum Leader asked. "What is his connection to the Central Intelligence Agency?" Castro, of course, knew all about Johnson and also knew that any U.S. president is in overall charge of all branches of the government, including the CIA. Daniel replied that he had never met Johnson.[5]

SHORTLY AFTER 3:00 P.M. that day, J. Edgar Hoover received an urgent telephone call from Gordon L. Shanklin, the special agent in charge of the Dallas office.* Lee Harvey Oswald, who was suspected of killing both the president and a Dallas police officer, had been arrested. Shanklin's office had a security file on Oswald, and the SAC quickly summarized its contents to Hoover.

Three hours later, *Air Force One*, bearing the body of the murdered president and his grieving widow, landed at Andrews Air Force Base outside Washington. Also on board was Lyndon Johnson, who had already been sworn in as the new president.

MEANWHILE, J. Edgar Hoover received a telephone call from former Vice President Richard Nixon, who asked: "What happened? Was it one of the right-wing nuts?"

"No," the FBI chief replied, "it was a Communist."[6]

WHEN *The New York Times* ran a banner headline, "Figure in Pro-Castro Group Charged," the Maximum Leader took to television and radio about the assassination. The crime could not conceivably have been committed by a Communist, Castro declared, although he conceded that Cubans hated the "imperialist and capitalist system." Most certainly the crime had to have been committed by right-wing reactionaries, like members of the John Birch Society or the Ku Klux Klan, or a McCarthyite, he asserted.

---

*Eastern Standard Time is used in the account of assassination events. Dallas was on Central Standard Time.

Those are people without "one iota of morality," Castro claimed. Was it not possible that Lee Harvey Oswald had been "an instrument chosen and prepared by the ultraconservative reactionaries of the United States, for a definite purpose of getting rid of a President who was not pursuing a more belligerent, more aggressive policy?"[7]

AT 3:15 A.M. on November 24, two days after Kennedy was killed, Gordon Shanklin, the Dallas SAC, awakened Hoover at his home. The FBI switchboard had standing orders to put any emergency calls through to him no matter what the time of day or night. Shanklin said that his office had received an anonymous phone call stating that Oswald was going to be shot when he was transferred from the Dallas Police Department to an undisclosed jail for safekeeping later in the day. Hoover instructed Shanklin to contact Jesse Curry, the Dallas police chief.[8]

About nine hours later, at 12:21 P.M., a Dallas nightclub owner said to have Mob connections, Jack Ruby, shot and killed Oswald in the basement of the Dallas Police Department building—live on NBC-TV before the entire shocked nation. At 2:07 P.M., Oswald died at Parkland Hospital, the same institution where President Kennedy had been taken.

IN WASHINGTON that afternoon, J. Edgar Hoover released a statement to the media. All available information indicated that Lee Harvey Oswald had acted alone, the FBI chief stated. "Not one shred of evidence has been developed to link any other person in a conspiracy with Oswald to assassinate President Kennedy," Hoover stressed.[9]

DESPITE THIS ASSURANCE from the FBI mastersleuth, Lyndon Johnson had hardly settled into the Oval Office before rumors began circulating in Washington that Jack Kennedy had not been murdered by a lone Communist fanatic. There were whispers that "sinister right-wing" groups were behind the murder. Other rumors were that Fidel Castro was the culprit.

Consequently, on November 29, only a week after Kennedy's death, Johnson appointed a commission headed by Supreme Court Chief Justice Earl Warren to investigate circumstances surrounding the assassination. Known as the Warren Commission, its blue-ribbon panel included Senator Richard Russell, Senator John S. Cooper, Representative T. Hale Boggs, Representative Gerald R. Ford, former CIA Director Allen Dulles, and John McCloy, former adviser to President Kennedy.

QUITE UNDERSTANDABLY, Bobby Kennedy was devastated by the loss of his big brother, whom he idolized. On December 9, Bobby and Arthur Schlesinger, Jack's former aide, talked far into the night. At one point, Schlesinger asked about Lee Harvey Oswald. "Bobby said that Oswald was guilty, but there was still argument if he had done it by himself or as a larger plot, whether organized by Castro or by gangsters," Schlesinger later stated. Bobby added: "The FBI thinks he did it by himself, but [CIA Director] John McCone thinks there were two people involved in the shooting."[10]

TWO WEEKS after Kennedy's death, U.S. citizens remained angry. Media reports continued to refer to Lee Oswald as a Castro agent, a Soviet agent, a Communist subversive, and a member of the U.S. Fair Play for Cuba Committee.

There were calls for an immediate invasion of Cuba by the U.S. armed forces to capture Castro and bring him to trial for the Kennedy murder. When Oswald had been shot to death in the basement of the Dallas police headquarters, citizens were convinced that the hit had been made to conceal evidence of Cuban or Soviet complicity.

Kennedy's death remained the primary topic among leaders in Communist countries around the world. In Moscow, after many days of deliberations, the Soviet leaders decided to launch a global propaganda campaign to convince people, especially those in the United States, that ultraconservative "provocateurs" in the United States and not an avowed Communist, who was a Castro devotee and had lived in the Soviet Union, had perpetrated the deed in Dallas.

34

A Naval Base under Siege

L ESS THAN TWO WEEKS after the thirty-fifth president of the United States was laid to rest in Arlington National Cemetery, fifty-two-year-old Rear Admiral John Bulkeley arrived at Guantanamo Bay to take command of the U.S. Naval Base. Twenty-one years earlier, Bulkeley, one of American history's most highly decorated warriors, had recruited Ensign Jack Kennedy into the PT-boat service, the Navy's "sea cavalry."

Shortly before President Kennedy's death, Bobby Kennedy had taken Bulkeley aside and said his brother was going to send the admiral to the Navy base to "put a muzzle" on Fidel Castro. For several weeks, the Maximum Leader had been howling stridently over Havana television and radio for the United States to get out of "Cuban territory," that is, Guantanamo. If it didn't, he implied, the Cuban armed forces would drive out the "imperialists."

"The President wants you to go down there and show that bastard with the beard who's the boss in this part of the world!" Bobby had told Bulkeley.[1]

Bulkeley's mission was clear: Defend the key U.S. bastion, stand up to Fidel Castro's threats, and avoid igniting World War III. In recent weeks, the U.S. media had been calling Gitmo a powder keg and a tiny American island in a sea filled with red sharks. *Life* magazine headlined a story: "The United States' Most Vulnerable Fortress."[2]

Only two weeks before Bulkeley arrived at Guantanamo, Nikita Khrushchev had noisily reaffirmed that should an armed clash break out between Cuba and the "Yankee squatters," the Soviet military would rush to the aid of Castro.

Americans at Gitmo were virtually surrounded, their backs to the sea and hemmed in on three sides by Castro's Frontier Battalion, his best troops, who were backed by artillery and mortars. A security belt, patterned after the Soviets' Iron Curtain in Europe, had been cleared of Cuban civilians to a depth of 2 to 6 miles. A network of roads had been built to provide greater mobility for Cuban tanks and motorized combat units.

Bulkeley had but 5,000 men with whom to defend the naval base if Castro were to attack with elements of his 250,000-man, Soviet-trained army and militia: a Marine battle group, sailors and Seabees (Navy construction men) trained as infantrymen, a squadron of Crusader jets, a few heavily armed helicopters, and the guns of warships that came into Guantanamo Bay on occasion during training cruises.

The scrappy Bulkeley was undaunted by the odds against him. At his first news conference, he told visiting U.S. reporters: "Gitmo is sure as hell not going to be another Pearl Harbor—for Castro or anyone else!" The "anyone else" was the Soviet Union.[3]

It was tough talk from a tough fighting man.

"Nothing fazes this man," a journalist cabled home. "Castro's going to find out he'll have his hands full—just like the Japs did!"[4]

Within a few days of the admiral's arrival, the Maximum Leader decided to test Bulkeley's resolve. Major Ramiro Valdes, Castro's minister of state security, sent Bulkeley a note by passing it through the fence along the base's perimeter. Valdes stated that 1,100 yards of the chain-link barrier on the western side of the base would be bulldozed down later that day by the Cuban army. Valdes warned that "it would be imprudent" for the Americans to try to restore the fence.

Bulkeley's square jaw tightened. "Well, we'll see about that!" he snapped to aides.

Major Valdes carried out his threat: Cuban soldiers bulldozed the fence. Within an hour, Bulkeley fired off a reply to Valdes by means of slipping it to Cuban guards on the far side of the base's northeast (and seldom used) gate. "That fence is going back up at ten o'clock in the morning," the admiral stated.

Just before the appointed time the next day, Bulkeley jeeped up to the site of the destroyed fence. If need be, he was ready to go to war. Wearing a steel helmet, combat boots, and battle fatigues, he packed a .357 Colt magnum pistol, and three hand grenades dangled from his web harness.

Dismounting, Bulkeley stood defiantly, glancing around at the muscle he had put in place. Two thousand Marines, commanded by Colonel George Killen, a hard-nosed veteran of Pacific battles, were dug in along the three-quarter-mile downed fence. Their rifles, machine guns, and rocket launchers were pointed toward the Cuban side.

High in the bright blue sky, Crusader jets circled like hawks ready to swoop down on prairie chickens. Maneuvering up and down the fenceline were six helicopters, their automatic weapons ready for action. Out of sight in Guantanamo Bay, crews stood by loaded guns on four destroyers.

It was an impressive show of force—one not lost on Castro's army commanders. The Cuban soldiers, who had been manning positions on the far side of the fenceline for months, had vanished from sight.

Seabees arrived with truckloads of fencing, cranes, and other construction equipment. Transits, double-checked for precise accuracy, established the true line of demarcation. By 4:00 P.M., a new chain-link fence had been erected.

Bulkeley knew that he had tiptoed a fine line between defense and provocation, and that his decisive action would result in a rash of nervous tics in the State Department. Nevertheless, in the first showdown with Fidel Castro, John Bulkeley had emerged the victor.

NO DOUBT HUMILIATED over his fenceline fiasco at Gitmo, Fidel Castro and his propagandists whipped up Yankees-get-out-of-Guantanamo hysteria. On January 13, 1964, thousands of Fidelistas rallied around the unoccupied U.S. Embassy building in Havana. It was a finely orchestrated demonstration. Cheerleaders with bullhorns led the throng in a defiant chant: *"Pim pam fuera—abajo Caimanera!"* (Get out of Caimanera, which is what Cubans called the naval base, after the nearest town to it.)

The frenzied crowd screamed its approval when an effigy of Uncle Sam was strung up by the neck from the balcony railing of the embassy. It roared triumphantly when a U.S. flag was torched and the burned remnants were trampled underfoot.[5]

THREE WEEKS LATER, the simmering Caribbean pot boiled anew. On February 2, a U.S. Coast Guard cutter was racing toward the Cuban ship the *Lambda 8* and three other Cuban fishing trawlers lying 1.5 miles off the Dry Tortugas islands, 60 miles west of Key West, Florida. The boats were violating the 3-mile U.S. territorial waters and would be warned away.

Suddenly, the Coast Guard cutter's electronic equipment picked up radio messages crackling back and forth between *Lambda 8* and Cuba. It seemed curious to the Coast Guard skipper that a fishing boat would have a high-powered radio and be in contact with a facility in Cuba. His suspicions grew when boarding parties discovered that the thirty-eight men on the four trawlers were clad in the olive-green uniforms of Castro's revolutionary movement. Not certain what the Cuban vessels were up to, the Coast Guard commander had the tiny flotilla escorted to Key West.

The state of Florida claimed that the Cubans had violated a 1963 law prohibiting vessels of Communist nations from fishing within 3 miles of Florida, a precaution against sabotage, and the crew members were hustled off to the Monroe County jail in Key West to await trial.

In Havana, Fidel Castro appeared on television and sputtered indignantly: "A stupid, provocative act by Yankee imperialists . . . An intolerable act of cold-blooded aggression!"[6]

In Moscow, *Pravda,* the Communist Party's newspaper, declared, "The [U.S.] pirates who are flouting international law must be called to order." The editorial was signed "Commentator," meaning Nikita Khrushchev.[7]

In Washington, a dispute between Bobby Kennedy and Thomas Mann, President Lyndon Johnson's expert on Latin America, broke out at an emergency session of the National Security Council. Mann declared that the Cuban fishing boats had been deliberately sent into U.S. territorial waters to test the mettle of the new president. Bobby scoffed at the assertion, dismissing the episode as little more than a "traffic violation."[8]

Bobby's sudden conversion from one of Washington's most tenacious hawks in the secret war against Castro to tossing off the electronic-equipped Cuban trawlers as mere traffic violators no doubt reflected the bitterness between him and Lyndon Johnson.

No longer assistant president of the United States, Bobby especially resented what he perceived to be a collusion between President Johnson and FBI chief J. Edgar Hoover to keep him from participating in key decision making. Johnson and Hoover, Bobby knew, had been longtime residential neighbors in Washington and held similar conservative views.

When Lyndon Johnson took over the White House, Hoover no longer made a pretext of going through his boss, Attorney General Kennedy. Rather, he communicated directly with the president. To confidants, Bobby sarcastically referred to the new circumstances as "the revolt of the FBI."[9]

In Key West, the Cuban "fishermen" went on trial before a Florida judge. The crewmen were judged innocent because they had been acting under orders, the jurist ruled. But the four trawler captains were found guilty of poaching, were each fined $500 (paid by the Czechoslovakian Embassy in Washington), and received suspended six-month jail terms. They were warned never to return to Florida coastal waters, then were put aboard their boats and sent home.

In Havana, Fidel Castro reacted angrily, even though the "fishermen" had received only a judicial tap on their wrists. He harped for two hours on television that the trial was "illegal, arbitrary, and inhuman."

Two days after the Cuban fishermen were released, the four trawlers chugged into Havana Harbor to a rousing heroes' welcome that had been arranged by Castro's underlings. Beaming broadly, the Maximum Leader was on hand to greet the men with bear hugs and a long-winded speech. "Your dignity and morale must have impressed the enemy," he declared. "This is a new generation of Cubans."

Shortly before the talk began, the captains of two of the trawlers almost threw a proverbial monkey wrench into the hoopla. They told Cuban reporters that their Soviet-made boats had many defects, something U.S. newspapers had been reporting. Consequently, in his speech, Castro castigated the American media for publishing these "deceitful accounts."

EVEN BEFORE news of the verdict had reached Havana, the Maximum Leader met with advisers to consider various means of retaliation. Castro said he could send a Cuban Air Force jet fighter plane to buzz low over the *Oxford*, a U.S. Navy spy ship loaded with sophisticated electronic detection devices, which hovered in international waters just off Havana Harbor. A sonic boom might break the ship's glassware and rattle the skipper and crew. Another option was to order one of the U-2 spy planes that periodically flew high over Cuba to be shot down. Or Castro could shut off the water flowing from the Yateras River pumping station in Cuban territory to the U.S. Naval Base at Guantanamo.

AT GITMO, Admiral Bulkeley was confident that he could parry, blunt, deflect, or defeat any Castro attack against the base for forty-eight to seventy-two hours, buying time for Marines to be rushed in from Camp Lejeune in North Carolina and Camp Pendleton in California, from Roosevelt Roads in Puerto Rico, and from the Atlantic fleet. His main concern was Gitmo's Achilles' heel—the freshwater supply. Average daily consumption on the base was about 2 million gallons, and Fidel Castro controlled every drop because the water was piped into Gitmo from the Yateras River, 4.5 miles away in Cuban territory.

Even during the Bay of Pigs and missile crisis confrontations, Castro had kept the water running, no doubt because his anemic pocketbook needed the $14,000 (equivalent to $140,000 in 1997) that Uncle Sam was paying monthly for the water.

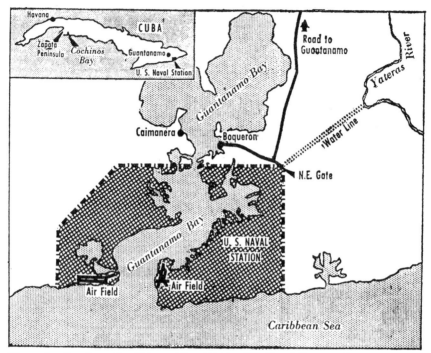

The water line from the Yateras River to the U.S. Naval Base at Guantanamo.

MORE THAN a thousand miles to the north on February 6, President Johnson was in New York City for some politicking and a speech. Before leaving his suite at the Carlyle Hotel for the New York Times Building on West 43rd Street where he would lunch with executives of the newspaper, Johnson received a telephone call from Secretary of State Dean Rusk: "The Cubans have shut off our water at Guantanamo!"

Grim-faced, the president replaced the instrument and left for his engagement, aware that a crisis pregnant with international ramifications had erupted in the Caribbean.

SEVERAL HOURS after Castro's soldiers had seized the Yateras River pumping station, Dr. Raúl Roa, the Cuban foreign minister, handed a diplomatic note to Swiss Ambassador Emil Anton Stadolhofer, who was representing U.S. interests in Cuba. The message was from Fidel Castro:

In view of the unusual, arbitrary, and illegal imprisonment of the Cuban fishermen forming the crews of the vessels piratically seized by the United States of North America in international waters, the flow of water will be halted . . . as a fitting reply to the imperial insolence.[10]

ON THE HOT SEAT at Guantanamo, Admiral Bulkeley promptly decreed Water Condition Alpha, a standby order to be implemented when "a serious casualty occurs in the water supply system that will require a shutdown for an extended period of time." Now each drop had to be measured. Marines were given orders to shoot to kill and rushed to protect freshwater reserves on the base from sabotage.

Bulkeley had to make certain that Castro had actually shut off the water. At 1:00 P.M., he and Navy Captain Zabisco "Zip" Trzyna, the base engineer, grabbed a doctor's stethoscope and rushed to the point near the main gate where water from two Yateras River pipelines entered the base. A native of Poland, Trzyna had a sunny disposition and a dry sense of humor; he was one of the most popular officers at Gitmo.[11]

Bulkeley and Trzyna put the stethoscope to the pair of 10- and 14-inch pipes. They could hear the rush of water; it would take several hours for the water already in the pipelines after the cutoff to complete its downhill run to Gitmo. Taking turns—it was tedious work—the two officers listened for five hours. At 6:00 P.M., Captain Trzyna got to his feet, took the stethoscope out of his ears, and with a straight face told Bulkeley: "Doctor, the patient has died."

Castro had indeed shut off the water. Bulkeley rushed back to his office and notified Washington.

DURING A WALDORF-ASTORIA DINNER to raise funds for the Chaim Weizmann Institute that night, President Johnson was grim. Mindful of this new crisis with Cuba and of Castro's tight alliance with Khrushchev and the Kremlin, he interrupted his prepared speech to say, "This is a world in which in only a matter of moments we could destroy one hundred million people in Soviet Russia, and they could destroy one hundred million people in Europe or the United States." However, the president added, "The United States will not be driven from Guantanamo."[12]

EARLIER THAT DAY, an upbeat Fidel Castro was holding forth at a news conference in Havana. Basking in satisfaction over the coup he had pulled off against Uncle Sam, the Maximum Leader was in a generous mood. Gesturing with a long black cigar, he told reporters that he would "allow" freshwater to flow into the naval base for one hour each day between 8:00 and 9:00 A.M., "for the women and children."

Told by news reporters of Castro's offer, Admiral Bulkeley exclaimed: "To hell with that bastard and his water! We'll furnish our own water."

Castro had been unaware that it would be impossible for Yateras River water to flow into the base any longer. Taking no chance that the Cuban dictator might poison the Gitmo water supply, Bulkeley had personally welded shut the intake water valves just inside Gitmo's main gate.

WASHINGTON WAS in an uproar. The Pentagon was ready to march. If Castro were allowed to grab Gitmo, the Soviets could base nuclear-armed warships and submarines only a stone's throw from the United States.

A White House spokesman, quoting a "high-level source," told the media, "If Castro thinks he can blackmail President Johnson out of Guantanamo, he has totally misread his adversary."[13]

That unidentified "source" was Lyndon Johnson himself.

Senator Barry Goldwater, who was expected to be the Republican nominee to oppose Lyndon Johnson in the fall presidential election, was politicking in New Hampshire. Speaking before a packed house at the Hampton High School gymnasium, he peered through horn-rimmed glasses and told a wildly cheering audience, "I hope that President Johnson will have the courage to tell Fidel Castro, 'Turn it back on, or our Marines are going to turn it on for you and keep it on!' "[14]

Nationwide headlines the next day blared: GOLDWATER CALLS FOR SENDING IN MARINES.

In Havana, Castro fired back. "If they [U.S. Marines] set one foot on Cuban soil, every last Cuban will die if necessary to defend the country," he told Tass, the Soviet news agency. "Goldwater is crazy. He should be in an asylum. Let him come in the first line of combat!"[15]

Goldwater, a major general in the Air Force Reserve, responded, "If Castro promises to be at the [Yateras River] pumping station, I'll lead the Marines' charge!"[16]

35

"We Won't Git!"

THE THREAT OF NUCLEAR WAR over Guantanamo reflected the awesome burden carried by U.S. presidents. If Lyndon Johnson had to give the order to launch missiles, he would have available elaborate communications procedures to ensure that his firing order got through to the button-pusher, even if the United States were afire and radioactive from a Soviet missile attack.

Sophisticated equipment was at Johnson's elbow at all times. Military officers of the Defense Communications Agency (DCA) were with him constantly in transit. They set up communications facilities at each stopover. *Air Force One*, Johnson's plane, was equipped with radiotelephone scramblers and a cipher machine for flashing top-secret signals. The president's custom-built Lincoln Continental limousine was followed in motorcades by a DCA car.

Alternately, five specially selected officers, carrying codes in a thin black case, shadowed Johnson night and day. When the president was working in the Oval Office of the White House, they hovered just outside the door. When Johnson slept, they maintained a vigil in the hallway outside his bedroom. If necessary, the president would use the codes carried by the briefcase officer. Both ends of the line could challenge or counterchallenge through a secondary code.

At the firing end of the communications link, two launch-control officers wore on chains around their necks 3-by-5-inch cards sealed in plastic. They were forbidden to ever remove these cards while on duty at the concrete-buttressed post deep underground at a location known but to a limited number of persons. The cards carried the secret firing codes.

Near to these two officers was a red telephone of the Primary Alert System (PAS). Its ringing (other than for periodic tests) could mean only one thing: The president of the United States had decided to go to war. Strict secrecy employed through the use of the codes was only to assure the launch-control officers that it was an authentic order.

If the telephone were to ring, a crackling voice would begin reciting letters in the phonetic alphabet: "Romeo, Tango, Mike, Yankee, Papa. . . ." This specified the target (or targets). Each control officer would write down the message independently, decode it, then confirm its contents with the other before beginning the countdown.

At the same time, another code would be flashed to the headquarters of the Strategic Air Command (SAC) at Offutt Air Force Base, Nebraska, and to flying command posts, which were airborne at all times in the event SAC headquarters was nuked. On receiving the "Go!" signal, the B-52 bombers would begin racing toward preassigned targets in the Soviet Union—but they were forbidden to proceed past a certain "fail-safe" point until they received specific instructions. Fail safe was a protective measure against the United States launching an accidental nuclear war.

MEANWHILE AT GITMO, the new flashpoint in the Cold War, Water Condition Alpha had reduced daily consumption on the base from 2 million to 1 million gallons. At the same time, a permanent solution to the shortage was in the works. On February 10 in Washington, Pierre Salinger, Jack Kennedy's press secretary who remained with Lyndon Johnson in the same role, announced a crash program to build a $10 million plant to convert saltwater into freshwater, making Gitmo "forever independent" of Cuban water.[1]

Fidel Castro's plot to drive the United States out of Gitmo was collapsing like a house of cards in a windstorm. A face-saving explanation was needed. So on February 13, water cutoff day plus seven, the Maximum Leader went on television to charge that Admiral Bulkeley had been using suction pumps to slyly steal some 14,000 gallons of water daily from the Yateras River pipeline. Had Bulkeley not been a thief, Castro declared, the United States would now be in the process of pulling out of Guantanamo and returning it to its "rightful owners, the Cuban people."

Reporters at Gitmo rushed to Bulkeley for his response to Castro's accusation. "Hogwash!" the admiral barked. "We're bringing in our own water [in tankers]. Our mains were sealed tight, so it is impossible for us to draw off water by suction pumps or any other method."[2]

Despite Bulkeley's heated denial that he was a water thief, Cuban newspapers, television, and radio continued with a barrage of charges against the base commander. Castro himself joined in the orchestrated chorus by exclaiming on television that Bulkeley had been "a member of [General] MacArthur's warlike clique" and that the admiral would "stoop to any evil act to gain his goals!"[3]

Under the drumfire of charges against him flowing out of Havana, Bulkeley told news reporters: "Castro's calling me a liar—and I'm mad!"

The Gitmo commander, who had not gained a chestful of medals in World War II by sitting back supinely and letting the enemy punch him in the nose, called in Captain Trzyna. "Zip, I'm going to cut the damned water pipe and end all this nonsense that we're stealing water from the Cuban people!"

Trzyna was instructed to rush an acetylene torch and two oxygen tanks to the water distribution station for imminent pipe surgery. A short time later, Bulkeley leaped aboard a jeep (he always drove himself) and raced to the site. Trailing in his wake were fourteen U.S. reporters who had been notified that "something big" was about to break.

At the water-intake station, about one hundred yards from the main gate, Bulkeley instructed three Cuban civilian laborers to start digging. Two hours later, a piece of the 14-inch pipe had been uncovered. Then work started burning through the pipe with the acetylene torch, and at dusk, a 300-pound section, 38 inches long, was hoisted from the excavation.

Across the fenceline, Cuban soldiers watched curiously. Now was the moment of truth: Which one is a liar, Bulkeley or Castro? If the pipe was dry inside, no water could have flowed into the base since the February 6 shutdown. The reporters pressed forward and peeked into the pipe—it was bone dry.

Bulkeley hitched up his trousers and remarked evenly, "Well, that's it—and to hell with *him!*"[4]

Most of the night, Bulkeley, wearing a steel helmet and combat gear, and armed with a rifle and a .357 Magnum pistol, trekked along the Marines' defensive positions along the fenceline, scrambling up one steep hill and down another. If Castro chose to retaliate for the humiliation that had been inflicted on him, the admiral was not going to be caught off guard. In the darkness, Bulkeley threaded past minefields, some real, some dummies, with their triangular warning signs. His bodyguard, a Tommy gun–toting Marine less than half Bulkeley's age, was hard put to keep pace.

On Suicide Ridge, a bluff not far from the main gate, the scene was World War II all over again. Foxholes and trenches honeycombed the rugged terrain. The moon was a luminescent fingernail paring, but by its mute rays Bulkeley could discern the helmets of Marines crouched alertly in the excavations.

On foot and by jeep, Bulkeley covered the entire eastern perimeter, the most likely sector for any Cuban armed assault on the base. It was not until 3:30 A.M., after being on the go for nearly forty-five hours, that he returned to his quarters and fell into an exhausted sleep—for two hours.

News of the pipe-cutting extravaganza rapidly spread around the world. The U.S. Navy was proud. President Johnson was proud. Americans were proud. Scores of U.S. newspaper and magazine editorials heaped praise on Bulkeley.

The Albany, New York, *Knickerbocker News* hailed: "Hurrah and three cheers for Admiral Bulkeley—the first man to put Castro in his place since President Kennedy called his bluff."

The *Arizona Republic* reported: "[Bulkeley] didn't present the all too frequent picture of the United States on its knees before some tinhorn dictator."

Almost overnight, John Bulkeley's hole in the ground near the main gate had become a sort of shrine, a Guantanamo Liberty Bell. With the admiral's gleeful approval, Captain Zip Trzyna had his men erect a large, hand-lettered sign next to the excavation:

U.S. ANSWER TO CASTRO . . . GITMO WATER LIBERATED
FROM CUBA AT THIS POINT

In the months ahead, no U.S. senator, congressman, general, admiral, cabinet member, or other VIP would visit Gitmo without having his or her picture taken next to the pipe-surgery excavation.

Clearly Castro had been made a laughingstock—and a liar—in front of the whole world. Consequently, his newspapers and broadcast outlets spewed a stream of vitriolic attacks against Bulkeley. *Revolución* carried a large front-page picture of the admiral being hanged in effigy from a balcony in Havana. The caption explained that the "blood-thirsty [Bulkeley] was promoting fenceline violences" at Guantanamo that could lead to a major war.

MEANWHILE IN WASHINGTON Lyndon Johnson, the consummate politician, had been closely monitoring the media's and public's reaction to the Bulkeley confrontation with Castro. He liked what he saw. So on February 21, the president, who was campaigning for reelection, told an audience in Los Angeles: "We have dealt with this challenge and provocation from Havana. . . . We believe it is far wiser to send an admiral [Bulkeley] to cut [Castro's] water off than to send a battalion of Marines to turn it back on."[5]

It was praise for John Bulkeley, but mainly a swipe at Barry Goldwater, who had been harpooning the president for "doing nothing" to respond to Castro's challenge to the United States. Actually, Johnson had applied some political sleight of hand. By using the term "we," he implied that the pipe-cutting maneuver had been his idea, whereas no one in Washington even knew about Bulkeley's maneuver until it was a fait accompli. Moreover, it had been not Johnson but President Kennedy, shortly before his death, who had sent Bulkeley to Gitmo to "put a muzzle" on Castro.

IN THE DAYS AHEAD, Fidel Castro appeared to have been forced into a change of heart about Guantanamo. On February 25, he told a group of foreign journalists in Havana, "There is no special reason now that the [Cuban] fishermen have been released to keep the Caimanera [Gitmo] water shut off." Pausing briefly and flicking an ash from his cigar, he added, "Of course, restoring the water supply depends on the United States of North America requesting it."[6]

Contacted by journalists for his response, Admiral Bulkeley snapped: "Mr. Castro can go straight to hell!"[7]

In Washington, State Department bureaucrats were appalled. Admirals of the U.S. Navy simply do not use such unvarnished rhetoric when referring to another nation's ruler. In the Gitmo powder keg, there was much glee over Bulkeley's terse response.

ON APRIL 1, 1964—All Fools' Day—work began on the huge desalinization plant that would forever free Gitmo from Castro's freshwater antics. Engineering and construction would be done by the Westinghouse Corporation, with the New York–based firm of Burnes and Roe Western Hemisphere Corporation to be subcontractor for field engineering and construction management.

The plant would be large and complicated, and nearly every pound of materials and most of the hundreds of trucks, cranes, tools, and other equipment and supplies would have to be rushed in from the United States. The construction pace was hectic; work continued around the clock. Progress was monitored daily all the way up the military chain of command and into the Oval Office of the White House. President Johnson had given the project the highest priority.

Despite the formidable obstacles, July 31—only four months away—was the target date for completion of the first unit of the seawater conversion plant (two other units would follow). However, at the request of Admiral Bulkeley, the target date was moved to July 26 to coincide with the big Cuban holiday celebration of Fidel Castro's 26th of July Movement. On that day, Bulkeley hoped to toast the Maximum Leader with a glass of freshwater, produced right in Castro's backyard.

Bulkeley had gotten under Fidel Castro's skin. Late in April, the Gitmo monitoring station recorded a speech given by the Maximum Leader in Havana. It was mainly a bitter tirade against Bulkeley, who was denounced as a "beastly assassin." Castro topped off his diatribe by putting a $50,000, dead-or-alive bounty on Bulkeley's head.[8]

In the meantime, construction of the desalinization plant had been moving at a spectacular pace. Engineers predicted the July 26 target date would be met. Then, out of the blue, came a series of instructions from the State Department:

> Desalinization plant not (repeat not) to be played up. Do not (repeat not) brag about our capabilities over Cuba in producing water. No (repeat no) flag waving of any sort. This has severe political overtones.
>
> Talk as little as possible about Gitmo. Keep it out of the public news.
>
> Planned July 26 plant ceremonies to be postponed. Under no circumstances (repeat under no circumstances) are you to take psychological advantage of Castro.[9]

Privately, John Bulkeley exploded over the State Department edict ordering him not to "take psychological advantage of Castro." A golden opportunity had been shot down for the United States to dramatize an infrequent Cold War victory. But an order was an order, so the unveiling celebration was pushed forward to July 31.

At three o'clock in the morning on July 26—Castro's biggest holiday—John Bulkeley and a few of his aides sneaked into the completed plant and, like mischievous schoolboys, drew several "unofficial jugs" and toasted the Maximum Leader with the freshwater.

Four days later, the formal unveiling of the plant took place. Nearly everyone in Gitmo was present. Although the State Department had sneaked in snoopers to keep a close eye on the prohibited "flag waving" and "taking psychological advantage of Castro," it was a joyous celebration.

IN SANTIAGO, the "cradle of the revolution," not far from Guantanamo, 250,000 perspiring *campesinos* (farm workers) were packed sardinelike in the main square under a broiling sun. They had been bused in from all over eastern Cuba for the July 26 celebration of the anniversary of Castro's movement. For nearly two hours, Fidel Castro hammered at the United States in general and Admiral John Bulkeley in particular.

Bulkeley had replaced Jack and Bobby Kennedy as Castro's most hated Yankee. "[Bulkeley] is a gorilla of the worst species!" the Maximum Leader thundered to the throng. "The interest of that gentleman is that we kill a few of his Marines to aid [Senator] Goldwater's campaign against President Johnson!"[10]

Pausing briefly, the Maximum Leader exclaimed that Bulkeley and Goldwater would "stoop to anything to stir up trouble at Caimanera [Guantanamo]!"[11]

One of the throng's greatest ovations followed Castro's warning that "our men will shoot back if these provocations continue [at the naval base]!"

A chant echoed across the pavement to the effect that "Fidel will hit the Yankees hard! Fidel will hit the Yankees hard!"

SIX DAYS AFTER his Santiago diatribe, Castro was holding court for a bevy of U.S. reporters at Varadero Beach, his favorite seaside haunt. He was ensconced in the once plush International Hotel. Castro lit a long black cigar, then opened a lengthy monologue.

"There are some who believe that an aggression against Cuba will not bring a world war," he declared. "But it will cause a world war, make no mistake about that!"

In reply to a question, the bearded Cuban said, "I would take missiles again. . . . The Soviet Union is seriously involved with Cuba."[12]

Three days later, thirty pieces of Soviet-built earthmoving equipment suddenly were brought up to the fenceline, and blue-clad Cuban "volunteer" laborers began clearing cactus and scrub brush to a depth of 300 yards along the entire 24-mile perimeter.

John Bulkeley was not impressed by the massive earthmoving operation. He called it "Mother Castro's gardening."

Six-ton Soviet-built flatbed trucks then hauled up conelike pillboxes, which were lifted off by huge cranes onto the top of holes dug in the ground by the "volunteers." Within a few weeks, the naval base was ringed by 141 bunkers, most of which were located on high ground.[13]

Throughout construction of the Cuban Siegfried Line, as Gitmo called it, Bulkeley provided the Pentagon with a running account of progress. Consequently, a Pentagon study concluded that the fortified belt had been built with Soviet military and engineering advice and heavy equipment—along with $15 million poured into the crash project by Nikita Khrushchev.[14]

Stateside reporters bombarded John Bulkeley by telephone for his views on the bunkers ringing the naval base. "Our Marine artillery is zeroed in on each pillbox," he replied. "So if Castro starts a ruckus, we'll blow his damned pillboxes to hell in a hurry!"

Responding to another journalist, the admiral said, "If we are ordered to break out of here, we'll go through the fortified belt like a hot knife through butter!"[15]

Bulkeley was constantly alert for a surprise assault. Each day, he flew in a helicopter along the base perimeter on the lookout for any telltale Cuban activity. Daily, he tramped the Marines' forward positions in full battle gear, toting a Tommy gun, ignoring the fact that he made a juicy target for any Cuban sniper only yards away on the other side of the chain-link fence.

In August 1964, Colonel Anthony "Cold Steel" Walker, a grizzled veteran of heavy action in the Pacific in World War II and later in Korea, routinely took command of the Marine battle group at Gitmo. On the first night, he brought up two tanks near to the fenceline, where they shone their powerful searchlights into Cuban positions. This action provoked gratifying reaction, with lights going on all along the Cuban lines. On occasion at night, the forty-seven-year-old Walker, a Yale graduate, sent helicopter gunships along the fenceline, with their landing lights on, looking like huge lightning bugs.

"All this was not frivolous behavior," Colonel Walker later recalled. "We wanted Reuben [Cuban troops] to know that we were alert, active, and ready if they wanted to take us on.

"Our mixed bag of Marines, sailors, and Seabees could have halted or slowed their tanks and infantry," Walker continued, "and the 2d Marine Division would have rushed in [from North Carolina] and driven the bastards all the way back to Havana."

Walker added: "Of course, Cuban artillery might have smashed things up a bit on the base."[16]

Time marched on at Gitmo. Almost daily, there was some sort of Cuban-inspired machination along the fenceline: rock-throwing, name-calling, infiltration of the base at night by armed Cuban patrols, random rifle shots, or loudspeakers hurling threats of looming armed assaults. Daily, the ten thousand Americans on the base were living in the front lines of this potentially explosive Cold War battleground.

The way Admiral Bulkeley stood up to Castro's bold challenge to the United States had triggered a deep pride shared by all hands—Navy men and Marines, women, children, and civilian employees. It was a kind of siege sentiment, a we're-all-in-this-together feeling. They realized the crucial significance of Gitmo in the greater scheme of things and the necessity for their being present in "the United States' most vulnerable fortress."

The Marines coined a defiant slogan: "They call it Gitmo—but we won't git!"

That motto precisely embodied the intention of President John Kennedy when he had sent Admiral John Bulkeley to the naval base flashpoint: Under no circumstances was the United States to "git."

36

Recruits for the Guerrilla International

ALTHOUGH BOBBY KENNEDY and Lyndon Johnson had long detested one another, there were whispers in Washington during the summer of 1964 that the president, a pragmatic politician, would select the attorney general as his vice presidential running mate to attract the vote of liberals in the fall. Johnson preferred to let the rumors fly, but privately he growled to aides, "I don't need that little runt to win!"

For his part, Bobby apparently was willing to swallow his pride and accept the vice presidential nomination. If elected, he would be but a heartbeat from the top job and would have a springboard from which to run for president himself in 1968.

When Johnson invited Bobby to the Oval Office to inform him that he had chosen Senator Hubert H. Humphrey, Kennedy noticed that the red light on the president's recorder was on, meaning their strained conversation was being taped.[1]

Bobby apparently was deeply disappointed by the rejection. Later, he remarked to a friend, "Johnson didn't want a cross little fellow looking over his shoulder!"[2]

After Johnson gained his party's nomination for the presidency in midsummer, Kennedy resigned as attorney general. On August 25, he announced that he would run for the U.S. Senate seat held by the veteran Republican Kenneth Keating. Republican leaders quipped that Bobby's motto was "Do unto others, then move to another state!"

Kennedy immediately plunged into nonstop campaigning and was promptly branded a carpetbagger by elements of the media and his political rivals. The charge had much credence. Bobby's only claim to New York residence was the Kennedy clan's elegant suite in Manhattan's posh Carlyle Hotel.

To establish the legally required official residence—and to give voters the perception that the Kennedys were truly becoming New York citizens—Bobby and Ethel signed a lease on a century-old, twenty-five-room mansion in exclusive Glen Cove, Long Island. However, Ethel already had enrolled her large brood of children in private schools in the Hickory Hill area outside Washington. She and Bobby spent little time at the Long Island estate. Bobby was mostly at the Carlyle, and Ethel spent much of her time at Hickory Hill.

November 4 was election day. But Bobby and Ethel were not registered to vote in New York, so they had to cast their ballots in Massachusetts, the couple's true home state.

New York voters, many of them still mesmerized by the Kennedy mystique, ignored Bobby's carpetbagger status and sent him to represent them in the Senate by a whopping margin over incumbent Kenneth Keating.

MEANWHILE on September 24, the Warren Commission released its report on President Kennedy's assassination. As the panel's investigative arm, the Federal Bureau of Investigation had conducted its largest probe ever. Eighty-six Bureau personnel had been sent to Dallas, some 25,000 interviews were conducted, and 2,300 reports, totaling nearly 30,000 pages, were prepared.

"Given the FBI's justifiable reputation as the world's most professional and respected criminal investigative agency, its effort in the Kennedy investigation was expected to be one of the highest degree of thoroughness and integrity," the House Select Committee on Assassinations stated in its final report. "Indeed, it was an effort of unparalleled magnitude."[3]

The Warren Commission concluded that Lee Harvey Oswald, acting alone, shot Kennedy from a window on the sixth floor of the Texas School Book Depository building. The panel also concluded that Jack Ruby acted alone in killing Oswald in a Dallas jail. No solid evidence of a conspiracy involving Oswald and Ruby was uncovered.

IN CUBA, Fidel Castro continued to wipe out any conceivable obstacle to absolute power. *Revolución*, whose editor was Carlos Franqui, a comrade going back to the Sierra Maestra days, was perceived by the Maximum Leader to be guilty of interpreting events in a way that differed from his own viewpoint. Moreover, *Revolución* was having occasional disputes with *Hoy*, the only other newspaper.

Castro met this "threat" by shutting down both publications and establishing in their place a single new daily newspaper, *Granma*.

Franqui fled Cuba and ultimately became one of the Maximum Leader's severest critics.

Appointed editor of *Granma* was Jorgé Enrique Menéndez, a long-time ally of Castro. There was a sole editorial standard: no criticism whatsoever of Castro or his regime.

Enrique Menéndez knew his role was to parrot the Castro line. Each day for years to come, he would telephone Celia Sanchez, Fidel's ever present confidante, to make sure what the Maximum Leader's views were at any given time.

By the fall of 1964, nearly five years since he had seized power, Fidel Castro had converted Cuba into a police state modeled after the dread Soviet version. Indeed, Soviet agents had helped create the is-landwide network known as the Comités para la Defensa de la Revo-lución (Committees for the Defense of the Revolution, or CDR).

Membership in the CDR would eventually number about three hundred thousand. These petty watchdogs spied on their neighbors, friends, even their own families. They were regarded by most Cubans as detestable symbols of dictatorship and oppression, much as most Germans regarded the *Blockwart* (block wardens) in Germany in the era of Adolf Hitler.

Castro's citizen snoopers were identified by small initialed flags placed over front doors and in the hallways of apartment buildings. The task of the informant was made easier because revolutionary "re-forms" made it almost impossible for a family to change its home, thereby dodging spying neighbors. Any acquaintance or relative might be a *chivato* (informer).

Supervising the CDR was the head of the Interior Ministry, Major Ramiro Valdés, who had ordered the Guantanamo naval base fence torn down in his confrontation with Admiral John Bulkeley in late 1963. Valdés instructed the civilian spies to keep a sharp eye open for "the enemy," which included imperialists, Bay of Pigs mercenaries, collaborators, agitators, laggards who avoided work or did not labor hard enough, chronic complainers, Catholic priests, Seventh-Day Ad-ventists, U.S. Marines, CIA agents and their contacts, Jehovah's Wit-nesses, "bandits" (anti-Castro guerrillas), Pentecostalists, Gideonites, "worms," slackers, social deviates, Baptist ministers, and anyone who kept his or her home lights burning late at night.

IN OCTOBER 1964, a brief item appeared in *Pravda*, the Communist Party newspaper in Moscow: "Comrade Nikita Khrushchev, at his own request, has been relieved of all Party and government duties, in view of his advanced age and deterioration of health."

Khrushchev would be replaced by Aleksei Kosygin as premier and Leonid Brezhnev as first secretary of the Communist Party.

A few days later, the new Soviet leaders, who had engineered Khrushchev's ouster, apparently had second thoughts and changed their cover story. Now *Pravda* charged Khrushchev with "harebrained scheming, immature conclusions, bragging, and phrase-mongering."[4]

At the same time, the newspaper published a document accusing Khrushchev of twenty-nine counts of political errors and misconduct. Leading the list was a scathing indictment of Khrushchev's fumbling of the Cuban missile crisis episode "which has caused the Soviet Union much embarrassment."

AS THE HEATED presidential race came down the home stretch in the late fall of 1964, Cuba and Castro were the focal point. Challenger Barry Goldwater charged that "even after the demise of Castro's good friend Khrushchev," the Maximum Leader still had a "firmly entrenched base of Communist subversion, guarded by Soviet troops and weapons."

Goldwater's running mate, William E. Miller, accused President Johnson of "coddling Castro," even though the U.S. government had the ability to seriously cripple the regime of the "Communist tyrant."

Lyndon Johnson, meanwhile, had assigned various hatchetmen to attack Goldwater and Miller so the president could act presidential and take the high road, seemingly above the tawdry fray. He stressed that he had taken a "vigorous but sensible" approach to Castro. At the same time, the hatchetmen relentlessly blasted Goldwater as a loose cannon bent on plunging the world into a nuclear holocaust.

In November, 60 percent of the Americans going to the polls cast their ballots for the Johnson-Humphrey ticket. Goldwater and Miller carried only Arizona and five states in the South. After his landslide triumph, Johnson let it be known that he would not "tolerate any more Cubas" in the Western Hemisphere.

A FEW MONTHS LATER in June 1965, much of the United States was electrified when an unexpected witness, Juana Castro Ruz, Fidel's older sister, appeared in Washington to testify before the House Committee on Un-American Activities. A year earlier, she had fled to the United States after becoming "disillusioned with the injustices conducted under [Fidel's and Raúl's] reign of terror."[5]

Juana told the committee that "Fidel's feeling of hatred for this country cannot even be imagined by Americans. His intention, his obsession to destroy the U.S. is one of his main interests and objectives."[6]

Toward this end, she continued, "Fidel has financed the trips to Cuba of the [New York–based] Student Committee for Travel to Cuba in order to create propagandists who will return to the U.S. and parrot the 'watchwords' of Cuban Communists."[7]

ON JANUARY 3, 1966, Fidel Castro convened the First Conference of Solidarity of the People of Africa, Asia, and Latin America, known in short as the Tricontinental Conference. Nearly 750 men and women, representing 82 countries, came to Havana as "delegates" to the event. Its purpose was to launch a massive assault against the "capitalist and imperialist nations," especially the United States, by forming what was called the Guerrilla International.

Castro was hopeful of stirring up unrest and violence among blacks in the United States and of triggering chaos and actions against the government by young persons who were starting to be alienated over an expanding war in Vietnam.

Among the delegates were the Vietcong, the new Palestine Liberation Organization (PLO) headed by Yasir Arafat, and such U.S. radicals as Jerry Rubin, Bernardine Dohrns, Eldridge Cleaver (head of the Black Panther Party), and Stokely Carmichael (chief of the Black Power organization). Cleaver, who was wanted in the United States for an alleged rape, was singled out for special treatment. He was provided a spiffy Cuban military-style uniform and beret, a chauffeur-driven automobile, and a Cuban army officer as an escort.

A principal instructor at the Tricontinental Conference was Huynh Van Ba, who had been the Vietcong's chief liaison officer in Havana since 1963. Van Ba taught his eager U.S. pupils how to organize antiwar demonstrations, how to encourage young men to resist the draft or to flee to Canada to escape service, and how to continually publicize the growing number of American casualties in Vietnam.

Instructing the delegates on terrorism tactics was Carlos Marighella, a Brazilian, a hard-core Communist, and a prototype of a professional revolutionist. He stressed that urban guerrillas had to attain two objectives: the liquidation (murder) of the chiefs and assistant chiefs of the armed forces and police, and the expropriation (theft) of government resources such as weapons and ammunition and the securing of funds from banks and other "big capitalists."[8]

Do-it-yourself kits for urban guerrilla warfare were distributed. These included instructions for making and using Molotov cocktails and spray cans containing the legend "Paint your policeman yellow."

In the wake of the Tricontinental Conference, revolutionary radicals built a support network for terrorism in the United States, providing services such as fake documents, safe houses, transportation, medical and legal aid, surveillance, and the supplying of weapons and explosives.

Among the most violent of the terrorist groups springing from the Havana conclave was the Weathermen. In Communique Number 1 published in *The New York Times*, the group proclaimed a "declaration of war against the United States." Revolutionary violence was the only way to fight "American imperialism," the communique stated. "Now we are adopting the classic guerrilla strategy of the Vietcong . . . to our situation here in the most technically advanced country in the world."

The Weathermen robbed banks and utilized various frauds involving traveler's checks, credit cards, and claims for welfare payments. Bombs were placed in military and law enforcement installations in Detroit, Chicago, New York, Washington, and San Francisco, killing one officer and wounding several others.[9]

In a raid against a "pad" of the Symbionese Liberation Army (SLA), another violence-bent underground organization, FBI agents discovered booklets by Carlos Marighella entitled *Minimanual for the Urban Guerrilla*, hundreds of which had been distributed at the Tricontinental Conference. These publications explained "action models" for perpetrating mayhem. No doubt adhering to these instructions, the SLA murdered Dr. Marcus Foster, the superintendent of schools in Oakland, California; kidnapped Patty Hearst, a media mogul's daughter (who soon joined her captives in their criminal capers); and robbed several banks.[10]

In Puerto Rico, the Macheteros, the largest of four active terrorist gangs whose leaders had taken their training in nearby Cuba from Carlos Marighella, destroyed most of the local National Guard's airplanes in an attack. The Macheteros also were thought to have been responsible for firing a ground-to-ground missile at an FBI facility in San Juan.[11]

37

A Tragedy in Los Angeles

DURING THE SPRING OF 1966, Fidel Castro and Lyndon Johnson were engaged in a one-upmanship duel, this time over the Central American and Caribbean games to be held in Puerto Rico. When plans for the athletic competition were being drawn up, the organizers in San Juan, no doubt prodded by Washington, announced that the Cubans would not be invited. Castro presumably appealed to the International Olympic Committee (IOC), which stated that unless Cuba were invited, the games would not be sponsored by the IOC.

Castro broke the deadlock by loading his men's and women's teams onto a ship that sailed to Puerto Rico. Then Lyndon Johnson made a countermove: Outside the San Juan harbor, a U.S. Coast Guard vessel halted the Cuban ship, and its captain was told that he could not enter. So the athletes climbed into lifeboats to continue into the harbor, at which point the miniconfrontation evaporated.

As expected by observers, Cuba's athletes carted off most of the medals. Back in Havana, a rousing welcome ceremony was put on for the athletes. Typically, Castro spoke for nearly ninety minutes, during which he declared that most of the judges had been CIA agents who had conspired to deprive the Cubans of even more medals.

Moreover, the CIA had brought to San Juan a large number of "beautiful women" to seduce, corrupt, and bribe the Cuban athletes, the Maximum Leader asserted. And there were CIA "thugs in priestly garb" to demoralize the Cubans.[1]

CHÉ GUEVARA, Fidel Castro's indispensable left-hand man, departed from Havana in October 1966 and, using a fraudulent passport identifying him as an Uruguayan, slipped into Bolivia. His mission was to energize a stalled effort by Cuban and Bolivian guerrillas to overthrow by force the government of President René Barrientos. Soon after Ché's arrival, Barrientos sent troops into the tangled wilds to track him down.

Guevara used a shortwave radio transmitter to keep in touch with Havana. Code names were used: Guevara was Ramón, Fidel Castro was Leche.

At dawn on October 8, 1967, Bolivian soldiers surrounded a small hut in which Guevara and a few of his men were sleeping. A brief fire-fight erupted and Ché was wounded and captured. He complained to the Bolivian officers that Fidel Castro had "failed me at a crucial time," abandoning him to "sink or swim."[2]

Twenty-four hours later, on orders from La Paz, Dr. Ernesto "Ché" Guevara, age thirty-nine, was executed by his captors. Not wishing to have a "Ché shrine" established in Bolivia, the government an-nounced that he had been cremated and the ashes buried secretly.

Within days, the "Cult of Ché" was born—in Cuba and around the world. At the University of Wisconsin in Madison, the University of California at Berkeley, and Harvard University at Cambridge, Mas-sachusetts, Ché T-shirts and posters appeared by the thousands. At Communist-orchestrated protest rallies in Washington, D.C., New York, London, Paris, Rome, Berlin, Tokyo, and other major cities, there were huge banners with Ché's Christlike image.[3]

SANTIAGO, CUBA, the "birthplace of the revolution," was being scalded by a boiling sun when thousands of Fidelistas gathered to hear Fidel Castro speak on the fourteenth anniversary of the 26th of July Move-ment. Seated on the platform as the guest of honor was Black Power advocate Stokely Carmichael.

Prior to the ceremonies, Carmichael told reporters that blacks in the United States were prepared to fight to the death in a guerrilla warfare campaign, and he predicted that the government in Washing-ton would be overthrown. Castro introduced Carmichael to the huge crowd as "America's most distinguished civil-rights leader."[4]

ON THE MORNING of August 7, 1967, Cuban government officials an-nounced that a "sensational" news conference would be held that af-ternoon at the Havana Libre (formerly the Hilton). Before a packed hall of journalists, Cuban security police hauled in five bedraggled, be-wildered men identified as "counterrevolutionaries." They had been sent to Cuba by the CIA to murder Castro, it was stated.

It was clear to objective U.S. reporters that the pitiful creatures had been badly beaten by the security police, and they promptly con-fessed their guilt. Then the reporters were shown their captured equip-ment and supplies: machine guns, radio transmitters, hand grenades, rifles, thousands of rounds of ammunition, bazookas, canned peaches, even several unopened bottles of scotch.

Laura Bergquist, a perceptive reporter for *Look* magazine, was highly skeptical. It looked like yet another phoney propaganda circus. How could so few men carry such a large amount of heavy weapons, ammunition, equipment, and supplies, presumably for many miles? she asked. Why did the "counterrevolutionaries" bring along a large supply of heavy canned peaches instead of the much lighter and more manageable military C-rations? And Bergquist said she had never heard of a secret raid in which the participants lugged several bottles of scotch.

Osvaldo Dorticós, Castro's puppet president, had been listening just outside the door. Like an angry bull, he stormed into the room, face flushed, hands visibly trembling. "You've heard the evidence," he shouted at the U.S. reporters. "Do you accept it or not?"

A female reporter for the Communist *Daily Worker* replied, "Of course." Others were silent. Bergquist said that a journalist needed more proof.

"Proof!" Dorticós thundered. Why did she not confront President Johnson and the CIA with the evidence? A male reporter from Uruguay yelled that she was obviously an apologist for the CIA or a CIA agent herself. Cheers and applause rocked the room.[5]

Meanwhile, Fidel Castro took to television to announce that he was going to "purify the nation' by wiping out the "last vestiges" of private enterprise. Nearly sixty thousand business firms, most of them mom-and-pop operations or those with a handful of employees, would be eliminated. Included would be such "exploiters of the people" as pushcart peddlers, small laundries, lunch counters, bars, repair shops, photo studios, and corner groceries.

These tiny enterprises had provided goods and services not available in the larger government-operated firms. Fruits, vegetables, and clothing almost vanished from stores. Black markets flourished. Evidence of great unrest surfaced, an unrest muted by the constant snooping of the CDR.

DURING THE EARLY SPRING of 1968, Senator Bobby Kennedy was mulling over the idea of following in the footsteps of his dead brother and running for president. Many of his advisers counseled him not to jump into the campaign, fearful of a repetition of Dallas. Young brother Teddy, convinced that the family was cursed, was in the forefront of this faction.

On the other hand, mother Rose Kennedy, who already had lost two sons to violent deaths, wanted Bobby in the White House. "He has lots of ideas, he's had them right along," Rose said.[6]

Bobby's ambitious, strong-willed wife, Ethel, who was pregnant with the couple's eleventh child, and the Kennedy sisters were urging the senator to throw his hat into the presidential ring.

At this time, President Lyndon Johnson's approval rating had dropped to a puny 21 percent. The country was ripped apart, in turmoil from the bloody war in Vietnam. Violence in the streets had become commonplace. Bobby knew he would be hammered as ruthless and opportunistic if he decided to run against Johnson, with whom he had been feuding for years.

On the morning of Saturday, March 16, Bobby stood at the same Capitol podium where Jack had announced his presidential candidacy more than eight years before. To a national television audience he stated, "I want the people of the United States to stand for hope instead of despair, for the reconciliation of men instead of the growing risk of world war."[7]

Watching Bobby's criticism of his stewardship in office from his living quarters in the White House, Lyndon Johnson fumed and cursed.

Senator Kennedy's decision came as no surprise to most citizens of the United States: They had long been convinced that sooner or later, Bobby would mount a white horse and make a charge on the White House.

Two weeks later, the television networks announced that President Johnson would make a brief address that night. Network executives and most Americans felt that he would announce some new development in the Vietnam war. Instead, Johnson stunned the nation: "I shall not seek and I will not accept the nomination of my party as your President."

Within hours, Bobby contacted Johnson's aides for a meeting with the president to determine what role Johnson would play in the campaign now that he was no longer a contender. Johnson was furious. "I won't bother answering that grandstanding little runt!" he growled.[8]

On June 5, eleven weeks later, Bobby was in Los Angeles after a vigorous campaign across the land. It was primary day in California, and television network projections had Bobby winning the state, which would be crucial to his nomination. Polls closed at 8:00 P.M. Bobby, Ethel, and a large gathering of supporters, including CBS's Roger Mudd and NBC's Sander Vanocur, joyously awaited the results in the Royal Suite of the Ambassador Hotel.

At 11:22 P.M., cheers rocked the Royal Suite: Bobby and the others knew he had won California over Senator Eugene McCarthy, the soft-spoken, antiwar candidate. Escorted by Bill Barry, a former FBI agent and now Kennedy's bodyguard, Bobby and Ethel took a service elevator downstairs to where hundreds of campaign faithful were celebrating raucously in the Embassy Ballroom.

Only minutes before, Barry had expressed concern that he would be able to react in time if Bobby got mixed up in a large, jostling crowd. What especially worried Barry was that Bobby didn't like for police to be around him because he felt the security would result in a barrier between him and the people.

Ten days earlier, Press Secretary Pierre Salinger had been warned by an acquaintance that Bobby could get himself killed unless he accepted more police security. Los Angeles Police Chief Thomas Riddin stated later that Bobby had refused offers to beef up his personal protection. "I got the impression that he wished to appear to be antipolice and not to need our help because politically it was the smart thing to do at the time."[9]

Pandemonium erupted in the huge ornate ballroom when Bobby, flashing a toothy smile of victory, stepped to the podium crammed with media microphones. Once a degree of silence descended, Bobby spoke, thanking "all those who contributed to this enormous victory." After flashing a V-for-victory sign, Bobby began wading through the throng on his way to give a press conference at the Colonial Room on the far side of the Ambassador's kitchen. In the crush, Ethel was separated from her husband.

While being shepherded through a pantry area on the way to the Colonial Room, a small, swarthy man edged up to the candidate and shouted, "Kennedy, you son of a bitch!" Then, twenty-four-year-old Sirhan Bishara Sirhan aimed a small-caliber pistol at Kennedy and emptied the chamber of eight cartridges. Two bullets struck Bobby in the head, and he crumpled to the concrete floor.

Bodyguard Bill Barry and two informal security men, former professional football tackle Rosey Grier and Olympic champion Rafer Johnson, pounced on Sirhan and wrested the gun away from him. Shouts rang out above the turmoil: "Kill him! Kill him!"

Sirhan, a Christian Arab who had emigrated from Jerusalem in 1957, seemed to hold Kennedy responsible for the troubles of his people. As he was led off to jail, Sirhan screamed, "I did it for my country!"[10]

Greviously wounded, Bobby, with Ethel at his side, was rushed by ambulance to Central Receiving Hospital, a mile away. At 1:44 A.M. on

June 6, Bobby was pronounced dead. A few days later, he would be buried near brother Jack's grave at the Arlington National Cemetery across the Potomac from Washington.

Teddy, the youngest of the four brothers, inherited the mantle of the Kennedy clan patriarch.

ACROSS THE UNITED STATES, Bobby's murder triggered a renewed rash of theories about who or what group was behind the assassination of President Kennedy in Dallas nearly five years earlier. Lyndon Johnson had his own theory about the mastermind, a view shared by many Americans. Before leaving the presidency, he blurted out to network-television anchor Howard K. Smith: "I'll tell you something that will rock you. Jack Kennedy was trying to get Castro, but Castro got to him first!"

ABOUT A YEAR after Bobby Kennedy was buried, an estimated 1 billion people around the world sat or stood transfixed to their television sets on Sunday, July 20, 1969. They were electrified as the U.S. astronaut Neil A. Armstrong climbed down from the landing module of the spaceship *Apollo 11* onto the surface of the moon. "The *Eagle* has landed!" a voice over television extolled.

Only a week later did Havana radio and television, which had long been trumpeting the Soviet Union's feats in space, tersely mention the moon landing, shrugging it off as "an effort by [President Richard] Nixon to disguise the ugly face of American imperialism, so rejected by the countries in Latin America."

No doubt Fidel Castro was personally chagrined by the U.S. space spectacular. Back in early 1962, soon after the Bay of Pigs fiasco, it had been the Maximum Leader's hated enemy, President Kennedy, who had urged Congress to launch a crash program to "put a man on the moon within ten years." Now the ghost of Jack Kennedy seemed to have arisen to taunt Fidel Castro.

Epilogue

I N MAY 1970, Alpha 66, the Cuban exile group based in southern Florida and the Bahamas, struck another blow at Castro. Several Alpha 66 members in a fast powerboat sank two Cuban fishing vessels and took the eleven crew members to a tiny, uninhabited island in the Bahamas. The exiles offered to exchange their captives for a like number being held in Cuban dungeons.

Castro was enraged. His underlings arranged a huge protest rally in front of the "Yankee lair" in Havana—the long-empty U.S. Embassy. Urged on by loudspeakers, the 100,000 demonstrators hauled in by horse, ox, cart, bicycle, automobile, bus, and truck waved huge placards that portrayed President Nixon as Adolf Hitler and the Central Intelligence Agency as "the new Gestapo."

The boisterous demonstration and Castro's threats paid off. Pressured by the U.S. State Department, the Alpha 66 leaders released their captives to the International Red Cross. In Havana, the Maximum Leader and thousands of Fidelistas were on hand to greet the returning conquering heroes.

In Miami, FBI agents raided the main offices of Alpha 66, but no weapons were found. Since the "kidnapping" had been mounted outside the United States, charges of violating neutrality laws were not filed against the exile group.

ON THE MORNING of May 2, 1972, J. Edgar Hoover was found dead in his home in Washington, where he had lived for all of his seventy-seven years, forty-eight of which had been spent at the helm of the FBI. Death was due to a heart attack.

Congress voted its permission for Hoover's body to lie in state in the Capitol Rotunda—the first civil servant ever to be accorded that honor. Previously, only twenty-one persons, eight of whom were presidents or former presidents, had received that distinction. The FBI chief's flag-draped coffin rested on the same catafalque that once had held the remains of Abraham Lincoln.

Thousands of tributes poured in from around the world. Senator Ted Kennedy, who had been fully aware of the clashes between brother Bobby and Hoover, nevertheless stated, "The nation has lost a dedicated and loyal public servant."[1]

Across the land, hundreds of media editorials praised Hoover. A few derogatory opinions were published, including a vicious one by the *Daily Worker*, the Communist newspaper in New York. It branded Hoover a "servant of reaction and repression, a political pervert."

THREE YEARS after Hoover's death, a U.S. Senate committee investigating assassinations of foreign leaders was preparing to subpoena Sam Giancana to tell what he knew about the Mob's plot to murder Fidel Castro more than a decade earlier. Two days later, the gangland boss was shot to death in his plush Chicago home by an unknown killer who pumped seven shots into him.[2]

In mid-1976, Johnny Roselli, who had been involved with Giancana in the scheme to kill the Maximum Leader, left his ornate Florida home to play a round of golf and disappeared. A few weeks afterward, his dismembered body, stuffed in a large oil drum, was hauled from Miami's Biscayne Bay.[3]

When Sam Trafficante, the third ringleader in the plot, heard that the Senate committee was going to subpoena him to testify, he fled to Costa Rica.

MEANWHILE, Ted Shackley, the young station chief at JM WAVE during the vendetta between the Kennedy brothers and Fidel Castro, had climbed the totem pole to near the top of the CIA hierarchy. After leaving JM WAVE, he had been the station chief in Laos and then held the same post in Saigon, where the CIA was becoming deeply involved as the war in Vietnam escalated steadily in the 1960s. Later, Shackley was promoted to head the Western Hemisphere Division of Clandestine Services and then became chief of the Far Eastern Division of Clandestine Services.

THROUGHOUT THE YEARS of the Cold War, Morris and Jack Childs (Agent 58 and Agent 69) performed invaluable service to the United States by acting as double agents. They were totally trusted by Fidel Castro, a succession of Soviet dictators, and other Communist leaders around the world. No doubt the crowning glory of the brothers' espionage mission came in 1975 when the Soviet Union proudly awarded Jack the Order of the Red Banner for exceptional services.

Through painstaking attention to detail, the FBI had managed to keep Operation Solo secret for more than two decades. Then, in 1975, came a haunting threat of exposure, not by the KGB but by liberal Senator Frank Church, who was widely regarded as unfriendly to the FBI. Church was chairman of a Senate committee conducting a far-ranging investigation of the Bureau.

When Church's probe unknowingly threatened to destroy the most valuable spying apparatus the United States had ever had against Cuba, the Soviet Union, and China, FBI Assistant Director W. Raymond Wannall was assigned to contact Church.

In a secluded room in the Capitol, Wannall showed Church a photograph of Leonid Brezhnev and his top leaders at a conference in the Kremlin. Pointing to a man seated next to Brezhnev but not identifying him by name, Wannall said, "Senator, here is our man, the one you are about to kill!"

Church seemed to turn almost ashen. His jaw dropped and he stared at Wannall in near disbelief for long moments. The senator finally said that the FBI official had put a heavy burden on him. Then the articulate Wannall declared, "Senator, we are counting on your honor and patriotism."[4]

Although the Congressional probe of the FBI continued off and on for most of 1975, Church never brought up Solo. Wannall's appeal to the senator's "honor and patriotism" had paid off.

In 1987, after the Childs brothers had been risking their lives as double agents almost constantly for more than twenty-five years, Ronald Reagan directed that the Presidential Medal of Freedom be awarded to Morris and bestowed posthumously to Jack, who died in 1980. Reagan wanted to personally make the presentation to Morris at the White House, but FBI officials involved in Operation Solo convinced the president that such an activity would be unwise because of security reasons. So Morris was decorated in a private ceremony at FBI headquarters by Director William Sessions.[5]

Perhaps it had been the first time in history that a U.S. citizen functioning as a double agent had received a decoration from both sides: the United States and the nation on which he was spying, the Soviet Union.

ALTHOUGH ADMIRAL JOHN BULKELEY had departed in mid-1966 from the U.S. Naval Base at Guantanamo, where he had been sent by then President Jack Kennedy and brother Bobby to "put a muzzle" on Fidel Castro, Bulkeley's name and spirit remain alive there. The Marine barracks area at Gitmo was named Camp Bulkeley after he left. The Marines also named an elevation Bulkeley Hill where the admiral had spent many nights in a bunker in anticipation of an all-out attack by Cuban armed forces. In 1989, a large new administrative building on the base was named Bulkeley Hall.

After his assignment to Guantanamo, when it appeared the world might have been on the brink of nuclear war, Bulkeley was sent to head the Naval Board of Inspection and Survey (InSurv). Bulkeley's mission was crucial: making certain that the six hundred Navy ships, along with airplanes and equipment, were combat ready at all times. Not until his seal of approval had been put on a new ship could it be accepted by the Navy.

Taking his InSurv team of experts, Bulkeley, in early 1973, flew to the U.S. Naval Base at Norfolk, where all of them boarded a huge new aircraft carrier. Loaded with an incredible array of sophisticated equipment, the vessel put to sea where Bulkeley and his technicians conducted exhaustive tests.

Once the carrier had passed muster, it proudly took its place as the jewel of the fleet. Ironically, the flattop's name was *John F. Kennedy*. Symbolically, the two Johns, Kennedy and Bulkeley, had been united for a third time.[6]

SIRHAN BISHARA SIRHAN, who had been charged with murdering Bobby Kennedy in Los Angeles in 1968, was tried, convicted, and sentenced to be executed. Later, the penalty was reduced to life imprisonment after the Supreme Court ruled that the California death statute was unconstitutional. Over the years, Sirhan has asked the parole board many times to release him from prison. Each time, his pleas have been rejected.

THE BLUE-RIBBON Warren Commission conclusion that Lee Harvey Oswald acted alone in assassinating President Kennedy has been disputed by numerous critics, most of whom refused to acknowledge that a Communist crazy perpetrated the vile deed. However, Bobby Kennedy and Teddy Kennedy have endorsed the Commission's findings.

During the 1970s, rumors of a massive conspiracy in the Kennedy murder became so prevalent that a special committee of the U.S. House of Representatives reexamined the ponderous amount of evidence and testimony that accrued during the investigations. Critics would later charge that for political reasons the Democratic-controlled panel put great credence in the testimony of acoustical technicians who claimed that shots were fired from two locations along the Dallas motorcade at almost the same time.

Consequently, in 1978, the House Committee concluded that the president "was probably assassinated as a result of a conspiracy." The report was silent on the identity of the alleged conspirators.

Hardly had the ink dried on the document than a galaxy of experts vigorously disputed the panel's findings. One of the most strident critics was the National Research Council, a scientific organization that disagreed vehemently with the testimony of the acoustical technicians.

During the nearly three and a half decades since the Dallas tragedy, a deluge of magazine and newspaper stories, television "news" reports and documentaries, books, and a Hollywood movie have flooded the United States. These fanciful accounts have largely ignored the findings of the Warren Commission and have resulted in a large percentage of Americans under forty-five years of age believing today that conservative groups joined with law enforcement agencies in a massive conspiracy to murder Kennedy.

No doubt the greatest impact on the American psyche in this regard was scored by Hollywood producer Oliver Stone's 1991 film *JFK*, which portrayed the Washington "establishment" as the conspirators. A high-budget movie with a marquee cast and splendid acting, *JFK* slickly blended known facts with fiction, conjecture, gossip, hearsay, and half-truths to create a grossly flawed but seemingly plausible scenario.

Few Americans have monitored the Kennedy assassination developments as minutely as Walter Cronkite, for many years the CBS-TV news anchor who had once been designated in a national poll as "the most trusted man in America." Cronkite had been a close friend and admirer of Jack Kennedy for many years (they had sailed sloops together on Cape Cod). In a mid-1996 television interview, Cronkite debunked the torrent of "conspiracy" books and articles. His heaviest criticism was of the Oliver Stone movie *JFK*, which he branded "garbage."

"There has never been one shred of credible evidence that anyone but Lee Oswald committed the murder," Cronkite stressed. "I had been in Washington for more than four decades, and I know that a secret there cannot be kept for as long as two days. It's utterly absurd to believe that scores of people could keep the secret for more than thirty-three years."

Anthony Lewis, a liberal syndicated columnist and also a longtime friend and supporter of Jack Kennedy, has stated the view of many: "The search for a conspiracy only increases the elements of morbidity and paranoia and fantasy in this country. It obscures our necessary understanding that in this life there is often tragedy without reason."[7]

Notes and Sources

1 Terrorist Plot: Blow Up New York

1. Author interview with W. Raymond Wannall, former assistant director of the FBI, April 1996.
2. Ibid.
3. *New York Times*, November 19, 1962.
4. *Washington Post*, November 19, 1962.
5. Declassified FBI documents, November 1962.
6. Ibid.
7. *New York Times*, November 20, 1962.
8. Ibid., November 21, 1962.
9. *Baltimore Sun*, November 21, 1962.
10. *Revolución* (Havana newspaper), November 23, 1962.
11. Author interview with Theodore Shackley, May 1996.
12. Ibid.
13. Ibid.
14. Ibid.
15. Ibid.

2 Machinations in Mexico

1. *La Calle*, June 4, 1955.
2. Testimony by Rafael Díaz Balart Jr. before the U.S. Senate Internal Security Committee, May 3, 1960.
3. Ibid.
4. Ibid.
5. Hugh Thomas, *Cuba* (New York: 1971), pp. 138–139.
6. Ibid.
7. Ibid.
8. Fidel Castro was never charged by Cuban police in the shooting of Leonel Gomez.
9. "The Real Castro," a series of articles in the *New York Daily News*, March–April 1960.
10. Ibid.
11. Willard L. Beaulac, *Career Ambassador* (New York: 1961), pp. 242–244.
12. *Daily Worker* (New York), April 12, 1948.
13. Carlos Franqui, *Diary of the Cuban Revolution* (New York: 1980), pp. 126–127. *New York Times*, April 26, 1959.

14. Thomas, *Cuba*, p. 886. *New York Times*, August 30, 1956. Ramon L. Bonachea and Nelson P. Valdes, *Struggle* (Cambridge, Mass.: 1972), pp. 285, 311–312.

3 A Blueprint for Gaining the White House

1. Bonachea and Valdes, *Struggle*, pp. 79–80. *National Review*, August 24, 1957.
2. Colonel Elliott Roosevelt, Franklin Delano Roosevelt's son, was piloting a plane nearby and witnessed the explosion that killed Lieutenant Joseph P. Kennedy Jr.
3. Joan and Clay Blair Jr., *The Search for JFK* (New York: 1976), p. 16.
4. Thomas P. O'Neill, *Man of the House* (New York: 1987), p. 158.
5. *Saturday Evening Post*, June 13, 1953.

4 A Hoax in the Mountains

1. Teresa Casuso, *Cuba and Castro* (New York: 1972), pp. 112–114.
2. *Bohemia*, December 27, 1959. *New York Times*, December 8, 1959.
3. Ruby Hart Phillips, *Cuba: Island of Paradox* (New York: 1959), p. 245.
4. *New York Times*, February 24, 1957.
5. Ibid., February 25, 1957.
6. *Philadelphia Sunday Bulletin*, August 3, 1958.
7. *Intelligence Digest* (London), August 1958.
8. Ibid.

5 Pulling Uncle Sam's Whiskers

1. *New York Times*, January 1, 1962.
2. Thomas, *Cuba*, p. 947.
3. *Washington Daily News*, February 3, 1961.
4. Earl E. T. Smith, *The Fourth Floor* (New York: 1962), p. 142.
5. Robert Murphy, *Diplomat Among Warriors* (London: 1964), p. 456.
6. John Dorschner and Roberto Fabricio, *Winds of December* (New York: 1961), p. 54.
7. Ibid., p. 153.
8. Ibid., p. 154.

6 "One Bad Apple for Another"

1. Dorschner and Fabricio, *Winds*, p. 159.
2. Memo, Christian A. Herter to President Eisenhower, December 23, 1958. Dwight D. Eisenhower Library, Abilene, Kansas.
3. Ibid.
4. Ibid.
5. National Security Adviser Gordon Gray memo, December 24, 1958. Eisenhower Library.
6. Ibid.
7. James Monahan and Kenneth O. Gardner, *The Great Deception* (New York: 1963), p. 8.
8. Peter Wyden, *Bay of Pigs* (New York: 1963), p. 107.

9. Veteran U.S. reporters compared the tumultuous welcome given to Fidel Castro in Havana to that American GIs had received when they liberated Paris in August 1944 during World War II.

10. *Time*, January 12, 1959.

11. Ibid.

12. Victor Marchetti and John D. Marks, *The CIA and the Cult of the Intelligence* (New York: 1974), pp. 304–305.

13. Ibid.

14. Allen W. Dulles, *The Craft of Intelligence* (New York: 1963), p. 178.

7 "Two Hundred Thousand Yankee Gringos Will Die!"

1. Nathaniel Weyl, *Red Star over Cuba* (New York: 1961), pp. 34–35.

2. Ibid., pp. 41–43.

3. Edwin Tetlow, *Eye on Cuba* (New York: 1966), p. 29.

4. Ibid., p. 31.

5. *Time*, January 19, 1959.

6. Casuso, *Cuba*, p. 35.

7. Ibid., p. 179.

8. *Time*, January 26, 1959.

8 The U.S. Power Barons Disagree

1. *Time*, March 16, 1959.

2. Tetlow, *Eye*, p. 145.

3. Dwight D. Eisenhower, *Waging Peace* (Garden City, N.Y.: 1965), pp. 522–523.

4. Richard Powers, *Secrecy and Power* (New York: 1987), p. 341.

5. Curt Gentry, *J. Edgar Hoover* (New York: 1991), p. 442.

6. Ibid., p. 443.

7. Senate Select Committee (Frank Church, chairman) to Study Governmental Operations with Respect to Intelligence Activities, Alleged Assassination Plots Involving Foreign Leaders. Published by U.S. Government Printing Office, 1975. Book III, p. 279 (hereafter referred to as the Church Select Committee Report).

8. After thirty years of service, William Sullivan left the FBI in 1971 after a quarrel with J. Edgar Hoover. Six years later, Sullivan was shot and killed in a hunting accident.

9. *Washington Evening Star*, January 14, 1959.

10. *U.S. News & World Report*, April 30, 1959.

9 A Safari to the United States

1. Casuso, *Cuba*, p. 211.

2. *New York Times*, April 19, 1959.

3. Ibid.

4. Tad Szulc, *The Cuban Invasion* (New York: 1962), p. 35.

5. Eisenhower, *Waging Peace*, pp. 402–403.

6. Richard M. Nixon, *Six Crises* (Garden City, N.Y.: 1962), pp. 214–215.

7. Eisenhower, *Waging Peace*, p. 403.

8. CIA report, April 23, 1959. Eisenhower Library.

9. Ibid.

10. Ibid.

11. Ibid.

12. Dwight Eisenhower diary, April 22, 1959. Eisenhower Library.

13. U.S. Army handbook, *Cuba* (Washington: 1978), p. 54.

14. Rufo Lopez-Fresquet, *My Fourteen Months with Castro* (Cleveland: 1966), p. 123.

15. Memo of conferences, September 28–29, 1959. Eisenhower Library.

10   "The United States Should Go It Alone!"

1. Monahan and Gardner, *Deception,* pp. 66–67.

2. Ibid., pp. 83–85.

3. Warren Hinckle and William W. Turner, *The Fish Is Red* (New York: 1981), p. 43.

4. Memo, Christian Herter to Dwight Eisenhower, April 30, 1960. Eisenhower Library.

5. Ibid., May 6, 1960.

6. Dwight Eisenhower diary, January 25, 1960. Eisenhower Library.

7. Stephen E. Ambrose, *Eisenhower the President* (New York: 1984), p. 557.

8. E. Howard Hunt, *Give Us This Day* (New York: 1973), pp. 184–185.

11   "Bobby's As Hard As Nails!"

1. *New York Times,* April 2–5, 1958.

2. Joe McCarthy, *The Remarkable Kennedys* (New York: 1960), pp. 30–32.

3. Jean Stein and George Plimpton, *American Journey* (New York: 1970), p. 42.

4. Victor Lasky, *JFK: The Man and the Myth* (New York: 1977), pp. 518–519.

5. William Robinson diary, July 21, 1960. Eisenhower Library.

6. Ellis Slater, *The Ike I Knew* (privately printed, 1980), p. 229.

7. Ambrose, *Eisenhower,* p. 597.

8. George B. Kistiakowsky, *A Scientist in the White House* (Cambridge, Mass: 1976), p. 402.

9. Arthur Schlesinger, *Robert Kennedy and His Times* (Boston: 1978), p. 18.

10. *Newsweek,* March 12, 1960.

12   A Secret Scheme Is Born

1. Thomas Powers, *The Man Who Kept the Secrets* (New York: 1979), p. 103.

2. David A. Phillips, *The Night Watch* (New York: 1976), p. 87.

3. In late 1961, Juan Orta fell out with Castro and fled from Cuba.

4. *U.S. News & World Report,* May 2, 1960.

5. Ibid., May 23, 1960.

6. *Newsweek,* July 25, 1960.

7. Ibid.

13   Intrigue and Covert Actions

1. Thomas P. McCann, *The Tragedy of United Fruit* (New York: 1976), pp. 93–94.

2. Albert C. Persons, *Bay of Pigs* (Birmingham, Ala.: 1963), p. 4.

3. *New York Daily News*, May 20 and June 20, 1975.

4. Frank Sturgis later was one of the "Watergate Burglars" in the 1972 break-in at the Democratic National Headquarters in Washington, an action that led to President Richard Nixon's eventual resignation.

5. *New York Daily News*, June 13, 1976.

6. Hunt, *Give Us*, p. 38.

7. Kistiakowsky, *Scientist*, p. 363.

8. Eisenhower, *Waging Peace*, p. 538.

14 Exercises in "Health Alterations"

1. Church Select Committee Report, p. 381.

2. Ibid., p. 382.

3. Hinckle and Turner, *Fish*, p. 30.

4. Ibid., p. 32.

5. *Time*, October 10, 1960.

6. Hinckle and Turner, *Fish*, p. 48.

7. Ibid.

8. *Time*, October 10, 1960.

9. Foreign Broadcast Information Service, September 29, 1960.

15 Spooks and a "Tweeping" Plot

1. The more than two hundred Castro agents was an FBI estimate.

2. Hunt, *Give Us*, pp. 47–54.

3. Memo, J. Edgar Hoover to CIA Director Allen Dulles, October 18, 1960. National Archives.

4. CIA memo for the record, May 14, 1962. National Archives.

5. Jim Hougan, *Spooks* (New York: 1978), p. 273.

6. U.S. Narcotics Bureau report, July 10, 1961. National Archives.

7. CIA planners did not use the code name Pluto. It apparently had been conceived by the Pentagon.

16 "Beardless, Ignorant Kids"

1. Schlesinger, *Robert Kennedy*, p. 229.

2. Hunt, *Give Us*, pp. 160–161.

3. Details based on Richard M. Nixon's *Six Crises*. Jack Kennedy's confidants have claimed that he knew nothing about CIA plans to invade Cuba at the time. "We only had a gut feeling," one former aide said years later.

4. Gentry, *Hoover*, p. 472.

5. *New York Times*, November 25, 1960.

6. Ruby Hart Phillips, *The Cuban Dilemma* (New York: 1962), pp. 265–274.

7. Dwight D. Eisenhower files, January 3, 1961. Eisenhower Library.

17 An "Evil Nest of Yankee Spies"

1. Herbert S. Parmet, *JFK* (New York: 1983), pp. 72–74.

2. Kenneth Galbraith, *Ambassador's Journal* (New York: 1982), p. 9.

3. *Saturday Evening Post*, September 7, 1957.

4. Paul B. Fay Jr., *The Pleasure of His Company* (New York: 1963), p. 11.

5. Clark Clifford, recorded interview, December 16, 1974. Oral History program. Kennedy Library.

6. *New York Times,* December 29, 1960.

7. *Wall Street Journal,* December 30, 1960.

8. Bobby Baker, *Wheeling and Dealing* (New York: 1975), pp. 120–121.

9. Hunt, *Give Us,* p. 66.

10. Memo of meeting, January 3, 1961. Eisenhower Library.

11. Ibid.

12. Affidavit by Alfred Naujocks, presented at the Nuremberg War Crimes Trials, November 10, 1945.

13. John F. Kennedy, *Public Papers* (Washington, D.C.: 1963), pp. 911–912.

14. *New York Times,* January 7, 1961.

15. Ambrose, *Eisenhower,* pp. 615–616.

16. Evelyn Lincoln, *My Twelve Years with John F. Kennedy* (New York: 1965), p. 237.

17. *Washington Post,* January 31, 1961.

18. *New York Times,* February 1, 1961.

18   Showdown on Guantanamo Bay

1. *Saturday Evening Post,* December 21, 1960.

2. The Navy Cross is the second highest award for valor in the United States.

3. Hunt, *Give Us,* p. 101.

4. Schlesinger, *Robert Kennedy,* p. 279.

5. Victor S. Navasky, *Kennedy Justice* (New York: 1971), p. 8.

6. Gentry, *Hoover,* p. 475.

7. Joseph L. Schott, *No Left Turns* (New York: 1975), pp. 192–193.

8. Arthur Schlesinger, *A Thousand Days* (Boston: 1965), p. 25.

9. Ibid., p. 259.

10. *Washington Post,* April 12, 1961.

19   "The President Said 'No Deal' "

1. Monahan and Gardner, *Deception,* p. 110.

2. Ibid., p. 111.

3. Hunt, *Give Us,* pp. 196–198.

4. Ibid., pp. 199–201.

5. Monahan and Gardner, *Deception,* p. 111.

6. Ibid., p. 112.

7. Thomas C. Reeves, *A Question of Character* (New York: 1991), p. 368.

8. Hunt, *Give Us,* p. 201.

9. *Time,* April 28, 1961.

20   "A Catastrophe Is at Hand"

1. *New York Times,* April 18, 1961.

2. Ibid.

3. Ibid.

4. *Washington Post,* April 19, 1961.

5. Monahan and Gardner, *Deception,* p. 127.

6. Schlesinger, *Robert Kennedy,* p. 445.

7. Ibid., p. 447.
8. Monahan and Gardner, *Deception*, p. 114.
9. Ibid., p. 116.
10. Ibid.

21 The Search for a Scapegoat

1. Schlesinger, *Thousand Days*, p. 281.
2. Ibid., pp. 285, 291.
3. Reeves, *Question*, p. 272.
4. *Baltimore Sun*, April 22, 1961.
5. *St. Louis Post-Dispatch*, April 21, 1961.
6. *New York Times*, April 17, 1961.
7. Wyden, *Bay of Pigs*, pp. 198–204.
8. Thomas Powers, *The Man Who Kept the Secrets*, pp. 113–116.
9. *New York Times*, April 21, 1961.
10. Richard M. Nixon, *Memoirs* (New York: 1978), p. 234.
11. Ibid., p. 235.
12. Ibid., p. 236.
13. *The Militant*, May 1, 1961.
14. Ambrose, *Eisenhower*, pp. 638–639.
15. *New York Times*, April 26, 1961.
16. Ibid.
17. *Robert Kennedy in His Own Words*, p. 247, Oral History program. JFK Library.
18. Schlesinger, *Robert Kennedy*, p. 291.
19. Robert F. Kennedy memo, June 1, 1961, RFK papers. JFK Library.
20. William Manchester, *Portrait of a President* (Boston: 1962), p. 35.
21. Haynes Johnson, *Bay of Pigs* (New York: 1962), pp. 194–195.
22. Fay, *Pleasure*, p. 186.

22 An "Assistant President" Emerges

1. The identity of the official in the White House suspected of treason by some CIA officials is known to the author.
2. *Harper's*, August 1975.
3. Ibid.
4. Thomas C. Reeves, *The Life and Times of Joe McCarthy* (New York: 1982), p. 149.
5. Jerry Oppenheimer, *The Other Mrs. Kennedy* (New York: 1993), p. 138.
6. Ibid.
7. Church Select Committee Report, p. 135.
8. *U.S. News & World Report*, January 28, 1963.

23 Eleanor Roosevelt: "A Silly Old Lady"

1. Kenneth P. O'Donnell and David F. Powers, *Johnny, We Hardly Knew Ye* (Boston: 1972), pp. 273–276.
2. Robert Kennedy interview by John B. Martin, April 30, 1964, RFK papers. JFK Library.
3. Reeves, *Question*, p. 276.
4. Schlesinger, *Robert Kennedy*, p. 489.

5. *Washington Post*, August 13, 1961.
6. Ibid.
7. *New York Times*, August 16, 1961.
8. Schlesinger, *Thousand Days*, p. 769.
9. Szulc, *Invasion*, p. 127.
10. Ibid.

24 Top Secret: Agents CG-5824S and NY-694S

1. Author interview with Theodore Shackley, August 1996.
2. Although in his fifties, William "Rip" Robertson played a key role in CIA undercover operations in Vietnam in the late 1960s.
3. U.S. Senate, Committee on the Judiciary, "Hearings on Scope of Soviet Activity in the United States," June 1957, pp. 107–108.
4. Ibid.
5. John Gates, *The Story of an American Communist* (New York: 1958), p. 110. Joseph R. Starobin, *American Communism in Crisis* (Cambridge, Mass.: 1972), p. 287.
6. Edward J. Epstein, *Legend* (New York: 1978), pp. 36–37, 263–264. Chapman Pincher, *Their Trade Is Treachery* (London: 1981), pp. 76–77.

25 The Dominican Republic Connection

1. Fulgencio Batista died of natural causes in 1977 while living in Spain with wife Marta and the couple's children.
2. Robert F. Kennedy interview by John B. Martin, April 30, 1964, RFK Papers. JFK Library.
3. Robert D. Crassweller, *Trujillo* (New York: 1966), p. 430.
4. Porfirio Rubirosa was killed in an automobile accident in 1965.
5. Crassweller, *Trujillo*, p. 439.
6. Zsa Zsa Gabor, *My Story* (New York: 1960), pp. 127–128.
7. Ibid., p. 133.
8. *New York Times*, July 27, 1957.
9. Tetlow, *Eye*, p. 287.
10. In the spring of 1996, former CIA Director William A. Colby told the author that John McCone was the best director the Agency ever had. Two weeks later, Colby died in a boating mishap.

26 A Green Light for Operation Mongoose

1. Church Select Committee Report, p. 139.
2. Ibid., p. 141.
3. Ibid., pp. 166–169.
4. *Washington Post*, October 10, 1976.
5. Philip Agee, *Inside the Company* (London: 1975), pp. 129, 168.
6. *New York Times*, September 25, 1961.
7. Johnson, *Bay of Pigs*, p. 262.
8. Church Select Committee Report, p. 1,451.
9. Monahan and Gardner, *Deception*, p. 184.
10. Ibid., p. 185.
11. *New York Post*, January 19, 1971.
12. Memo, Special Agent in Charge, Los Angeles FBI field office, to J. Edgar Hoover, March 5, 1962.

13. Gentry, *Hoover*, pp. 515–516.

14. Ibid., p. 517.

27 Tension Grips Washington

1. James G. Donovan was not related to William J. "Wild Bill" Donovan, legendary founder of the OSS, although both were New York lawyers and had other similar traits and backgrounds.

2. *Harper's*, August 1975.

3. *Revolución*, August 26, 1962.

4. *New York Times*, August 27, 1962.

5. David Detzer, *The Brink* (New York: 1979), pp. 103, 114–115.

6. Roswell Gilpatric, Oral History program. JFK Library.

7. Elie Abel, *The Missile Crisis* (New York: 1966), p. 58.

8. Ibid.

9. The Monroe Doctrine was set forth by President James Monroe on December 2, 1823. It said that the Western Hemisphere was "henceforth not to be considered as a subject for future colonization by a [foreign] power."

10. *Saturday Evening Post*, December 8, 1962.

11. Robert F. Kennedy, *Thirteen Days* (New York: 1965), p. 28.

28 "Our Blood Ran Cold"

1. Thomas Powers, *The Man Who Kept the Secrets*, p. 329.

2. Joseph S. Burckholder, *Portrait of a Cold Warrior* (New York: 1976), p. 37.

3. *Time*, November 2, 1962.

4. Associated Press, October 22, 1962.

5. *New York Times*, October 23, 1962.

6. Polls showed that 74 percent of U.S. citizens approved of the actions outlined in President Kennedy's televised address.

7. *Washington Post*, October 24, 1962. Foreign Broadcast Information Service, October 24, 25, 1962.

29 "If We Want to Meet in Hell"

1. Kennedy, *Thirteen Days*, p. 35.

2. *New York Times*, November 18, 1962.

3. Ibid.

4. Ibid.

5. *U.S. News & World Report*, December 16, 1962.

6. Robert McNamara served in the U.S. Army Air Corps as a statistician in World War II and held a colonel's commission in the Air Force Reserve.

7. Abel, *Missile*, pp. 154–155.

8. Despite his most able handling of the Navy's role in the missile crisis, Admiral George Anderson had fallen into disfavor with the top civilian leaders in the Pentagon. When his term as chief of naval operations expired in June 1963, he was not reappointed.

9. Kennedy, *Thirteen Days*, pp. 75–76.

10. Ibid., p. 97.

11. *New York Times*, December 23, 1962.

12. *Washington Post*, October 29, 30, 1962. Foreign Broadcast Information Service, October 29, 1962.

30 Shake-up in the Secret War High Command

1. *Time*, December 16, 1962.
2. *U.S. News & World Report*, December 23, 1962.
3. United Press International had obtained a copy of the original text of the Ché Guevara interview with the *Daily Worker* of London.
4. O'Donnell and Powers, *Johnny*, pp. 276–277.
5. *Miami Herald*, December 30, 1962.
6. *Newsweek*, January 14, 1963.
7. Ibid.
8. Church Select Committee Report, p. 173.
9. Robert Kennedy memo to John Kennedy, March 14, 1963, RFK Papers. JFK Library.

31 Shooting Up a Soviet Ship

1. *New York Times*, April 21, 1963.
2. Ibid.
3. Interview by Marquis Childs of the *St. Louis Post-Dispatch*, March 12, 1963.
4. Schlesinger, *Robert Kennedy*, p. 544.
5. Navasky, *Justice*, pp. 87–89.
6. Author interview with W. Raymond Wannall, former assistant director of the FBI, 1996.
7. Ibid.
8. Ibid.
9. *New York Times*, October 29, 1976.

32 "We Must Do Something about Castro"

1. *Revolución*, June 4, 1963.
2. *Washington Post*, June 5, 1963.
3. *Revolución*, June 7, 1963.
4. Church Select Committee Report, pp. 172–173.
5. Maurice Halperin, *The Rise and Decline of Fidel Castro* (Berkeley, Calif.: 1972), p. 258.
6. Church Select Committee Report, p. 87.
7. *New York Times*, September 9, 30, 1963.
8. Church Select Committee Report, p. 14.
9. *New York Times*, October 8, 1963.
10. CIA reports, 1963–1964, *Newsweek*, November 7, 1963; Hinckle and Turner, *Fish*, pp. 137–142.
11. Church Select Committee Report, p. 174.
12. Ibid., pp. 16–20.

33 "The President's Been Shot!"

1. Schlesinger, *Thousand Days*, p. 1,024.
2. Ibid., p. 1,025.
3. Schlesinger, *Robert Kennedy*, p. 608.
4. Philip L. Geyelin, *Lyndon Johnson and the World* (New York: 1966), p. 4.

5. *New Republic*, December 7, 14, 1963.
6. Nixon, *Memoirs*, p. 252.
7. Halperin, *Rise and Fall*, pp. 343–344.
8. Gentry, *Hoover*, p. 543.
9. *Baltimore Sun*, November 26, 1963.
10. Schlesinger, *Robert Kennedy*, p. 643.

34 A Naval Base under Siege

1. *Life*, December 22, 1963.
2. Author interview with Vice Admiral John D. Bulkeley (Ret.), April 1993.
3. *Male*, July 12, 1965.
4. Ibid.
5. *New York Times*, January 14, 1964.
6. *Washington Post*, February 11, 1964.
7. Reuters news agency, February 6, 1964.
8. Stein and Plimpton, *Journey*, p. 128.
9. Schlesinger, *Robert Kennedy*, p. 657.
10. U.S. State Department office of Public Affairs bulletin, February 7, 1964.
11. Navy Captain Zabisco "Zip" Trzyna died in the early 1980s. His good humor and love for his adopted country resulted in the epitaph on his tombstone: "Born in Poland, Died in the United States, God Bless America."
12. *New York Times*, February 7, 1964.
13. *St. Louis Post-Dispatch*, February 8, 1964.
14. Ibid.
15. United Press International, February 7, 1964.
16. *Washington Post*, February 8, 1964.

35 "We Won't Git!"

1. *New York Times*, February 11, 1964.
2. *Boston Herald*, February 15, 1964.
3. Declassified intelligence bulletin, U.S. Naval Base, Guantanamo Bay, Cuba, February 14, 1964.
4. *Time*, February 24, 1964.
5. *Los Angeles Times*, February 22, 1964.
6. Reuters news agency, February 26, 1964.
7. Author interview with Michael L. Infante, Bulkeley's aide at Guantanamo, May 1990.
8. *Male*, July 1964.
9. Declassified intelligence bulletin, U.S. Naval Base, Guantanamo Bay, Cuba, July 1964.
10. Declassified intelligence document, U.S. Naval Base, Guantanamo Bay, Cuba. Translation of Fidel Castro speech, July 26, 1964.
11. Ibid.
12. *Chicago Tribune*, August 1, 1964.
13. *Philadelphia Bulletin*, August 26, 1964.
14. *Norfolk Star-Ledger*, August 29, 1964.
15. *New York Journal American*, August 28, 1964.
16. Author interview with Colonel Anthony Walker (Ret.), USMC, April 1990.

36 Recruits for the Guerrilla International

1. Schlesinger, *Robert Kennedy,* p. 658.
2. Ibid., p. 661.
3. Gentry, *Hoover,* p. 550.
4. *New York Times,* October 26, 27, 1964.
5. Report of Committee on Un-American Activities, House of Representatives, June 1965.
6. Ibid.
7. Ibid.
8. Declassified FBI document, 1984.
9. Ibid.
10. Ibid.
11. Ibid.

37 A Tragedy in Los Angeles

1. *New York Times,* June 8, 14, 30, 1966.
2. *Nation,* November 20, 1967.
3. In August 1996, twenty-nine years after Ché Guevara's death, the Discovery Television channel in the United States ran a documentary on him.
4. *New York Times,* July 26, 27, 1967. *Time,* August 7, 1967.
5. *Look,* December 12, 1967.
6. *Washington Post,* March 18, 1968.
7. *Baltimore Sun,* March 17, 1968.
8. Jules Witcover, *85 Days* (New York: 1969), p. 47.
9. *National Enquirer,* October 26, 1976.
10. *Los Angeles Times,* June 6, 1968.

Epilogue

1. *New York Times,* May 3, 1972.
2. Sam Giancana's murder was never solved officially.
3. Johnny Roselli's murder was never solved officially.
4. Author interview with W. Raymond Wannall, former assistant director of the FBI, September 1996.
5. Ibid.
6. Author interview with Vice Admiral John D. Bulkeley (Ret.), May 1993.
7. *New York Times,* September 25, 1975.

Index